Move, Love and Learn

A Compilation of Sermons

Reverend Albert Gani

First Edition

MOVE, LOVE AND LEARN

Reverend Albert Gani

Published by: Reverend Albert Gani
207 S. Commons Ford Road
Austin, Texas 78733

ISBN 1-882853-12-1

$20.00

About the Author

Reverend Albert Gani is the author—publisher. For the past 26 years he has helped people find purpose and meaning to their lives, motivating them towards the pursuit of happiness through ethics and faith. His work has taken him from coast to coast in the United States, as well as Europe and Mexico. It is said of him that he motivates people and organizations to effect major changes through the application of spiritual and ethical principles.

Reverend Gani brings to his teachings a keen wit, a versatile knowledge of world history and politics, proficiency in languages, great knowledge of music and of philosophy. In this way, he challenges, entertains and provokes people to rethink and restructure their lives.

He uses his own crises and struggles as examples in his teachings. Perhaps most apparent and aspiring of all of his qualities is his courageous, ethical, and loving stance for the truth, regardless of the outcome.

This book is dedicated to

Vicky Linsalata

for her great devotion
to this Church and to this faith.

Acknowledgments

Gratitude may be repeated, but, for me, and in this case, cannot be repetitive. Immense gratitude is felt by me, and will be felt by many, first and foremost, as usual, to my wife, Robin, for her tireless and loving dedication to my work, and particularly here to this book. Great blessings to you, Robin, for all you do.

Great and many thanks to all my friends of this faith who contributed to the corrections, the suggestions and the live examples that have inspired this material.

Last, but not least, much gratitude and acknowledgment is due to Vicky Linsalata's study questions, which, due to their volume, will be published separately.

Table of Contents

Warning—Disclaimer

This book is an invitation to spiritual introspection. It is sold with the understanding that it, or anyone involved in publishing or marketing it, makes no claims of healing of any kind.

The purpose of this book is to inspire you to a spiritual and ethical life. The author, or anyone else involved in publishing or marketing it, will not have any liability and desists themselves of any responsibility to any person or group or company for any damage or loss incurred in any way by the contents of this book.

Foreword

Here is more of the wisdom of the ages adapted to our faith here at the Church of the Path.

As Boileau once expressed, everything has already been said, and we come many centuries late, rewording and reinterpreting old wisdom. This is not incompatible with the fact of the progress of humanity. Although the new is the old in new form, there still is progress in cyclical evolvement. It is the same circle which is being retraced on higher and more accelerated levels.

Let no one arrogate ownership of the Path through this wisdom. It is the Path to God. It is fact. It is yours and ours. Blessings on every step you take in this way.

Reverend Albert Gani
October, 1998

Part I

Motion

Chapter 1
Get Cracking

In the spirit world there are points of high focus which consist of entities, experts in their fields, that are trying to communicate with the human world. They do so:

1) By direct contact with us humans.

2) Through our spirit guides.

They guide our way. They try to show us the way whenever we let them. All of the concepts that I have given you come from such a source.

The spirit guides prepare you to receive these concepts. They are making it possible for you to be ready for them. That's why you so often get the feeling that a sermon has been particularly prepared for you. It fits and you understand it so well. It answers so many questions in so many new ways for so many different people.

The common commitment to the truth is what binds us together. This bond creates a collective entity which draws the light to us, guiding and protecting us. Our commitment to the truth entitles us to this light, brought to us by experts. The vocabulary used in these sermons is meticulously studied and chosen to fulfill our need.

****

We now approach a subject broached before: **Motion.**

Now, life is motion. Yet, we defend against it in so many ways. We know that non-motion is death. We also know that inanimate objects also move. They are made out of atoms which move at a slower rate than in an animate being.

So, **life is a function of motion.** The more there is life, the more motion. Evolution is also a function of motion. The more evolved a being, the more he is capable of motion.

This doesn't mean that the more a person travels, the more he is evolved. This would make airline pilots and stewardesses the most evolved beings in the world! No. A person may move while being very still. I am in a dynamic state of motion right this minute, as I write this. You are in a dynamic state of motion when you listen or read this. A tree has an intense inner life.

You move when you feel. Your openness to change is motion. Resiliency is motion. Potential for betterment, joy and happiness is motion.

So, there is inner motion, as described above, and outer motion. Both must flow harmoniously. If one is cramped, you may displace onto, and therefore, intensify the other. Thus, busy bodies who are super busy, over busy, are stopped, petrified, unmoving inwardly. Conversely, there are others who totally abhor outer motion. They cocoon themselves, thus, intensify their thoughts and feelings to the point of paranoia.

We can also reflect on healthy and unhealthy motion, just as we can reflect on healthy and unhealthy stillness.

Travel

We often dream of trains, or boats, or planes, and, as many of us know, they symbolize our life.

The very valid allegory of the train, so useful in the past, can now be replaced by the allegory of the plane which would perhaps be even more valid. Indeed, when we speak of plane, we not only visualize an aeroplane, carrying us from departure to destination, but also a level of consciousness. One must be on a particular plane on the inner level in order to catch a particular plane on the outer. Planes move; so does our life. If we are on the plane, the motion is easy and effortless. If we miss the plane, we feel disconnected. Our life has no direction. We must catch up with it, so we run, we strain. All straining to learn something we don't know, to acquire a skill we don't have, corresponds to a missed plane. At some point in the past, we did not want to move or to change. Consequently, we missed the plane, the opportunity. Now we must strain, run, in order to catch up with it. If the motion is natural, no plane is missed. The person feels as if he is gliding through a joyous and fulfilled life. Things seem to fall into place, with a minimum of effort. The inner plane of our Cosmic Life Force is carrying us everywhere, as long as you maintain the appropriate and the corresponding level/plane of Cosmic Consciousness.

Inner Motion

Travel inwardly by discovering new places, new states, states of mind, of feeling and of spirit. You confine yourself into what is, to you, familiar and seemingly safe. This creates, at the same time, a feeling of boredom and anxiety. You feel that there is a lot more to you than you can experience and manifest. You know that you are not living out to your full potential. You are wasting your life and your time. An oft-mentioned question is: "How do I set in motion my full potential?"

Inward motion and travel must happen before this untapped potential can be realized. It is waiting for you in the next **state**, inner state, wherein you will find a new landscape, new ways, new tools, new interaction, which will draw out of you potentials you never even knew you had. However, this requires the risk of leaving the old state behind. It also requires learning new ways, new habits, new customs, new thinking and feeling, new interactions, even a new language.

The cleaner you are—the freer of old baggage—the easier will this inner travel be. Trust that you will find all you need in the new state. Don't over prepare, over pack.

Let yourself be transported by the excitement of discovery. Let yourself tune in to the rhythm of your plane. Dance with it. Attune to the rhythms found in your mind, your emotions, your body, your job, your sexuality, your car. Be aware of the continuous change in all of them.

You can see here the **receptive aspect of motion.** Let go and attune. Yield inwardly and outwardly. No motion is possible without this yielding. Don't confuse yielding with collapse. See it as a dynamic phase of motion.

Your growth and maturity are direct functions of your capacity to move. An infant's world is more limited than a child's, which in turn is more limited than an adult's. What is true outwardly is also true inwardly. You are as capable of exploring the infinite vastness of the inner world as you are spiritually developed. Your capacity to move—and therefore, your freedom—is a function of your development. This is true on any level. And, consequently, your reaching out, exploring and making new worlds yours, makes you wiser, greater, closer to God. And you still want to go back to childhood!

Now consider the consequences of hindering this motion on the outer level. Consider preventing yourself from motion. You would be a prisoner behind your own bars. Consider the fact that, although you allow yourself motion on the outer level, you hinder your travel on the inner level. You put yourself behind inner bars. This considerably damages you, shrivels you up into childhood, puts you in a straitjacket, in baby clothes. So:

- You feel deprived and empty, no matter how many vacations you take.
- Your life feels pointless and wasted.
- You are invaded by inexplicable and disconnected fears, anxieties, longings. The Cosmic Life Force, hindered, has turned against you; the Cosmic Consciousness, numbed, distorts your thinking and feeling.
- You feel pain in an irrational and unjust Universe.
- You create secondary and tertiary issues to which these states can be attributed in order to get at least a false sense of causality and avoid the pain of injustice.

****

The dwelling in the Hall of Ignorance will confine you. Any distortion, freeze, violation of Spiritual Law will decelerate, i.e., stop your natural motion, disconnect you from the plane.

The stopping or deceleration of your motion itself is a violation of Spiritual Law. The volition to not move is also.

"I want not to know." We have abundantly explored this during our past retreat. Now, see how it confines you to old and obsolete states, spaces, clothes. Realize that you have outgrown them. You need new ones. Which means traveling to get them. They are waiting for you at an adult store, not a baby store. Go get them.

"But I can't afford them." See how you say that inwardly and outwardly. Meditate on this **self-imposed prison of self-indulgence.**

Afford them. Earn the energy. Yes, you have it already in

you. Revive what you already have and you'll get there. Which means remove the cobwebs and burst out into life. Just do it. Everything else will fall into place.

****

Teach you inner child inner travel. Invite him to inner exploration. Send him to new states, new countries, new planets. Conceive of new spaces and states for it. If you can conceive them, they already exist.

Detect the blocks as you go. Connect them to personal experiences, freezes, mistakes, bad habits. Take the necessary steps to correct—dissolve—them, in order that your inner child be free. Realize, as you meet these blocks that you are free to choose to obey or dissolve them, creating your own funeral or resurrection, respectively.

Caution; wishful thinking: True motion is through the blocks, not around them. Going around the block means giving up on it, leaving it in stagnation and deceleration. The movement away from it becomes false—an escape, an illusion, a wishful thinking from which you find yourself not wanting to come back. A good vacation is one at the end of which you want to go back home. Good inner motion and travel activates your desire to dissolve your blocks and freezes and dissolve your problems.

Motion Versus Dying

Motion and change, being on the plane of my life, will always give me a sense of Eternal Life. This is reality. Now let's study the illusion that contradicts this:

- I want happiness and Eternal Life.
- I don't trust that changing and moving will bring it to me. The present state seems safe enough.
- I will confine myself to the present state—or to a state, or

to an idea, or to the Bible, Koran, or Bhagavad-Gita—and attribute to it Eternal Life and permanence.

- I will prevent myself from traveling.

Consequently

- Having disconnected myself from the motion of life, I am now dying.
- Fear of dying starts.
- I try to escape it by moving even less; from this decelerated and disconnected viewpoint, any motion appears to precipitate death. Travel can only mean death. Passage of time means death. Change means death.
- I have substituted life for death by attributing to death that which belongs to life. Motion, travel through time, change, all constitute life. Yet, I want to see them as death.
- I become increasingly disconnected; my life is meaningless; my pain is increasing.
- Having slowed down, I have not accomplished my task; that makes me fear death even more, the agonizing fear of not having lived, experienced, achieved, moved, changed, grown so much more.
- I slow down some more, confining myself further;
- I now feel stifled in my confinement; I have killed myself out of my fear of dying. I have killed myself out of my fear of living.

Conversely

- I am in motion; I totally live every moment of my life.
- I revive the dormant parts of me.
- I discard and destroy the obsolete within me and without.
- I joyously seek my blocks and my problems, willingly and with caring, dissolving them without wasting time.
- I cannot fear death because death doesn't exist for me; death doesn't exist when I am in motion; setting myself in

death doesn't exist when I am in motion; setting myself in motion sets me in perpetual motion; nature moves me; God lives within me, changing me continuously, transforming me.

• At some point, I will have to shed my body, changed planes; I am not afraid of this because I see it as a phase, an opportunity to **organically** move to another state.

Caution: Death of the body in this case will happen naturally, not forcefully. Remember, suicide or interference with nature dangerously worsens the situations, regressing and immobilizing the soul.

Perhaps each lifetime, or each phase of our lives can be seen as one plane trip, starting at one specific point, taking an opportunity—a plane—along with a bunch of other souls like us, and landing at the end at a destination. While on the plane, I am 100% committed to this voyage. Anything less than that is not only regressive, but suicidal for myself and perhaps for others. Indeed, if I get off the plane in mid-air, I would be totally disconnected, suspended and accelerating my death. I would also be endangering the other passengers when I break my commitment by opening the plane door.

One hundred percent commitment must be given to your here and now. What does this mean for you here and now?

Truths

• Motion does not accelerate you to your death; it prolongs even the life of your body while giving you a taste of Eternal Life.

• Immobility is death, inner and outer, so there cannot be pleasure in it.

• Motion through time does not accelerate death; motion, accelerated, transcends time; this is true, down to the physical level, as Einstein demonstrated.

death, on all levels; including the physical.
- Motion brings pleasure and the bliss of flow with nature; deceleration and immobility conflict with nature, and therefore, are the authors of all pain.
- Halting motion to conserve life is dumb, evil, contrary to nature, and produces pain; otherwise, there is nothing wrong with it.

Leave

Motion means going from one place to another. You cannot hold on to the past and move into the future. **Motion requires letting go, sacrifice.** I cannot move to Texas as long as I still hold onto New York.

What, in your old state, is preventing you from traveling into a new state? How are you holding onto it? What would be the implications of giving it up?

When you go on a trip and you pack light, you know you must leave most of your possessions behind. You can't move your entire dwelling place with you.

Where would you like to go with your life? What is it that must be left behind?

<u>Caution:</u> Escaping a problem by geographically traveling represents the antithetical distortion. It is just as bad. It is another refusal to change. If I have a problem in one state, inner or geographical, and I move to another without resolving the problem, I am decelerating, and regressing. I don't want to change that in me which created the problem. That's why I am not solving it. So, I move, geographically, emotionally or mentally. Geographical motion is self-explanatory here as an escape. The corresponding pseudo-motion on the emotional level occurs when, refusing to deal with a particular emotion, I superimpose another over it.

The same is done with thought—superimposing one

thought, which I like, over another, which I don't. Beneficial thinkers are masters at this deception. Hypnotists have made a profession of it. Other religions have their own way of facilitating this pseudo-motion.

****

We have recently seen how destructive is individual stagnation at our Church. When you don't move or change, i.e., when you don't practice this faith, you sink in a self-made quicksand, and you draw with you those who are close to you, in your family, in your group, or in your Church. You also form self-protective cliques which exclude others from the benefits of entering this faith that has given you so much.

Deadwood must be cleansed by you on the inner level or you will be moved out to make room for others who are more willing to be in motion, the ones that you block out by your immobile presence. I mean it. Move or move out. Find your way to God.

Chapter 2
Hindrances to Motion

You are sitting in a grounded plane ready to take off. The delays are getting greater and greater. The promises heard on the loud speaker are repeatedly broken, one after another. You think of your destination, of the consequences of your delay, and you become increasingly frustrated. You finally numb yourself into a stupor.

You are sitting in an old state, complaining that you are not moving, that you are not getting to the new and fulfilling place/state in which you know you'll be much happier. Yet, you still hold on to the old state, refusing to change, perpetrating your old harmful habits. There is despair on both sides—despair in holding on to the old and despair about not reaching the new. **You** are holding on to the past. **You** are the dishonest pilot, promising to take off and never doing it. **You** are keeping yourself grounded.

You are straining in two different directions at the same time. You are operating in both forward and reverse modes.

You don't release the old. You grab onto it, or to some deified aspect of it. This refusal to release the old is a non-giving, non-loving aspect. Indeed, you believe that, by holding on, you have more and by letting go, you will have less. Yet the holding on prevents you from receiving . **Your hands are**

too busy holding on; they cannot reach out. Consequently, motion is imparted and you are dead, petrified in your old possessions.

To what are you so attached, so greedily and tightly?

• To your love, or feelings.
• To your possessions, or your money.
• To your energy or time.

You fear yielding all of this because you lack faith. You have invested your faith in an unjust Universe, a cruel one. Your mistrust of anything outside of yourself is a reflection of your mistrust of your own self. It is yourself that you mistrust. **You** are the life that you don't trust. Your opinion about life is your opinion about yourself.

Moi?

You, you are so generous, have been in the past, are in the present! How can anyone say that your lack of motion and fulfillment is due to your ungiving? This is your protest.

Well friend, you lie to yourself, as the airline lies to you about their delays. You may be very generous—a good person; "who? Me? A bad person?" However, as long as there is one area where you hold back, the plane cannot go. All it takes is one problem to ground it. And the fact that it is not taking off means that a problem exists. It is as simple as that. The fact of your stinginess and greed is demonstrated by your lack of movement. Now, if you deny this and defend against it with a "Moi?" you will be adding dishonesty to your avarice and mistrust, insult to injury.

And so, when you are in a "Moi?" state you are being both dishonest and withholding. Oh, there is no question about it!

Meanwhile, back within, you know that you are cruelly withholding. The "Moi?" confirms it.

What's more is that you are condemning yourself and continuously punishing yourself for it, which makes you feel even less entitled to the next and better state. Inside, you feel that you are 100% withholding, while actually only part of you is. So, you disproportionately punish yourself, which adds to the pain.

Because you withhold and are unloving, you must also believe that the entire Universe is too. So, the Universe is perceived as bitter; you experience rejection; you resent the guardedness of others towards you. "So, that's life!" you say. And who, in his right mind, would want to "live and move and have his being" in it?

The Little Self Attached to The Familiar

I remember, as a young child, wanting my father to tell me again and again the story of Ali Baba and the 40 Thieves. I did not want a new story. I wanted the same old one. I enjoyed it the first time, and I wanted to hold on to and reproduce that same enjoyment. I did not trust that I would experience it with a new story.

I often mention Saint-Exupery's fox who teaches the Little Prince how to tame him by sitting at the same spot, at the same time of the day, for the same amount of time, until the fox finds the courage to, one additional step a day, get closer and be touched.

So, there is something touching about that little self in us, stingy, greedy and mistrusting as it is. If we could admit that it exists, and that it is merely a finite part of us, rather than condemning it and ourselves, we could perhaps open our hearts and give to it. If we could do this inwardly, the world will transform and we will move in it freely, joyously and lovingly.

If we could only stop idealizing this little self! If we could only stop punishing ourselves for it!

Sacrifice as Giving

See it that way, as generous giving. Sacrifice first and the magnetic void will let in the new and infinitely rich reality of life. Let go in order to make room for God. I let go of the old, not knowing what the new will be. I practice an act of faith. I bravely face the unknown and the insecurity.

You have already done this in the past. Look for the many ways that you have changed, leaving behind your childish toys, your adolescent attachments. They all seem petty to you now. It is clear now that, had you not sacrificed these things, you could not enjoy your adulthood, your freedom. Besides, what you got as an adult far surpasses in pleasure, meaningfulness, and power, anything in childhood and adolescence.

You sacrificed your toys. You gave them to God. New aspects replaced them which, in turn needed to be sacrificed, given to God. And the ritual perpetually continues. When you sacrificed your toys, you sought other, higher things. You conceived other interests. You perceived new goals. Do the same now, trusting in this faith that carried you up to now, your inner plane of evolution.

For The Veterans

You have greatly cleansed yourself. You have accomplished a lot. You have transformed your life. You have, therefore, created greater happiness in a shorter time than you thought possible. Your cleansing continues.

However, beware of stagnation. Even this better state must be given up, or it will become stale. The same courage that elevated you to the present level, must be enlisted to elevate you to new heights. You must move on to bigger and better states. Your inner motion—plane—is, now, going there.

You have sadly witnessed the demise and regression of

those who stagnated. They have left us, failing to maintain their divine inner motion.

Caution: This next step is not motivated by yuppy upwardly mobile distorted ambition. This is a Genuine Need, the need to continuously improve. It is a natural motion of your inner plane.

So, don't make it a pressured, intensified function of your deified self. Let yourself glide, on your plane to the next state, traveling light, sacrificing the old, with serenity, with joy.

If you connect with you inner motion, with your continuous motion of evolution (see sermons entitled "The Divine Movement of Evolution"), you will elegantly sacrifice **and** move to the next state. My favourite painting, Antoine Watteau's[1] *Embarkation for Cythera* represents this readiness to embark for another country, space, plane, incarnation. There is a lightness about it. There is no forcing. There is elegance and yet excited expectation.

If you get used to constantly listen in and yielding to this, you will "go places" as it were, and effortlessly at that. You are meant to ever expand in capacity for calmness and serenity, for joy and ecstasy, for power and creativity.

"I Take on All of The Sins of The World"; Leadership

This necessity to move on helps us understand leadership and followership. Here we encounter Christ's saying that He suffered and died, thus expiating all of our sins. It is as if He, being the leader of all of humanity, bore the brunt of all of our mistakes. How does this enter into this material?

When you are in a position of leadership, you are supposed to be more developed than those who follow you. This is true in all cases. If, for instance, because of your

---

[1] French painter, 1684-1721.

wealth, you find yourself at the head of a project or of a group, you must be capable of handling any of the problems of your followers. If you are not, those will become **your** problems.

The leader is a channel for the sum total of all the energies, beneficial or harmful, of a group. As a channel, he receives guidance from superior beings which he passes on to his followers. However, he also receives the sum total of the distorted selves of his followers. They must be filtered through him in order to be purified. Therefore, the leader runs the danger of expressing and magnifying all of the distortions and qualities of the group. So, if the leader's distorted self is not being purified, there will be unhealthy collusion between leader and follower.

Suppose the leader is incapable of clearing himself of a particular distortion. All of the similar distortions in the group will go to reinforce the leader's, colluding with it and creating distortions and unhappiness.

Since the leader is unwilling to **move** in a particular area of his personal life, since he holds on to and deifies some of his distortions, he will be unable to help others when it comes to the same problems. Since, being the leader, he is invested with power and energy commensurate to the power of his group, he will commensurately create distortion and wreak havoc in his own life, let alone what he will do to his followers.

Conversely, if cleanses this problem, he will neutralize it. He may not even have to resolve it to do so, as we have demonstrated elsewhere. The mere cleansing it with commitment, will neutralize the problem, preventing collusion, allowing for confrontation. But, in doing so, he also has to reveal to his followers that he, too, has this problem. He must learn how to do this **and,** at the same time, confront others on their mistakes, risk their dumping, and still stand steady in the light, moving towards the truth and guiding others in the process.

This job only seems difficult. It becomes difficult if the leader rests on his laurels and abuses his achievements, deciding that there is no need to grow any further, that he has made it. Unfortunately, this is a stance adopted by the overwhelming majority of leaders, making them dangerous.

The teacher who is continuously in **motion** on his evolutionary plane, has no problems doing this. He sees that being the focus of other's distortions is a greater opportunity to further cleanse. If his problems are going to be magnified, so much the better, because he will be that much more motivated t dissolve them.

If his followers quit him because he has shown his distorted self to them, good riddance. This demand for perfection from their leader reveals that they don't want to move and change. They want the perfect leader to do it for them. They want to build cases to denigrate their own evolutionary progress, their own inner plane, which requires effort and pain.

Let them go to the false, pseudo-perfect teacher who cannot teach them anything but stagnation.

The continuous changes effected by the leader in his own personal cleansing will draw the followers to effect their own changes, move in their own lives. So, indeed, by clearing himself, he clears others through him, meaning of course that the followers have to do as he did in order to be saved.

Unfortunately, organized bigotry has distorted all of this. Christ dying for our sins has come to mean that we don't have to **move, change,** struggle and cleanse, as He did. He did it for us.

Here, I say again: no self-respecting teacher or saviour or prophet, in his right mind, would deprive you of riding your plane, of moving, by merely offering instant salvation. Only the devil does that. By distorting this principle of leadership, organized religion has, therefore, been doing the labour of the devil, debilitating, diminishing, numbing and ossifying their followers.

So, whether you are leader or follower, it comes back to the same thing: how much are you willing to move, change, sacrifice, commit, in your **personal** life? Everything hinges on that. It's just that for a leader, the task's difficulty is increased by the number of his followers or by the magnitude of the distorted selves which he is helping. It's as clear as that!

Believe it and practice it and you will find, within yourself, the unmistakable presence of God!

Chapter 3
Three Defenses

Every time I sacrifice an old state, a magnetic void is created, making room for a new one. Having sacrificed the old, I am freer to **move** into the new one. Visualization, as motion, allows me to get into the new state.

So, sacrifice as motion, change as motion, visualization as motion, propel me into ever new, ever improved states of being.

Resistance to Motion
I. **Collusion:** But, my resistance to motion, my greed against sacrificing the old, **collude** with my fear of the unknown and visualize a harmful new state. I fear that the new may be harmful, worse than the old state. So, I freeze myself into the old.

There are many harmful forces labouring here:

A) **The path of least resistance,** defending against any effort, any motion or change.

B) **The greed,** grabbing on to the old so as not to lose it, never sacrificing anything.

C) **The fear,** convinced that anything new is unknown, therefore, bound to be worse.

D) **The conceit,** convinced that any yielding to the

evolutionary motion is humiliating.

There may be more. See if you can find them. Anyhow, however many there are, they feed each other's case against motion.

Examples:

- The path of least resistance convinces the greed to tightly hold on to the old out of reluctance to exert itself.
- The greed magnifies the fear in order to avoid sacrifice.
- The fear enhances the conceit by saying,"How can you want to move and change when you have based so much on the old state, the old way of thinking? You will look so foolish when you demonstrate that, what you clung to so much, was wrong, that you were wrong!"

More examples can be found with complete permutations of all the harmful aspects and how they influence each other. You should try that and complete the exercise on your own and for your own distortions.

Reality: The reality is that none of this is true. Being alive, the liberation of the Life Force, effected through the sacrifice of what is obsolete, must naturally lead me to greater happiness. The Life Force carries and is carried by consciousness. Left to its own devices, liberated, it is bound to create better states. What's more, if I help it with my conscious awareness, my *I am*, if I deliberately visualize beneficial states to replace the obsolete ones, I am bound to succeed.

So, question this conviction that the new will be worse. It doesn't make sense. It makes a lot more sense that the new will be a lot better.

But wait. It gets even better. After all, your change, your motion, your sacrifice have been effected with good will, caring and intelligence. You committed yourself to doing what's right when you decided to thus move. You enlisted and activated the best in you. **Therefore, you are entitled to the best. The best has been earned by you. You gave. You sacrificed. All the goodness in the world is yours. Claim it. Take it. Not doing so is also defense against motion and change.** Doing so, far from being greedy is, on the contrary, a giving to the Universe. Indeed, having done the cleansing, you justly get rewarded, which:

* Convinces you to continue doing it.
* Inspires others to do the same.
* Makes it possible for the goodness of the Universe—the Kingdom of God—to penetrate your life.

There will be no question about the Law that says, "Give and you shall receive." It will become an experiential reality for you and for your environment.

Full commitment leads to full happiness on all levels. Giving merges with receiving as effect merges with cause to whoever totally commits to this faith.

Conversely, let your imagination soar. Dare to visualize the best. Then, look at the defenses against moving to the newly visualized state. Either way works.

****

However, sometimes the accumulation of blocks will prevent you from visualizing, even from praying or longing, or needing. So, the clean up must come first. Sacrifice must precede even visualization because the old has become pervasive enough as to block your vision of what could be.

So, soar in your imagination. Extend it as far as it can go. You can always correct it and ground it later.

Remember that reality is always better than illusion. If you move, sacrifice and change, whatever you visualize in your new state will be far surpassed by reality, which will always be fuller than your personal imagination. However, you must then let your imagination itself grow further, inspired by your newly found abundance. And so, you will have created a benign circle, ever more capable of visualizing and sustaining happiness and pleasure.

****

II. **Displacement:** Your soul makes motion available to you. If you don't move, what do you think is going to happen to this gift of motion? It will become unhealthy and displaced on the other areas within, areas that don't need it.

Suppose you resist moving in the areas where you should. You will become compulsive in an area that has heretofore been healthy. And, you'll wonder why. You'll feel victimized, unjustly treated because you disconnect from:

A) Your lack of motion in the other area;

B) The displacement onto the area which has become compulsive.

Sleeplessness, anxiety, piddling, restlessness, disproportionate worry, compulsive substance or food abuse, obsessive fear, all exist out of non-movement in, very often, seemingly unrelated areas.

So, incapacity to be serene and still is also a consequence of defense against motion.

So is jumping from one thing to the next, never bringing a task to completion. Consider the spiritual butterflies here, hopping from one workshop to the other. They all are avoiding the same thing: motion in an area where there is poisonous retention.

Retention as Anti-Nature

What is obsolete is waste and must be eliminated. Retaining it is anti-nature. It will poison you. What is true of your body is also true of your emotions and thinking. Think about it.

The Good Is Immortal

Conversely, what is good in you cannot die. Good is infinite. You will not lose any goodness by sacrificing obsolescence. So, stop holding on and compromising. You will never progress—travel—to the new and better state if you do so.

Avoid throwing baby and bath water by making sure the baby has been removed from the bath water. Disconnect the beneficial from its harmful attachments. It is only the harmful that must be discarded. The beneficial will not die unless you kill it.

Interim; up in the Air

You have taken off, sacrificed your old state. You are now up in the air, in between two states. This need not be a miserable time. On the contrary. Settle down and expect, visualize, anchor yourself in expectations of what is to come. Give it your best volitionality. Replenish yourself in preparation of what is to come. The trip itself has its infinite rewards.

****

I yield to the Will of God.

I open my heart and let the love of God move through me to others.

I give the best of myself and sacrifice the obsolete.

I claim the best with dignity.

I devote myself to the highest cause.

I am blessed and at-one with God.

Chapter 4
More Insights

Motion and Soul Essence

Let's go back to the soul, releasing into your personality the essence needed to deal with the changes in your life. We are dealing here with:

1) The essence, which a) effects the change or b) is attracted to the need for change; see if you can visualize both at the same time.

2) The personality—the form—a) changing as a result of the impetus of the released essence, and b) as attracting its coming through longing, through desire to change.

The essence itself is divine. Unimpeded, it will transform and transfigure, bringing grace, beauty, bliss, knowledge, wisdom and more.

But, all of this means **motion.** If motion is impeded, the personality cannot change. However, the motion of the soul essence continues, on another level. Ultimately, the personality dies. Less drastically, part of it dies. Any obstruction of motion results in some form of death.

This obstruction constitutes a disconnection. From what do we disconnect? From the Life Force, from life. That's why we die. Meanwhile, the Force continues to live on another plane.

Consider now your refusal to change and see in it the

process of death. What is it that you don't want to change?
- A habit of thought?
- A perpetrated and manipulated feeling?
- A manipulation of others and of yourself through offensiveness, docility or escape?
- A state of victimization?
- A _moi?_ defense?
- An obsolete belief system?
- A bad habit, an addiction?
- A glamour?

Any improvement means change, which means motion, which means volition to move. Why are you so frightened of change, of motion? You erroneously believe that you are holding on to life by not moving. Actually, you are holding on to death. Identify:

1) The desire not to change, an unnatural block to life, an obstruction, which is mistaken for life itself.

2) The desire to change and move, which is real life; this is much more important to find and cultivate. It is perpetual motion and eternal vitality. Don't let it pass you by.

Caution: Too much change, change as an escape, change as a spiritual butterfly, is not change at all. It is a defense against real change. It is change in appearance only. It is in effect, regression. As the French say: _Plus ça change, plus c'est la même chose._ This means: "The more it changes, the more it is the same." Change that makes sameness more the same, regresses.

The most insidiously difficult distortions to dissolve are the ones that are covered up with and justified by glamours. It then appears as if it is very much to our detriment to give up a distortion, as we would be giving up an advantage or a self-idealization. These stubbornly held habits of thought and feeling eventually become diseases. Conversely, every disease or physical discomfort is connected to a glamour.

Glamours Are Connected to Diseases

This insight came to me when I realized that I was losing my glamour of France this summer. It was incredible, even to me, that after two and a half weeks—exactly at the end of our pilgrimage—I wanted to go home. There was nothing else I wanted to do in France. This feeling contagiously influenced Robin and, free of my glamour, we came back to Austin and did good work on getting *Immortality Through Honest Doubt* ready for the press.

Simultaneously, I noticed that I was free of a stomach problem which had been bothering me for five or six years. When I shared this wonderful healing with Robin, in spite of my enormous brilliance, I was defending against connecting it with what caused it. She actually made that connection for me, linking it with the dissolution of my French glamour, which, of course, was connected to food and was ruining my stomach.

Glamours constitute a double evil. At the bottom is a distorted self aspect volition towards evil. The glamour covers it up, idealizes it, perfumes it, embellishes it, deifies it. At the bottom was my distorted self volition to follow my path of least resistance and over eat and drink. The glamour glorified the eating and the drinking, ennobled it and idealized it. At the bottom of my disease was an unwillingness to feel the pain of hunger, which, itself, is an unwillingness to feel inner emptiness. I filled myself with food and drink and my stomach was paying the price.

The dissolution of the glamour liberates healing energy which organically restores the natural and healthy state. **Every disease is perpetrated by a glamour and corresponds to it.** Make a list of all of your ailments. Connect them to the corresponding glamours within you. This step is not always easy. It was not for me. You will need the help of your friends and teacher.

Once this is done, go below the glamour and identify the evil. It is usually an unwillingness to go through a particular pain, an opting for the path of least resistance. Match this with the specific feelings that pertain to the ailment you are examining.

In many cases, you may know all of this. It may take deep cleansing, time, a trip or an event on an inner or an outer level for the glamour to dissolve to the point where the necessary healing energy will do its work. I, for instance, was aware of my French glamour and of my greed. It is through patient and continuous work that I finally was able to, through this trip, let go of it.

It would also help if, during your vacation, you undertook a pilgrimage to the places where these glamours originated. The feelings, the people, the scents in the air, the atmosphere of these places will help deepen your awareness of having created and nurtured these distortions and the glamours that cover them up.

Caution: Don't go on trips every time you find a discomfort within yourself. A lot of inner cleansing is needed first in order to make the trip worthwhile. Also, an outer trip may not at all be necessary. An inner trip always is, however, and it is cheaper.

Don't be too quick in treating the painful symptoms of your diseases. Removing them too quickly robs you of the pain that reveals both glamour and underlying evil. Don't fall prey to the established "professions" who, through their legitimized greed, will rob you both of the healing pain and of your money. Give first a chance to your own power of self-healing. You can always go to the "professionals" later.

Commitment Abused For The Purposes of Slavery

Another unfortunate consequence of resistance to motion is to be felt in the area of commitment and relationships. Indeed, a commitment made by the Divine Self is abused by the distorted self. The following will explain and expand this.

Let's treat this subject first from the point of view of a marriage or a relationship. Concepts are always clearer when they can be translated into sexual terms.

The Divine Selves of the two people commit themselves to each other in marriage. The distorted selves abuse this commitment as follows:

- Since you are now committed to me, I can parasite off of you.
- Since you are now committed to me, I can make you into my maid or servant.
- Since you are now committed to me, I don't have to love you.
- Since you are now committed to me, I can dump on you.
- Since you are now committed to me, I can take you for granted.
- Since you are now committed to me, I can belittle you and your value.
- Since you are now committed to me, I can safely dump my hostilities on you.
- Since you are now committed to me, I can betray you.
  It works the other way too:
- Since I am now committed to you, I don't have to be attractive.
- Since I am now committed to you, I don't have to improve myself.
- Since I am now committed to you, you will bail me out.
- Since I am now committed to you, you are responsible for me.
- Since I am now committed to you, I will make you feel

guilty.

All of these distortions are caused by non-motion, resistance to it.

Now that you have been able to identify this on the sexual level, see if you can generalize it. The same is true the minute you feel comfortable in a friendship, in a group, in an organization, at a church, in a job, in a country, in a state, or in a family. They all get taken for granted, abused, distorted. They all get dumped on. In that relationship, you dump on yourself, neglecting yourself and sinking, decelerating into apathy and regression.

A well-known distortion sets in:

- **I will conform to what you want of me. In return, you will owe me.**

  Then other freezes come along to fuel the problem:

- **If you love me, I will unhealthily depend on you; you must welcome that state as a proof of your love for me; I will test you.** *Love* = *distorted dependency,* **misnamed co-dependency.**

- **I will only love you if I can enslave you and dominate you.**

- **Independence means lovelessness.**

- **Commitment and responsibility mean enslavement and loss of freedom.**

All of this, of course, is wrong and evil. To the degree it exists in any relationship, it is poison to it. Either it gets removed or it kills the relationship.

The truth is that love is a function of independence. **The more a person is independent, the greater is his capacity to love.** As we know, freedom is a function of responsibility and vice versa. Distorted dependency is a child's tendency.

There is no room for it in an adult.

Slavery and coercion negate a relationship. They are the enemy of commitment. They imply that the commitment doesn't exist on a real, inner level.

Therefore, a commitment is only valid if it is made to a set of principles, not to a person. When two people are married, they commit themselves to both follow a set of principles together. This is the foundation on which the marriage is based. The other oaths contained in a marriage rest on this bedrock. If this base is destroyed, the rest is bound to crumble.

This also applies to any relationship that you have, whether to an organization, a church, a job, a company, or a set of friends. It is important to define what are the principles that bind you to your friends and your friends to you, you to your job and your job to you, and so on. Define, in writing, those principles, and whenever appropriate, send a copy to the other party. For example, **it is very appropriate to make those principles clear to your boss or to the organization for which you work, on whom you depend for your livelihood. Nothing is healthier than a well-defined job description that sets these principles on paper and is agreed upon all around.**

Wherever you sense that there is lack of clarity, clarify, specify. Take the initiative in doing so. It will not come from the other side. Confront the place in you that does not want this clarity in order to abuse the relationship in the ways that we described above. Confront also the corresponding volition on the other side. In the cases where it can not be done directly—outside of your friends at our Church, for example—find ways to do it diplomatically, but just as sharply. Of course, at our Church, you can do it as directly and as bluntly as you would like to. The more it is done directly, the better.

****

Liberate your soul essence and let it move you into the spirit of commitment. As a side effect, your body will heal. Conversely, listen to your body and let it guide you through its diseases and discomforts to the discovery of your lack of movement, your holding on to death. Thus, you will come to life and you will be at-one with God.

Chapter 5
Time and Death

Fear of change created death. It decelerated the Cosmic Life Force because of its limited consciousness. So, it became necessary for an organism to die. The energy expenditure necessary to fix the old and decelerated organism, exceeded the energy necessary for abandoning it and acquiring or creating a new one.

Fear of change, the association of change with what is harmful, therefore, is an ancient human evil. It hinders your growth on the emotional, mental and spiritual levels. What would happen if you hinder the growth of a child's body? It would be grossly distorted. In some parts of the world, they still do this, glamourizing these outrages into standards of beauty. The greater part of the world has now become wise enough in its young adulthood to do away with these barbaric practices on the physical level.

However, they still persist on the other higher levels for the majority of humanity. Those distortions through hindrance of motion and change are just as hideous on the emotional and mental levels as are a distorted foot in a Chinese or Japanese woman, or an elongated cranium in other cultures. These aberrations which repel us on the physical level are perpetrated by all of us on the other bodies, the mental and emotional ones.

Seeking Justice in Anger

The heavy handed demand for justice, accompanied by rage and anger, is supported by fear and cowardice. It will not bring peace. If you find yourself dwelling in that trap, you must let go and dive into the underlying fear, saying, as in the "Mantram of Fire," *The way of fire calls me with fierce appeal.* You should not seek peace and earth. You should seek fire and respond to its appeal. When you are stuck in anger, you are escaping the appeal of fire which exists below your fear.

So, we have three levels:

1) On the outermost level, the anger and rage which demands peace now; this escape, if not deepened, leads to insanity, or to suicide—a misguided attempt at finding serenity.

2) The next level, supporting the anger which escapes from it, is the fear—fear in the fire of level three; fear of squarely facing the problem expressed by the fire.

3) The fire, which is seen as death and which is feared for its destructive powers. Actually, when faced and integrated, this fire becomes inner light, immunizing the entity from danger.

The anger and rage are a short lived fire which must collapse because of its disconnection. The fear will never dissolve if it escapes the fire. On the contrary, it will transform itself into love if it yields to it. The fire is the bottom line, the problem itself, which always yields blessings when faced in a straightforward manner.

****

Fear of change created death, not the other way round. Death is not the cause of fear of change. Seek within yourself the fear of progress and change because you are convinced that you thus are drawing closer to death. "If I progress and

change, I'll get closer to dying; if I remain the same, I'll never die." This misconception is wrong on two counts:
- The certainty of death.
- The belief that immobility is eternal life.

Death is not a certainty. It is an inevitable consequence of deceleration of life. So, contrary to common belief, deceleration and immobility are death and bring on death.

Therefore, if you keep moving, you don't have to die. You know that; you feel it whenever you are changing. Extend this feeling, this state to the physical and you'll create the possibility of Eternal Life in the body. This, by the way, is your goal, spiritually, mentally, emotionally and physically.

Believing that death is the cause of fear of change is putting the cart before the horse, seeing the Universe in reverse. Where else do you put the cart before the horse? Where do you make the cause into a consequence and the consequence into a cause?

Look at yourself in your fear of death:
- I am afraid of death because it is inevitable.
- Besides, I don't know what will happen after death, and that frightens me.
- So, I fear the unknown.

This is illusion. What is real is:
- I fear the unknown in any change.
- I have decided that **what I don't know must be harmful,** and I have made myself terrified of it.
- Consequently, I have warped my bodies through hindrances of motion.

And what is even more real is:
- Change through cleansing must bring improvement since

I am increasingly eliminating the harmful creators. I am a better person so I am bound to change for the better.
• I can help my cleansing by **choosing** to plan, visualize, anticipate the beneficial.

When you cook a recipe for the first time, you are apprehensive about its outcome. However, if you are used to cooking, you are no longer afraid of new recipes, or new ideas. You know what is going to come of it because you are moving in that area of your life.

When you first learn how to drive, or to make love, or to operate a piece of equipment, you are rigid and apprehensive, expecting and attracting the worst. When you start accelerating the flow of your practice, you improvise, take liberties, become creative and are always confident of the outcome which you already have visualized.

Creation of Time
Just as you created death, you created time. Time is born out of deceleration, out of fear of the future, out of wanting everything to remain the same, in an illusion of safety.

The illusion which creates time says: "What remains the same is immortal; therefore, I mustn't change or move; I mustn't grow or breathe; it is dangerous to do so and it leads to death."

Perpetual change transcends time. Acceptance and flowing with change brings Eternal Life and eliminates time. Experience yourself when in the center of change. Time stops and the bliss of eternity—the wonder of it—is experienced.

Fear of death disappears when you are within that state. When you can extend that state, fear of death disappears in a commensurate fashion. As long as you are in that state, there cannot be fear of death. How do you feel in it?

- Limitless in your potential
- Infinitely patient
- Intolerant of any waste
- Free of baggage
- Free of distorted dependency
- Free of desire to enslave

Time, Death and Schedule

If you change your beliefs about time and death, they will both disappear from your reality. It takes courage and honesty to live in reality. Nevertheless, it is the natural state and it is our birthright.

It also requires the same honesty and courage to modify your life, to trust the inner motion and take the risk to change. To what extent are you committed to doing the right thing regardless of circumstances or of apparent outcome? To the extent you are, you will eliminate from your life the illusions of time and death.

For some of us, change means letting go of a cushy but obsolete state of peace. *Naught in me seeks the way of peace*, as the "Mantram of Fire" says.

For some others, change means making the right decision, staying on the side of truth which may appear to be a rigid position to take. Far from being rigid, uncompromising truth is most resilient and adaptable. It is the lie that is dead and immobile, appearing to be flexible. When a lie appears to be flexible, it is merely hiding its deadness.

Let's take a simple example involving time. The truth is that any conflict you experience with your activities at this Church are a) created by you and b) your expression of hostility, your defense against our faith. There is no question about this. There is nothing rigid about this either. You create your own reality; that includes your conflicts. The fact that you are unconscious of this is a function of your voluntary amnesia (see the sermon bearing this title). This is the way you choose to conduct your life.

When you take responsibility for your harmfulness towards this faith and its lessons you will experience the volition in creating these conflicts, and they will stop, as they did for me and for all of my friends of old at our Church. The conflicts stopped regardless of how demanding their profession or any of their lives were.

Now watch what happens when the defense steps in, and it particularly and unfailingly does with **all** our new friends without exception:

- They place other aspects of their lives above the activities here, in terms of importance. That's a **rigidity;** what's more, it is an admitted setting of **double standards.** They essentially are staying that the other aspects **must** take precedence.
- Consequently, they expect our Church to bend to their rigid demands. That's arrogant.
- Then, when they don't get their way—and trying to, no matter how cleverly it is expressed, through sweetness, meekness or victimization, or through vehemence, or through pouting—they accuse our Church of being inflexible. That's an outrageous lie that covers up their own inflexibility and double standards.

Even in psychotherapy, time conflicts and lateness are correctly identified as acts of hostility. You wouldn't expect less from spiritual training would you?

Conflict With Spiritual Activities
When a conflict arises between an activity and a concern and your spiritual activities, a triple hostility exists:

A) Hostility against your spiritual pursuits.

B) Behind it, a problem, a deadness in the part of your life that conflicts with your spirituality, that opposes it, that doesn't flow with it.

C) A volition to not penetrate this side of your life with spiritual material.

Many stay stuck in a victimized pretense of helplessness. Soon, being stuck in A) they have created such well-entrenched cases against doing spiritual training that they must drop it. This is a pity, perhaps even a lost incarnation.

On the contrary, those who accept the challenge and who let themselves be penetrated by this spiritual principle, will continuously benefit by these conflicts which will always reveal a deep hindrance in their life.

Generalized, this principle demonstrates the **harmful volition** behind any time conflicts in your life, with anyone, anywhere. All the excuses against this—cultural, professional, physical, cataclysmic, critical—are defenses and are rigid at that. They resist change and motion. They restrict. They are dictatorial. They want to dominate and subjugate. They deform your bodies. They negate the Law of Cause and Effect, and therefore, life. They create death. When you believe and defend them, you create death, you are dictatorial, rigid and uncompromising, however mild, meek and victimized you appear to be.

Anything untimely hides harmful volition. Anyone late for an appointment commits an act of theft of somebody else's time and Life Force. Any defense against that is a hurtful lie. It creates death.

Any delaying of right action, of taking a position, of uttering clear statements, of discharging obligations, of paying debts, of fulfilling commitments, however subtly expressed, constitutes a double hostility:

• The unwillingness to do what's right.

• The denial of this unwillingness, a lie.

This delaying, procrastinating, avoiding, ambivalence is the worst defect in the people at our Church. It corresponds to a glamour in Ray II, the Ray of Love, the glamour which negates right action, which denigrates action altogether. The Ray of Love, being the dominant and the most powerful Ray in our Universe, its glamours are the most harmful, the most damaging.

Landmarks at Our Church

Whenever your life hits one of these obstructions, and particularly if you find yourself defending against it, rest assured that you have come upon a major problem.

Now, a problem is good news and bad news. The good news will come when you decide to think, feel and act the right way. The bad news will be created if you don't. Any problem is a gold mine, a rebirth, or a calamity, a funeral, depending on **you.**

When you start this spiritual cleansing, you soon collide with the important issues of your life. The fact that you collide with them is good news. You never collided before because you allowed your life to be missed by these problems without opposing them.

Therefore, see the conflicts as opportunities. Open yourself to help. At the beginning, you must admit to yourself that you don't know, that you are "powerless," that you need help. Avail yourself of the help here. Commit yourself to it and it will yield results. The rest is up to you, between you and God.

Chapter 6
Your Next Task

Fear of Death And Personal Growth

The dissolution of fear of death must come with personal growth. It must be the result of the dissolution of the harmful within us. If it weren't, no fear of death would perpetrate the distortion. Indeed, why should I progress if I am fearless and immortal? If none of my bad habits will kill me, I will perpetuate them. They will magnify to the detriment of the beneficial.

Oscar Wilde's deep understanding of this process created *The Picture of Dorian Gray.* In it, through the effect of a magical oath, young Dorian Gray unwittingly displaces the effects of all of his distortions onto a portrait of himself. He keeps his youthful looks while the portrait acquires all the ravages of life. Sure enough, because of this impurity, youthful looking Dorian Gray accelerates his evil to a monstrous degree, while the portrait acquires all of the consequent hideous deformations and while he remains youthful. Finally Dorian attempts to destroy the portrait and kills himself in the process.

The apparent advantage of youthful looks was abused because it was disconnected from the Law of Cause and Effect. The abuse did not make Dorian happier; it only made him more self-indulgent, destructive to himself and others, which promoted rampant laziness, deceleration and living death.

So, thank God for the Law of Cause and Effect. It protects me from my own distortion through its experienced consequences. Thank God also for the fear of death which has beneficial aspects to it. Looked at from the point of view of reality, fear of death can be seen as a desire for living, a function of the Instinct of Self-Preservation. "I don't want to die; I want to live fully and accomplish my task. I want to fulfill all of the potentials in my soul."

Caution: Don't misinterpret this to mean that fear of death is a motivating factor. This would be regressing into the belief of a punishing God. No.

The **experience of the pain** of the fear of death heals it and transforms it into a enlivening desire for motion.
- Fear of pain causes our problems.
- Pain is the result of our problems.
- Experience of pain heals our problems and dissolves.

Shrinking away from pain creates more pain. Raising our awareness of pain dissolves it and yields pleasure supreme, blissful life, blossoming and moving.

Do this and you will develop implicit and explicit trust in the Universe, total self-confidence, faith in changes, motion and the future.

Interestingly enough, when I complete my seed plan—my soul plan—I loose the fear of death.

Magnetic Attraction of Next Task

However, does that mean that I am ready to die when I accomplish my task? What if I finish early? Will I be wilting and dying? If so, what is the point of progress, of accelerated cleansing and growth?

When I am finished with the seed that I brought in and my vehicles are still vibrant, I attract a new life, a new soul, a new seed plan. I move into my future life. I give birth to my new incarnation without dying physically and taking on a new body.

Accelerated growth accelerates the task. At the end of it, a vacuum—a magnetic void—is created and a new seed is attracted. This means that the individual suddenly manifests new desires; new talents appear, as if out of nowhere. The new person is difficult to be recognized.

Some of my friends will begin to have a glimpse of what that state might be like. What will your next incarnation be like? To what extent do you, in this life, begin to bring this on?

All of this suggests acceleration of motion into the future. It is an invitation to trust the future and to move into it.

Actively meditate on this daily. Move in your thoughts and feelings into the future. Visualize the creation of the most shining life of light, love and power. What would that be like?

Real And False Security

As you do this visualization, you will find yourself not wanting to leave the old and secure places in which you now dwell. This hinders your progress and deadens you. Living means changing, which means venturing **out** of your present/past limits. It means a constant dissolution of your rings-pass-not, your self-imposed and collectively supported, straitjackets and limitations.

If you don't venture out, you will self-destruct with your old and obsolete dwelling.

Therefore, what appears safe and secure is actually dangerously explosive.

By contrast, the new places, apparently dangerous at first, become safer and more secure once we make them our own.

Of course, it is a gradual way to mastery (see the sermon "Mastery" in my book *From Crisis to Mastery and Ecstasy*). **What appears frightening in the future is actually your new home beckoning you to take it, make it yours, inhabit it.**

So, include your new home in your visualization. See yourself becoming familiar with the new state, owning your new talents, skills, spaces.

Any yet, you'll find yourself still gazing at the old. Perhaps what holds you back is unfinished business, debts to pay, restitution to be made, settling unfinished issues. This, then, is part of the old seed plan that hasn't been completed. This incompleteness often only becomes clear when we have started moving into the future. From the new vantage point, we clearly see what still holds us back into the past. As long as we clung onto the past, we couldn't see our ties to it. Moving into the future makes those ties clear. It also motivates us to dissolve them.

Fear of Death Summarized
Here is in summary some of the basis for this great fear:
1) Being terrified of abandoning one's body.
2) Terror of the unknown.
3) No faith in Eternal Life.
4) Fear of loneliness—being without those we love.
5) Materialistic attachment to three-dimensional life.
6) Identification of self with it.
7) Old and obsolete creeds about the fires of hell or the dullness of heaven, making of them two undesirable alternatives.
8) Mistrust in the future.
9) The Instinct of Self-Preservation.
10) Fear of pain, physical, emotional, or mental.
11) Fear of failing in one's task.

Take each one of these seriously. Search deep within yourself for their existence. Remember that, emotionally, you are largely a child. So, for example, what you were taught as a religion is still largely believed by the child within you. To what extent, in a state of extreme danger, will you resort to old ways of thinking and praying that you were taught as a child?

How deeply are you attached to your body? To your house? Etc.

How afraid are you of not having accomplished your task? Of accomplishing it too soon?

Remember also that death is one of the most familiar activities in human experience. Indeed, you have died hundreds of times. You have died more times than you have done a lot of other things. What's more, the process of falling asleep is a yielding similar to death. So is the ecstasy of orgasm, the yielding to union with another.

Here are some exercises that will help relax our fear of this transcendence:

1) Learn to focus and concentrate. Specifics can be found in the first step to meditation. However, concentration can be practiced every moment of the day by fully abandoning oneself to what one does.

2) Before you undertake any activity, ask yourself a) how am I serving through this and b) how am I being egocentric? Then prioritize appropriately, keeping in mind that, in the last analysis, what is good for all is good for me too.

3) Watch yourself coming into and going out of sleep. The violent starts and abrupt ends of it should be examined and related to the existence of deep distorted self conditions. The dissolutions of those conditions will make going in and out of sleep a smooth transition. Knowing how to do this helps conquer the fear of the unknown, and therefore, the fear of death.

****

Accelerate your growth. Accomplish your task. Dissolve the old ties of guilt by discharging all your debts on all levels. Reincarnate in this incarnation as many times as you can and you'll make room, not only for all your souls but for your spirit that creates them which is you as living God.

Part II

Learning

Chapter 7

Innate and Acquired

Learning is the process of acquiring knowledge, and therefore, through it, we raise ourselves from the hall of ignorance through the Hall of Knowledge, to the Hall of Wisdom.

In our own dualistic world, education is seen and must be experienced in two ways: **innate** and **acquired**. Let us focus on each one.

Innate: Here we are concerned with the discovery of what is already contained in the individual's soul, his uniqueness, what he personally is to contribute to humanity. He will express in his own way a unique talent in his field. All of these potentials must be drawn out by this individual.

Acquired: Here we are concerned with input as in a computer. This is the well-known didactic western style education.

Distortions

Now, some people favour one at the expense of the other. The **"innates"** exaggerate the fact that all knowledge already exist within in order to indulge their path of least resistance, their base for inertia. This is the eastern mistake and it resulted in ignorance, demise, poverty. This is also the old "New Age" way which has given us a "Great Society" generation of functional illiterates and has regressed the level of literacy of this country to number 48 in the world.

By contrast the **"acquired"** ones exaggerate the truth of the need for outer discipline in order to negate the discovery of inner knowledge wich they fear. They fear yielding to it.

So we have here:

1) **The Innate Camp:** Idealizing inner knowledge for the purpose of denigrating outer knowledge because of fear of effort.

2) **The Acquired Camp:** Deifying outer knowledge and negating the inner—*tabula rasa* theory—because of fear of loss of control in yielding.

Reality

No learning is possible without both. The understanding and assimilation of the outer is merely relating it to the inner. I cannot acquire any knowledge that does not relate to what is innate.

Conversely, what I learn from the outside draws out of me what is innate. If I shelter myself from the outside, I will never challenge my inside to meet what is outside. Furthermore, it is my inside which draws the outside, which creates it.

Both must be utilized in a rhythmic fashion, sometimes drawing from the innate, sometimes acquiring input.

Both must be taught. We must give equal time to learning how to drop into the inner levels of our reality, to attune to the inner spaces and knowledge. We must teach this to our children. If we don't, they will dry up. Knowledge and its acquisition will become stale and irrelevant.

We must also equally emphasize the **acquisition** of knowledge, the input. There is nothing old fashioned about that. However, if it is linked to what is already there, it will acquire greater meaning. The child will be excited by what he is learning.

This linking of inner and outer will reveal Spiritual Law from within. So, our teachings will become an experiential, inner and outer reality. **Needless to say, the fundamental teachings must be based on Spiritual Law**. We have demonstrated here, in this community, that they can successfully be taught and they can create magnificent human beings. A child must and will be taught how to attune to the voice within, how to recognize it and how to link it to the world out there.

So, education will consist in knowing Divine Selves, distorted selves and deified selves. The first and foremost task will be to detect and dissolve the deified selves, instead of reinforcing them. Once this is done, the exposed distorted self will be much more easily dealt with, in a truthful atmosphere of generosity and tolerance.

These elements of truth will be part of the regular school curriculum. It will not merely constitute Sunday School. It will also consist of an ongoing subject, taught from the lowest to the highest levels of education.

It will be understood by everybody that the externalization of the Divine Self must be the primary goal in life. Thus, everything else, including the development of the intellect, must be subordinated to it.

This doesn't mean that intelligence should be neglected. On the contrary, intelligence will blossom when the development of the intellect is subordinated to the spiritual . Let us remember that a good intellectual understanding is essential in the search, discovery and externalization of the Divine Self.

Parents stuck in self-indulgent false New Age education which excludes intellectual challenge should ask themselves with what tools will the intricacies of the Divine, distorted and deified selves be understood if not with intelligence? A good brain is essential. It remains the principal organ in the human body. There will never be a brain transplant.

Reason must be taught about the existence of the inner world. Once taught, the individual is ready to experience its reality.

Spiritual Law must be taught intellectually first. Emotions and the body will thus fall into place. You can see this when it comes to physics or math or chemistry. However, it becomes increasingly hazy when you consider the less "hard" subjects.

Take history, for instance. It is not taught as it should be—as a demonstration of Spiritual Law through the ages. Consequently, it is seen as an irrational continuum of events, in which some are victims of others and in which all are victims of cataclysms. What a waste! History is a fascinating tool for the understanding and the application of the Laws of God in the human realm. It will be taught that way in the future. It will become a way for self-exploration and self-identification. Indeed, any civilization, nation or city, or creed, will be seen as an entity, with a soul, traveling through a cycle, revealing its Divine Self, forming distorted and deified selves, disconnecting from its divine source and dying. It will be a mirror of the student's self, a place where he will learn about himself.

Consequently, a President, or any leader educated in such a manner will profoundly understand right and wrong courses of action. Unlike in the present, he will not be and live in denial. He will be incapable of lying since he will know the futility and the debilitation of lies. He will have the honesty to own up to his distorted self, thus neutralizing the press and/or any other people with evil volition. He will understand that, what feeds morbid curiosity is the hiding of evil, inner or outer. He will know this by experience, having himself in the past committed evil in thought, feeling or actions. He will have experienced the liberation of the cleansing of this evil, and, through the undefended revelation of it, he will have rendered himself immune to the judgement and the criticism of others. All of this must be learned and will be.

Those who consider themselves the victims of judgement and of public opinion, those who blame the "paparazzi" are those who have not learned the value of cleansing and of revealing all secrets from rooftops. There are no innocent victims. This applies to Princess Di as well.

Motivation in Learning

The **Instinct of Enquiry** will be kept alive when innate and acquired learning are linked. And here is the secret to motivating children to learn. The student will be filled with the Cosmic Life Force as he explores the world of knowledge. Thus, he will want to devour knowledge with an endless hunger and thirst for it. The excitement will be found in the establishment and sustenance of the link between inner and outer. Infinite Life Force will pour out and assimilate the outer world in an attempt to own it, to move in it, to govern it.

Start now by:

A) Encouraging your child's questions.

B) Creating this atmosphere by reviving the child within you, with its endless questioning.

C) Remembering that Eternal Life is available through honest doubt. Honest doubt is questioning. Questioning is learning.

Answer **all** of your children's questions. If they ask, it means that they are ready to learn. If they want to know, quench their thirst. **You** are blocked when you don't, when you easily dismiss them, telling them easy answers or lies. **You** then have a problem, not they.

If this thirst is frustrated, it will be displaced onto unhealthy pursuits, create unhappiness and **die.** That's how the child then loses his thirst for knowledge. School, and by extension, work or life, become dreary, drab prisons. Those are the recipes for substance or sexual abuse, for rebels without a cause, for rampant child or adolescent monsters.

Children's questions should make parents happy. They should be encouraged and answered joyously.

Now, watch for your egocentric know all self. Suppose a child asks you a question which you don't know how to answer. Perhaps you don't know this because you warped your own attitude towards learning, thus missing out or blotting out what you were taught. That's possibly why you can't answer some of these questions.

In this case, be honest. Say, "I don't know." Say that they will learn this in school. Say that the child should ask their teachers this question again. This humility is very healthy. It means that it's ok not to know. If it's ok not to know, it is ok to ask. But if I constantly have to pretend that I know everything, I will learn nothing and I will teach nothing. Actually, I will teach that it is ok to pretend to know and it is not ok to learn, to search and to ask.

By not knowing, you humbly teach your child a truthful and open energy system. Remember, you are the prime role model.

It would also be good if, not knowing, you find out and come back to the child with the proper answers. Take the trouble to do it, for both their sake and yours.

These early questions may be the gate to the child's task. Answered and taken seriously will facilitate the unfoldment of this task. Stifled and treated with disrespect, they will take refuge behind false pride, deified selves, attitudes which will unhappily hinder the unfoldment of their divine task. If you don't encourage and answer a child's questions, he will become a know-all teenager.

Desire For Incarnation

It is a function of curiosity, a sense of adventure that makes us want to penetrate this reality and master it. Coming here with a task is a wonderful adventure story in the making. Encourage the discovery of this unfolding story within yourself and with your child.

How do we reconcile this notion with the notion that we need to reincarnate because we still have distortions that must be purified? Aren't we irresistibly attracted to incarnation because of our still existing distorted self?

Any distorted self constitutes ignorance and desire for ignorance. Inside any distortion is the healthy longing for liberation. In that longing is to be found the healthy curiosity, the sense of urgency to learn correctly and to integrate the lower parts of us with the highest. The dissolution of the distorted self **is** a process of learning as we all know.

****

See your distorted self as darkness ready to be illumined through learning the light of God.

Chapter 8
Freedom and Personal Discipline

Let's begin by a quote by Sir Walter Scott:[1]
* *All men who have turned out worth anything, have had the chief hand in their own education.*

Freedom, the capacity to choose what we learn or what our children learn should be cultivated **whenever possible and appropriate.** The element of punishment should be present as a last resort, not as a daily regimen. Pleasure in learning should be enhanced.

Of course, it would help if the atmosphere were conducive to it. Here are some guidelines:

Requirements for a Learning Climate
1) **Love:** To dissolve fear and eliminate the desire to be careful about what is said; in which the child doesn't have to be shy.
* Courtesy, respect must be cultivated.

2) **Patience:** To allow the blossoming of inner light.

---

[1] Scottish novelist and poet, 1771-1832.

- To provide answers to all questions and problems.
- To enhance and encourage the Instinct of Enquiry.
- To prevent irritation, both of student and of teacher. The Tibetan says that so many lives are destroyed through irritation.

3) **Order** and rhythmic activity facilitates learning and assimilation of spiritual, emotional and mental food. Order promotes responsibility and commitment. Repeated activities at particular times cultivates a sense of responsibility, and demonstrates the ease and pleasure involved in commitment. This should be extended to service, when the person is ready for it.

4) **Acceptance and understanding:** Through instilling a sense of recognition of motives for actions or feelings or thoughts.

- Which doesn't necessarily mean approval of them.
- Cultivation of the Law of Cause and Effect to rationally connect inner with outer.

5) **Parents in our faith.**

- If the parents are open and, themselves, in a continuous spiritual growth.
- If they dissolve the temptation to appear to know everything, the child will respond in emulating them in this healthy and joyous way of learning. If the parents cleanse and dissolve **the freeze of equating work with pain** and the **anti-freeze of equating apathy or non-work with pleasure,** the child will be a lot less likely to pick this up. The climate of freedom from that glamour will be absorbed by the child.

Pain Not a Price to Pay for Pleasure

Here we encounter a huge misconception that escapes just about everyone, including mundane psychology and those who call themselves motivators: "I must pay a price of pain, by working, in order to earn my pleasure; so *work* = *pain* and *pleasure* = *sin*; so I work in order to sin; the world is a continuum of desire for pleasure which is bad, and punishment for it by working, which is good."

The effect of this on the student—or the person at work, for that matter—is the death of the healthy pleasure and curiosity in learning and working. Even if there initially is a **natural attraction and desire to learn a particular subject** or doing a particular work, it will dissipate under the glamour of this freeze.

Freedom and Personal Discipline

Most people operate under the **illusion that freedom is negated by discipline and that discipline negates freedom.** Exactly the opposite is true:

1) Nothing is possible in life without **discipline.**

2) This includes the achievement of **freedom**—because it is indeed an achievement, obtained through discipline.

You are free to speak, walk, fly, travel and succeed **because** you have disciplined yourself.

Therefore, **there is no freedom without discipline.** However, also, **true discipline is the one we freely choose for ourselves,** not the one imposed on us. The point, therefore, is to teach children to **choose to apply discipline to themselves, to learn how to cultivate and enjoy personal discipline.**

This is taught through:

1) Obviously setting limits, a necessary step in the beginning.

2) Less obviously by example, by demonstrating the beauty, serenity and dignity of self-discipline.

When personal discipline has not as yet been learned, or when it has been lost, then **outer discipline must be imposed**, until the entity learns how to discipline itself, freely and personally. **Freely chosen personal discipline is the only true one.**

This must be taught to children so that they can gracefully and resiliently accept outer discipline when it is given to them.

Freedom is erroneously associated with the path of least resistance. Actually capitulating to the path of least resistance is slavery, not freedom.

Discipline is erroneously associated with numbness and lack of pleasure. Actually, dullness and numbness are the products of chaos, not of discipline. Order and discipline produce life, joy, serenity, brightness, and are produced by it. Order facilitates the flow of the Cosmic Life Force. Chaos obstructs it. Order makes the inner and greater order of the involuntary, of nature, shine and flow through us, enlivening and energizing us.

All of this can and must be taught to children. You will find that in many ways, they are closer to accepting this than you are.

This is taught through:

A) **The clear differentiation between freely chosen and imposed discipline.**

B) The clear understanding that the imposed kind is the sword of Damocles that will come down if the freely chosen one is lacking.

When, an individual's distorted self is rampant, creating damage, then outer discipline is necessary to protect this individual, his environment and the members of his community.

Generalization: Human Laws Created

It is the lack of discipline on the part of humanity that has created the need for human laws on the outer level. Indeed, limits are needed for the protection of humanity. The disconnection of humans from Spiritual Law creates the necessity for human laws, albeit imperfect. The disconnection from the perfection of Spiritual Law creates the necessity to adopt and impose imperfect human law.

The demand that human law be perfect, that there be perfect justice in the Universe corresponds to a refusal to discipline oneself in the obedience of Spiritual Law.

Think of it. It is lack of discipline that disconnects humans from perfect Spiritual Law and that necessitates the creation of imperfect, human law. Then, in that disconnected state, humanity demands that the imperfect law that they perforce created, be perfect. That's putting the cart before the horse. It is that lack of discipline that has created outer, imperfect law. Only the return of personal discipline will call back perfect law and remove the necessity for imperfect human law. So, it is unfair to:

1) Lack discipline

2) Which disconnect from perfection and introduces outer imperfection.

3) Blame this imperfection for our unhappiness.

4) Accuse the world for being bad because of it.

Whoever lives in accordance with Spiritual Law is beyond the need and the reach of human law. Look around you for examples here. Discuss this with your teacher if you disagree. **Therefore, when humanity will have embraced voluntary discipline, human laws will become irrelevant and will disappear.**

Remember, human law tries to imitate Spiritual Law.

Sometimes it succeeds; sometimes it doesn't. When human law contradicts Spiritual Law, it must be fought, disobeyed. By contrast, Spiritual Law should always be obeyed.

Caution: Beware here of misusing this truth for the sake of your evil volition. The overwhelming majority of laws of this country are good laws. The very few bad laws are usually not enforced. McCarthyism is a thing of the past. Prevent its return by asserting the good existing laws and by dissolving your "shame" of this Church or of your belief in God.

This shame blacklists us and you to your entire environment. **You** become the blacklisting Joe McCarthy, and your blacklist, which includes you and us, is **contagious.**

Post-Law Future

There will come a time when human laws will no longer be needed. It will first happen in isolated areas of humanity, namely wherever this faith is practiced. This community is a good example. We learn here how to apply the Laws of God to our lives on a voluntary basis. We do this, not out of fear of the human policeman. We dig deep within ourselves and find there the **desire** to discipline ourselves, on the outer, most mundane level, as well as on the inner and more subtle levels of volitionality. Thus, this little nucleus of ours prepares to teach the masses of people when they will be ready. Imagine how beautiful and great the task of this church is. There are, hopefully, others who also are preparing themselves to dispense this type of training.

In this future that we are ushering in, we will be free of crass criminality. We will be well-anchored in our Divine Selves to **want not to** commit crimes, lie, cheat. This discipline will be seen as desirable and the lack of it as undesirable.

You can, therefore, see the immense value existing in the

voluntary disciplining of ourselves on all levels. You can also see the great necessity to spread this word, how beneficial it is for everybody.

Note: Sometimes, although we, for ourselves, understand the value of personal discipline, we must recognize that others aren't there as yet. For them, fear of the policeman is the only possible morality. We must accept that state and allow for the imposition of human law. We must see this imposition as being beneficial, constructive, necessary, divine, on this level. The punishing God was needed for humanity in its childhood. Here, we must again recognize two extremes:

1) The **acquired ones** who will be too severe, enjoying the inflicting of pain on the outer level through the policeman.

2) The **innates** who:

A) Harbour resentment and rebellion against **any** discipline;

B) Hide that behind a pretense of teaching inner discipline; what gives them away is their denigration/hatred of the value of outer, albeit imperfect, discipline;

C) Deny the child—who sometimes could be their boss—the fact of their need for the policeman, for outer imposed discipline, for the goodness of imperfect human law.

Personal Discipline Protects You

If, through personal discipline, you learn how to live in harmony with Spiritual Law, you will immunize yourself from the perils and injustices in human law. Remember, you create your own reality. Any injustice you attract corresponds to an injustice you commit, inner and outer. You may harbour emotional or mental double standards which you refuse to give up. This alone, being an injustice on the inner level, will attract you injustice on the outer. Of course, an inner injustice usually has outer level manifestations. If you harbour a double standard, there must be ways that you act it out and create injustice out there. The discovery of this will make it easier to understand how you attract injustice.

Take, for instance, the **great injustice** of the "shame" of this church or of your belief in God. It is unjust because you are dumping, displacing your need for confronting the devil on to this church or on to God, both of whom are taken for granted and abused. The mere existence of this condition on the inner levels, even if it doesn't appear to be acted out, will attract injustice on the outer level, even if it is merely out of punishment for guilt of biting the hand that feed you.

And, the dissolution of this problem, learning total personal responsibility, living on all levels in accordance with Spiritual Law, will immunize you totally from injustice on all levels. As distorted as human justice is, it will not affect you.

****

Embrace the requirements for learning. Embrace personal discipline. Let the Laws of God mould you. Be blessed in God.

Chapter 9
Inspiration and Personal Discipline

Personal discipline tends to be erroneously associated with rigidity and lack of imagination. Wrong. The truth is that:

1) Rigidity is a reaction against chaos and fear of chaos. **Discipline cultivates resiliency,** i.e., neither the brittleness of rigidity nor the collapse of over malleability.

2) Inspiration, imagination and spontaneity are all the result of Cosmic Consciousness flowing through you. For that, order and discipline are needed.

3) Creativity, creation is cosmic sexuality. (See my sermons on all these subjects.) Sexuality is a function of order and of personal discipline.

Therefore:

- **All beneficial aspects and attributes are creating and are created by one another.**
- When we distort them, they create their harmful components.
- These then create each other but cannot tolerate one another's presence. Those two laws govern good and evil.

Insights
Learning about his Divine Self, distorted self and deified self makes the child increasingly perceptive of these layers in

others. Here are points to remember as parents and teachers concerning this:

1) We recognize that we ourselves went through the same way of becoming increasingly perceptive with the expansion of self-knowledge.

2) However, whereas we used to fear others' distorted selves, we less and less do; it is the same with children who must learn to perceive and accept their faults, learning at the same time how to perceive and accept others'.

3) This increase of perception must be encouraged, nurtured and cultivated. Children are very sensitive to others' moods, states, interests. We must learn to listen and encourage this perception. We must teach them the necessary vocabulary to express what they perceive. We must call it "understanding life," or something simple like this. Perhaps we should start calling our Sunday School, Life School.

4) We must learn and teach about feeling states, moods of different kinds. Even our poor vocabulary contains enough to learn and to teach. However, new terminologies will be created and we must help by creating our own.

5) With greater and greater self-knowledge, self-acceptance and dissolution of distortions, our perception also increases in clarity and reality. It becomes less and less biased, distorted by our own little distortions and harmful volitions. It is the same with children whose perceptions are sometimes amazingly correct. *La vérité vient de la bouche des enfants:* Truth comes out of the mouth of children. Amazing lies, too—and don't we forget it!

6) Insights go beyond what is expressed in words or deeds. We learn to detect and sense people's inner lives. We literally **see inside them**—insight. That, too, is true of children. That, too, should be cultivated and not dismissed.

7) As we gradually gain clearer perception we are still

hindered by our own distortions which interferes with it. It is important for us to learn and for us to teach the difference between the truth and the obstruction of the truth created by our own private little distorted selves and deified selves—our distortions. This means a balanced approach which respects our own and our child's insight, without being blind to the possible influences of our distortions.

8) This means honest and caring enquiry; reserving the right to make a decision or take a position only when we are ready. This enquiring stance should be encouraged everywhere and with everyone.

9) However, it also means trusting our gut feelings; recognizing the right ones from the wrong ones.

Responses to Insights

The freer you are of distortions, the more easily and elegantly you will deliver your insights. Being comfortable with your own distorted self, having cleansed your judgements of yourself, you will accept others with their faults. Consequently, your approach to them will be kinder and lighter, creating less friction.

This state, although not intense, is more certain, more grounded in its perception than the anxious and intense one, which is insecure.

In this state, you are not a slave to your insights, being either too eager or too afraid to share them. You are able to choose the way, the manner and the time to give them.

In this state you also **allow the other the freedom** to react as he pleases, whether with gratitude or resentment. You **do not manipulate** or demand a particular response.

Anger, Teaching and Learning

Do not fall into the syrupy trap of unilaterally banning

anger.

Do not confuse healthy anger which is relaxed and explodes freely, with the tense, intense and pretentious anger which manipulates and demands. Healthy anger makes no demands and does not manipulate. The tension and intensity of demands takes no risks and manipulates. Healthy anger is honest giving of your feelings. The other is dishonestly trying to obtain its little way in spite of the truth.

So, it may appear that someone is in distortion because of anger, while in reality he may be expressing his Divine Self. Remember, the Christ was angry without distortion.

Backlash

Your freedom to perceive what the other hides without being involved, as well as your freedom to express or not to express what you perceive, will trigger a very intense primitive resentment. It will be violently expressed to you.

You see, whether you reveal your insight or not, his **distorted self feels your light, knows it is being seen and knows that it cannot hide.**

This reaction comes from very deep levels of the individual. He is used to hiding and to being believed for what he wants to show you, not for what he hides. He is used to being believed for his pretenses and lies.

What's more is that he has **convinced himself** of his pretense. The light you are shedding illuminates material that he is unconscious of. **You, indeed, know him better than he knows himself.**

So, his enraged response is a mystery to him, too. Thus, he must build cases against you to justify these reactions. His goal is to wipe you out, personally. It becomes a matter of personal vendetta when cases are built.

You see, he cannot attack your light. So, he attacks you in your weaknesses.

Generalization: Now that you see this on a one on one basis, with another human being, see also that it is true with:

1) Spirit entities around you who are reacting in this same manner to your light; those are the cling-ons of our past sermons.

2) Organizations and creeds with whom you interact.

3) Family and friends who are not accustomed to your newly found perception; they will blame the church—calling it a cult—for your change and your greater insights, for your refusing to play the old games because you now see right through them.

The Light Prevails

Nevertheless, you must realize that you can only be hurt where you still are in distortion. **Your lower and deified selves are not just your weakness,** they are also their ammunition.

And, remember, you too are doing the same thing to us, in reverse, blacklisting us to them, denigrating us, building cases against us. So, in doing so, you want to agree with them. You collude with them. You want to call us a cult, since it adds to the ammunition you seek to feed your resentment for being unmasked.

All of those who left have done this. They have made our imperfections into their ammunition, out of unwillingness to face what was being revealed through our light.

However, **the more you cleanse, the less ammunition they have.** So, the suffering that must be temporarily endured accelerates the motivation for growth. **The more they attack our weaknesses, the more pain is inflicted, the more we will want to cleanse ourselves, thus immunizing ourselves.**

Thus, they are our allies against our own distorted selves. This makes them our dearest friends.

Therefore, this stage of suffering, of being under attack, of being scrutinized is temporary. As cleansing progresses, this state wanes.

But, also, the light shines ever brighter, blinding them and scaring them. This includes those who were once close to you. They will go away. They won't be able to reach you, nor hurt you.

Later, they may come back, but only to learn from you, no longer to manipulate, control and hurt you.

****

This way immunizes you. Immunize your children through it as well. Become the invulnerable loving light which is God.

Part III

Communications

Chapter 10
Word as Explosion of a Spiritual Atom

The importance of the spoken word is monumental. Let's examine its importance on a comprehensive level. Here are several quotes for meditation and appreciation:

I. From the Bible:

- *But be ye doers of the word and not hearers only.*
  —James 1:22
  This exhorts us to walk our talk. It also points out the connection between the word and the deed. A word is a deed.

- *As newborn babes, desire the sincere milk of the word.*
  —Peter 2:2
  Emphasizing the need for sincerity both in the childlike desire for learning and in the generous and loving response in the word of instruction.

- *Thy word is a lamp unto my feet.*
  —Psalms 119:105

- *In the beginning was the Word, and the Word was with God and the Word was God.*
  —John 1:1

- *And the word was made flesh and dwelt among us.*
  —John 1:5

II. From Horace, *Ars Poetica:*
- *Many words which have now dropped out of favor will be revived, and many of those which are now fashionable will now drop out.*
  —Line 70

- *... the word once out cannot be recalled.*
  —Line 388

III. From Victor Hugo, *Contemplations I:*
- *Car le mot, c'est le Verbe, et le Verbe, c'est Dieu.*
  (For the word is the Verb, and the Verb is God.)

IV. From Shakespeare, *Merchant of Venice:*
- *She speaks poniards and every word stabs; if her breathe were as terrible as her terminations, there were no living near her; she would infect to the North Star.*

In the beginning was the word, and the word was God. We are still living God's word, His AUM. This is as old as time.

The word is born in the **spirit**, as a flash, an explosion of a spiritual atom. It then penetrates the **mind** and creates a **thought**, which creates a **feeling** which then penetrates the body and the word is uttered.

So, the word, born in spirit, triggers a causal devolution **from** the higher **to** the lower levels of manifestation.

Once uttered, the word engenders consequences on the outer level, creating responses in others, flashes in their own psyche, resulting in their own creation.

Therefore, the word is:

- A fact, an act, a creation,
- Influencing and starting other creations.
- You don't just communicate with the word; you also **create**.
- It is a seed in which there is a **preparation** for further action and creation. It is, therefore, a **visualization.**
- It is an imparting of knowledge, albeit distorted at times.
- It is a commitment to a belief.
- It expresses volition, beneficial or harmful.
- It gives a feeling or, in distortion, an emotion.
- It reveals and raises consciousness, albeit warped.

Therefore, the word engendered and still engenders All That Is.

****

Obviously, you have taken your word for granted. Think of all the words that are being continuously uttered by all the parts of yourself. **You**, your experience, job, relationship, wealth or poverty, all of your life has been created by your utterances, your words on all of these levels.

If you can govern your utterances on all these levels, you can govern your life, your creation. Therefore, you must make all of these utterances conscious. Listen to and write all the words uttered by your various bodies. You will have to wade through the garbage and the noise, constantly produced by you. You can't clean it up unless you face it.

Incidently, the environmental disasters created by our outer level garbage are consequences of our inner, collective utterances of garbage. Inner pollution creates outer pollution.

The litanies indulged in by the various parts of yourself have become unconscious and are now polluting your air waves, much like the utter nonsense polluting most of our radio and television air waves. Unfortunately, the gentle and limpid voice of your Divine Self—your divine guidance—is lost among the garbage. By maintaining the busy plethora of words all over you, you therefore trash the Word of God which is trying to guide you every moment of your life.

Thus, your utterances to others also becomes mostly garbage. Garbage in, garbage out.

****

Become aware of the words you speak on all levels of your being. If you do this, you will:
• Greatly calm down, experience a level of serenity that you have never known before.
• Become concise and clear in your word and in your communication.
• Transform you life the way you want it.
• Influence others in transforming theirs.
• Listen and speak the truth of your guidance thus becoming a dispenser of light, a restorer of salvation.

****

The various parts of yourself oppose each other with their utterances. The resultant forces emerging out of these conflicts leave you with very little energy.

See how you confuse yourself and others, how you hide behind a smoke screen of words, how you avoid the incisive power of your words, how you deny the effects of your beneficial or harmful utterances.

Let yourself listen clearly to the truth. For example, instead of making excuses, realize that lateness is **theft** of another's time. **Theft;** what a word! You do not want to hear it. You make all kinds of excuses for your lateness. Yet **theft** best describes what you have done. Hear it, say it, heed it. The pain of it will heal your volition to be hostile through lateness.

Breaking a commitment is **betrayal.**

Fear of the truth is **cruelty.**

Despair is an imposition, a **demand.**

Not telling the truth is **lying.**

Bring down the truth, **the one central utterance that is responsible for the current unhappiness. Precipitate the one word responsible for your situation.**

****

Why aren't we talking about beneficial words? For many reasons:

- They would be trite before the harmful is sharply faced and cleaned up.
- They would cover up the harmful, and therefore, become perfume over garbage, or excrement. That's what the so-called positive thinkers do.
- They would, therefore, facilitate the rampage of the harmful; they would enhance and perfume it; you can see how regressive this would be.
- They would split and neutralize the individual not unify him and restore his power.
- To use the correct word that describes this: it would be **hypocritical.**

Consider the ones who utter beautiful concepts, words of love and wisdom, words of power without, themselves, having cleansed their distortions, thefts, cruelties, betrayals.

They are:

- **Hypocritical** in their denial.
- **Slothful** in the refusal to cleanse.
- **Irresponsible** about their harmful creations, albeit unconscious.

- **Faithless** in their reluctance to reveal their distortions.
- **Chaotic** in their victimization.
- **Out of reality** in their daydreaming.
- **Conceited** in their overdone goodness.
- **Cowardly,** lacking the courage to face their own selves.
- **Dishonest,** lacking the honesty to do it.
- And so on and so forth.

Otherwise, they are great swamis and great popes and great teachers of spirituality and wisdom!

****

Your word will have power to create once again when you descend/ precipitate the salient harmful words, take responsibility for them, feel the pain that you are creating. Only then can you disconnect the power invested in that harmful creation, and allow it to return to the Word of God.

****

3) **The real you.** The major factor of an effective communication has nothing to do with what you say and how you say it. It has to do with **the real you.** The real you completely supports or overrides what you say or how you say it. If someone talks to you and informs you of something that sounds good, you will believe it only if you trust his credibility. If you trust him you will believe what he says. If you don't, you won't, even if he says the truth and even if it sounds like the truth.

The best compliment I have ever received was hearing my boss say, "If Albert Gani said it, it then must be true". He didn't know I was listening. We were standing back to back in a crowded room. Therefore, **the key to improving communication lies in improving yourself.**

A better self emanates confidence. Thus, he convinces better, comes across more powerfully and magnetically.

Self-improvement involves:

A) **Your reputation, your professionalism, your consistency, the degree of your intelligence.** It takes time to build these up. They are all based on a great deal of integrity. The inner state of **integrity** goes beyond telling the truth for the sake of the truth. When you cultivate this you will radiate confidence. People will intuitively know they can trust you, and therefore, will value what you say. Communication mostly occurs on an unconscious level. The reasons why people like or trust each other are 90% unconscious. The person of integrity is more likely to develop personal power and magnetism.

B) **The sum total of your past experiences;** your emanations, accomplishments, all influence and energize who you are and how you communicate that to others.

C) How you have assimilated, interpreted, digested your experiences; whether they have served the building of your distorted cases, creating obstacles; or whether they were cleansed and integrated in Divine Law.

D) Aside from all of this we seem to be influenced by the **personality types** to which people belong. They remind us of people we have known, with whom we have had beneficial or harmful experiences. Therefore, to be an effective communicator, one has to study character types and be aware of how they interact. Two questions should be considered: What personality type am I? What personality type is the person with whom I am communicating?

These personality types can be detected on mental, physical and emotional levels. For instance, we know that we have encountered people who remind us of a parent, relative or teacher. Our reaction to these people depends on what we have learned from the original communication with the person they remind us of. In preparation for the study of the personality types, make a list of the people with whom you usually communicate in your professional & personal lives and try to identify them with powerful and influential figures.

Self-Worth and Self-Love

The power of your utterance is a function of your self-love. You cannot lie, steal, lack the courage of the truth without doing damage to your self-love. This damage exists whether you like it or not. Having damaged yourself by disconnecting from the truth, your word is weak because you are weak. Who you are is weak; therefore, what you say and how you say it will be weak.

This weakness is actually experienced as **slime.** You do not trust someone who gives you this feeling, no matter how beautiful is his word. Of course, if you, yourself, are slimy, you will not only trust them, but love their presence. You will engage in a relationship that will bring you unhappiness and pain, that will regress you.

There are many around you that emit slime. Yet, you are reluctant to confront them and call them on it because, up to now, you have been close to them. Having raised yourself from the slime, you haven't got the courage and the honesty as yet to denounce theirs and renounce your relationship to them. These people are real or substitute parents, close friends, family, etc. They are connections that you have formed in the past out of your own blindness to your own slime. Now that you are clean of it, you are shedding light on their dirt. The situation is worse. You are unnecessarily putting up with a great deal of suffering.

Let go. Let them go. Liberate yourself by creating new

and cleaner relationships. The pain of tearing yourself away from the slimy ones will cure you of the residual slime within yourself, the slime that still keeps you attached. Soon, their tentacles will not reach you because you will be shining the powerful Light of God.

Chapter 11
One-Pointedness

We are still examining the third factor that influences your communications with others: **the real you.**

The real you, of course, influences your sense of self-worth. In turn, your word is empowered or debilitated in accordance with your sense of self-worth. The more you value yourself, the more your word has value and power. If you emanate self-worth, you will be listened to. Your words will have commensurate weight.

Now, your self-worth and your self-love depend on the degree to which you have at least honestly reckoned with—if not outrightly purified—your distortions, your marred integrity, i.e., your distorted and deified selves. You cannot love and value yourself as long as they are denied, and, as you know, the harder you try to deny, the worst you feel about yourself. Consequently, the less you will be believed; the lesser the value of your word.

Nor can you claim what is your birthright of happiness, grace and ecstasy. If you try to claim it before cleansing, you will be hostile, intense and phoney.

As long as you haven't faced your distortions, you will, behind the pretense of claiming the best, be anxious, despairing because you will, inside, be convinced of your worthlessness. Defending against revealing your worst is, as you know, condemning yourself for being the worst at perpetuity.

And, if you temporarily acquire any goodness without cleansing, even if you have legitimately earned it, you will not feel deserving of it. You will cling on to it on one hand while destroying it on the other. This has been abundantly observed in those who are born rich, who marry for money or position, in short, who obtain anything without cleansing. It is also true of those who succeed without cleansing.

As long as you haven't purified, as long as you haven't unified with yourself inside, you will continue to emit, transmit, utter contradictory messages. Your "affirmations" will be superceded by the affirmations of that in you which you denied.

And the word spoken by your unconscious has more weight than the word spoken by your consciousness. This is particularly and painfully true to the degree you deny your distorted selves and your deified selves. The more you deny them, the more power their word will have and the more unconsciously that power will create.

That is the cause of all your lack of faith, all your fear and all your pessimism. That is also why you perceive the world as being made of disconnected parts, why things don't make sense for you. Therefore, that is also the consequence of your lack of faith. Lack of faith creates the problem; in turn, the problem creates even more lack of faith, which means more insecurity, more anxiety.

****

Our faith, therefore, provides you with the tools to make your communications a one way street, i.e., to unify your word. Unified, it will shoot like an arrow. Your whole being will be launching it, aiming at the center of the truth in others. It will not miss because:

A) It will be propelled by unified volition, the combined forces in you.

B) It will be attracted by its own target, since its target is the truth.

One-Pointedness

As the Tibetan calls it, one-pointedness is the manner in which the person in our faith seeks to express himself.

The Tibetan sees it as the result of cleansing.

Patanjali confirms it in Books II and III of the Yogasutras.

One-pointedness, being of one word, is the goal of our way of meditation.

In short, walking this faith is living and uttering the word in a one-pointed way. This can only be achieved through cleansing. You must expose your false and conceited worthiness, puncturing it and revealing your hidden self-depreciation. This is the only way to find the self-love necessary to express the salient, angular, enlightened challenging truth.

One-pointedness is characterized by:

- Serenity; an absence of scatteredness of thoughts and words.
- Unification of all the chakras and their cooperation with each other; this can only happen in truthfulness.
- Caring; the losing of oneself in service.
- Self-appreciation; the claiming and assertion of the actualized self.
- Cultivation of quiet and silence.
- Steady commitment.
- Ease in **right posture**, not only physical, but emotional and mental as well; meditate on this.
- Rhythmic, committed effort, practiced without intensity,

easily, lightly.
- Unification of all volitionality.
- Mind government.

One-pointedness results in:
- Understanding in depth of all duality.
- Power to resolve all conflicts.
- Clear perception in all subjects.
- Openness to inspiration and solutions from other divine sources.
- Wanting to love; the will to love is triggered and sustained.
- Capacity to communicate with higher spheres. **One-pointedness in word reaches bull's eye inside and outside.**

Honest And Dishonest Questions

Often, questions are not at all what they appear to be. Instead of being the humble expression of enquiry, they can actually:

I. **Insinuate an insult,** disguising it and making it appear to be a benign question. The Christ was painfully aware of this. He was a master at exposing the harmful volition disguised by question.

II. **Be traps,** drawing you through their false hood, to utter the false word and thus sully yourself.

Examples:

1) Shortly after the Waco incident in which the Branch Davidians' compound was destroyed, I met an acquaintance at a concert, a Catholic woman. She had come to our Church and had reacted defensively to our material—probably because the one-pointed message hit home in her distorted self. So, she

greeted me and smiling, asked me, "I thought you might have been particularly affected by Waco; what do you think of it?" With this utterance, by associating us with Waco, she was accusing me and us of:

- Contemplating mass suicide at our church.
- Abusing children and women.
- Amassing armaments to oppose authorities with violence.
- And all the other atrocities committed by the Branch Davidians.

Thus, her question was both an insult and a trap. Of course, being Catholic, she was a lot closer to the Bible thumping doomsday believing Branch Davidians than we can ever be.

Being in public and knowing that she was capable of hysterics, I simply said that we do not relate at all with any of this, and that it didn't particularly concern us. And I walked away.

2) Someone at tennis asked with a sarcastic smile, "What do you think of the huge Bible church that is being built about a mile away from yours?" The question reeked of at least contempt for our smallness. It also implied that we might feel threatened by the proximity and the competition with a huge edifice dedicated to the Bible.

Actually, he is a hypocritical yuppy. He wants to come to our Church. He expressed this to me many times. Only he doesn't. It would challenge his false life at its core. He prefers to confine himself to the status quo of conventionality and preserve his false life. However, deep down inside, his soul is confronting his hypocrisy. And he feels the pain. And he hates the fact that our little Church stands with dignity and humility, simply bringing the truth to Austin. He resents the fact that he wants to be part of it, knowing that it would be the right thing.

So, he insults our smallness by asking his question. "What

do you think of the big Bible church?" And I replied, "But I do not think of it." And, it is true. I/we do not compete with Bible churches. I/we actually send people to them when they call us looking for a "Bible-based" church. However, they resent us and compete with us in a hostile manner because we puncture their deified self and expose their obsolescence. We are the real Christians, and they know it.

3) The mother of a member is visiting Austin for the holidays. Our member friend told her that she planned to spend the holidays attending our activities, services, meals, etc. She told her mother that she was welcome to come if she wanted to. If her mother didn't, our friend made it clear that her plans wouldn't change. At that point, her mother asked, "They won't try to recruit me, will they?" There are several distortions in this question. Let's see if we can find them all.

A) **"Recruit"**: Accusing us of behaving like the selective service system did; it accuses us of forcing people to join. Which is a presumptive lie. We never solicit people in any way to join us. We invite them if we feel a convincing interest on their part for our teachings.

B) **Conceit:** is implied, making her desirable and making us desirous of her. Wrong. **We** are doing **her** a favour by **allowing** her to be our guest.

C) **Contempt** for her daughter's gracious invitation; instead, there should be an expression of **gratitude**.

4) This very same friend of ours, along with many other friends, are themselves guilty of the same offense. In their case, however, it is considerably worse because they claim to be members of our Church. Indeed, when the recent mass suicide of cult members occurred—I forget their name and I don't want to dignify this any further by looking it up—I was asked by these members, "When I heard of this mass suicide, I thought of you and of the Church of the Path. What do you

think of this?"

This is an obvious and blatant insult by associating us with those people whose belief is so diametrically opposed to us! How can members of our own Church compare us with a cult that denies life on earth to the point of committing the worst possible murder—suicide—in order to be rescued by mythical spaceships? Haven't they ever heard of our repeated stressing of looking inside for distortions, of taking full responsibility for this reality here and now, of our preaching that it is a good Universe and of our views on suicide being a great evil? The volition to hurt us here is so blatant as to be comical.

****

Can you find other examples? To how many such questions have you capitulated, i.e., colluded with? Why?

These questions must be exposed for their dishonesty. Your light of honesty, your sharp word must penetrate and denounce this. Reply by saying, "What you ask is not a question; you are making a statement; your actual statement is . . ."

Questions for Yourself

Honest question are truthful, constructive, instructive. They give while asking. Question your questions. Cleanse them of distortion. Doubt, by all means, doubt. As you know, it is the surest way to faith. But do it honestly, one-pointedly, not deviously and in a duplicitous way.

So question yourself. And do so in more ways than one. Use the word in the precise questioning of your own self:

- Question your self-assertion; it might be or contain conceit and arrogance.
- Seek the self-contempt behind the arrogance and conceit.
- Expose your self-contempt; see how you permanently act it out.

- Test the value of exposing your worst.
- See how it liberates your best.

****

Make your word as penetrating as the Light of God.

Chapter 12

The False Seeker

Dishonest questions lead us to study dishonest seekers.

The truth is your natural state. Originally, in that state, you were all knowing. You fell from that state. As a seeker of truth, how often you forget that! It is the closest thing to you. It is your reality here and now, only you choose to look away from it.

You will find the truth when you stop lying, marring your integrity. It is as simple as that. **If you are not in truth, you are in untruth, in the lie.** You are selling out, or manipulating or playing games. You are making demands. You are attempting to be desired, to get approval, to manipulate in some way.

There is a kind of pseudo-seeker of the truth who idealizes his quest, his doubt. When you answer his questions, he never is satisfied, attempting to draw you into his games. His words may be expressed as folly. "No, this is not quite it, keep feeding me, keep desiring me by trying to convince me, and I'll continue to derail what you are telling me, thus feeling superior and making you feel inferior." This is particularly and painfully true when it comes to religion. "Make me believe; convert me" seems to be the challenge of the false seeker. We answer them as follows:

1) Little do you know that seeking, as noble as it can be,

is still a state of ignorance; therefore, in that state there is a desire not to know, which is lying.

2) It is your ignorance, not mine; therefore, making me responsible for it makes you dishonest.

3) Being conceited about seeking is a double dishonesty; you are superimposing the lie of idealization over the lie of not knowing.

4) Your seeking should be **humble**, as humble as the thirsty person in the desert, willing to drink even if there might be impurities in the available water, putting away the demands for the perfect kind; this type of humility is loving and grateful, not conceited and full of contempt.

5) Your lack of humility reveals your demands that I satisfy you without your really trying. Thus, you are not really seeking.

6) Which means that you are protecting deep distortions, deep issues which you are not examining, and which are poisoning your life.

7) Do not try to poison mine as well; if I let you, I am capitulating to you out of my own lie, duplicity and duality.

If you see his deep issues—they usually are revealed by his characterology—go ahead and tell him about them, even if your perception is vague. Give it to him.

Perceiving and denouncing falsehood requires a solid anchoring in your own truth, a solid sense of who you are. Be who you a really are, which is God.

Warning: Because you have found here in this Church so many wonderful answers, your desire for the truth within may tend to wane. Because you find, you stop seeking and develop a sense of self-satisfaction, taking these teachings for granted.

On the contrary, what we find here must serve as a springboard to the infinite well of knowledge, connections and goodness that we have within us. Each idea we get here should be absorbed and applied to our lives to the point of kaleidoscoping it into an infinite of new ideas, each of which will parent an infinity of new ones. We are divinely infinite, each one of us.

Self-Defamation

We have seen so many times that the defense against revealing the distorted self content constitutes the condemnation of that distorted self. It is a function of an active despair that has decided that part of our self is hopeless, worthless, impossible to reform, too vile to reveal. This means that we are actively, consistently and permanently deforming ourselves. We utter words of self-defamation, of assassination of our own character. We continuously reinforce our bad reputation towards ourselves. We call ourselves names. These words of defamation must be found and exposed. They create constant damage to ourselves and to others. They diminish us and our effectiveness. They neutralize and implode our power.

Most of these words are unuttered. They lurk within, creating an inner fog so as not to be detected. Once in a while they reveal themselves when we become aware of our self-contempt.

Only the honest search within will make it possible for us to discover the words of self-defamation and maligning.

Nevertheless, in their unuttered state, these words monopolize considerable energy, forming inner black holes in which a lot of goodness is sunk in despair. This concentration of heavy deadness weighs you down. On the outer level, you wonder why you are tired, why you lack courage and honesty, why you are unable to love or want to, why your outer word doesn't carry.

If you find and shed light on the bottom of those black holes, if you get in there and experience their reality and utter their hidden word, you will explode them. You will liberate and release the sunken energy of self-destruction and self-defamation they contain.

You need to feel, taste, smell, experience the quality of energy within those black holes of self-defamation. Only with this consciousness will you be able to unleash the right utterance that characterizes them. That utterance explores, exposes and explodes them.

Once again, utter the word that defines every quality of energy within you.

"Who You Are" Distorted

One can indeed distort that too. The harmful aspect of investing a lot of credence into, "who you are" can take many forms:

1) You can abuse "who you are" to get your way when you use your **assets,** i.e., your sexuality, your talents, your attractiveness, your achievements to make people do what you want them to.

2) You can betray your own truth and your own honest search by **succumbing to the lure of the glamour of title and position,** relying on "who they are." "If they have credentials, if they are ordained by organized religion, if they are a cardinal or a pope, if it is the Bible, if Walter Cronkite said it, then it must be true." No. You know that you are trying to sell out to get approval, to be taken care of. Actually, you are not being taken care of. You are being taken.

3) This must degenerate into **sensationalism and personality cults.** People are no longer searching for the word of truth, but for escapes from themselves into other people's lives. It is reminiscent of aping as opposed to healthy emulation.

You may want to give more trust to sources that have, in the past quenched your thirst, but their word must resonate with something within, even if it is merely on the intellectual level at first. It makes sense even if I yet don't feel it. Or, depending on your character type; it may **feel** right even if it doesn't make sense. The choice must remain yours and must come from autonomy.

All Philosophies and Religions Are Found on the One and Only Path

The Path to God combines all the philosophies and religions of the world. Since it is found at the base of all philosophies and religions, this faith unifies all of them. It is a way to reinterpret them, give them new meaning, a new boost.

This principle doesn't confine itself to the realm of thinking and conceptualizing. The **practice** of the Path to God is the basic practice of all philosophies and religions. As we cleanse, we find a way to the genuine beneficial aspect of all of them. Look closely in our faith and you will find Plato, Socrates, Aristotle, Seneca, Aquinas, Augustine, Montaigne, Descartes, Pascal, Hume, Newton, Montesquieu, Voltaire, Rousseau, Hegel, Sartre, Husserl, as well as Buddha, Patanjali, the Christ, Mohammed, Moses, to name a few. Look for them. Communicate with them. They all are realities here and now. They all brought different interpretations of the same truths. Therefore, they all taught their own angle of communications. By discovering them all within your faith, you make it possible to communicate:

A) With all human beings;

B) With all parts of yourself.

****

Walk the Path to God. Find all philosophies and religions in it. You will be blessed and find at-onement with God.

Chapter 13

From One-Pointed Word to Drivel

The one-pointed word has the most power. It unites the individual and finds its mark without fail, as does a heat seeking missile.

It may be uttered or not. It will still have power, being one-pointed.

From there we descend into lesser realms:

1) **A harmful word:**

- Has power to the degree it is well-grounded in the self.
- This power can never equal—is always inferior to—the one-pointed word; only in the beneficial can the one-pointed word exist and have full power.

2) **A positive expression disguising a harmful one:**

- Of course it is weaker than a one-pointed expression.
- Even if it initially is stronger than the harmful one it covers up, it will diminish in strength, feeding the harmful below it.
- It is sometimes expressed in intensity to compensate for the underlying distortion.
- And sometimes it is expressed softly, pseudo-lovingly, or in a victimization mode. In any of these cases, it is gradually weakening.
- It is doomed to die, covering up what it tried to hide.

3) **Drivel:** The meaningless chatter that never ends:
- Fogs the unuttered word which has much more power and which remains unexpressed, whether it is beneficial or harmful.
- Fills inner emptiness.
- Escapes an inner problem or unresolved conflict.

All of these create. Your life is the sum total of their effect. If you seek and reveal all of them, if you become aware of all the levels on which there is expression and creativity, you will be on the road of unification and one-pointedness. Detect and reveal all of these levels, both in yourself and in others.

Connect the inner expressions with the outer realities of your life. Every event, state, object, person in your life, corresponds to a word you emanate, whether you utter it or not.

You could make a list of people in your life, from important to unimportant and realize that each one of them is there because of a word within yourself.

You could make a list of all that has ever happened to you and is still happening to you, and realize that it has all been brought to you by words within yourself.

Consider your physical body, your emotions, your addictions, your faults, your knowledge, your thinking and see how it all is the effect of words within yourself, words of power, uttered or not.

You need to clearly liberate the pronunciation and the enunciation of these words, shouting them from roof tops. You need to meditate on them, take responsibility for them. Then you need to decide which ones to keep and which ones to abandon. This is the road to unification. Use the truth as a yardstick, the magnetic, loving, good willed truth, ever present and permanently expressed by your God self.

As long as you persist in the emanation of words that contradict your God self, you will continue to create duality, self-propelled distortion, addictions, self-depreciation and self-idealization. And you will feel a human wreck, thrown to and fro in the currents of these self-contradicting falsehoods.

However, when you become aware of the creative power of your word, beneficial or harmful, you will want to exercise your choice to utter words of love and truth in all of yourself.

Cynicism And Nihilism

The deep conviction in a chaotic Universe without laws or justice, without order and without a creator is arrived at as follows:

1) I do not want to believe in the creative power of my word; it is too good to be true; I do not want to believe that I deserve such power; I may feel this consciously or unconsciously. It is a self-condemnation, debilitation, depreciation.

2) Therefore, I cannot believe that this power exists for any other individual, or for all of the Universe.

3) I deny the Law of Cause and Effect because I refuse to experience it within myself.

4) Therefore, the Universe is chaotic.

5) It is easier to accuse the Universe of chaos than to face the pain of rejecting myself and the power of my word.

6) At first, I feel an undefined pessimism; I find myself afraid without knowing why;

7) Insecurity develops; I feel disconnected from everything around me.

8) I feel disconnected from everything within me.

9) I must find a reason for all of this—because, by the way, causal connections heal, justice heals.

10) So, I make sense of what doesn't make sense by

believing that the Universe is chaotic at best, bad at worst. I find relief in believing that there is no God, that injustice rules, that I must be Machiavellian to succeed, that the sun may not rise tomorrow. I must destroy that which makes sense and heals in order to feel good and heal. That makes sense to me.

Actually, I am protecting myself from the pain of having condemned myself in the first place. Little do I know that this pain is very small compared to the pain I will create with a cynical nihilistic belief system.

All wrecking balls of self-destruction, all rampages of distorted self, all attempts at derailing the truth, love, healing, personal power and choice, all are based on this system. Study it. Look for Hume's wrecking ball in your own life. It is there, I assure you, in everyone of us.

The Evil of Palliating

Here is a good word to describe an oft-practiced evil. We use the denigration of the Universe as a palliative. It palliates the pain of self-contempt, of self-depreciation.

Palliate; verb to: (from the Latin *pallium*, a cloak) 1. to lessen the severity of without curing; 2. to make an offense appear less serious; excuse.

For example, misappropriation of funds is a palliative for theft; ignorance as a palliative for manipulation or for lying, etc.

You do it a lot. It is done even more around you. It actually colludes with the harmful which it tries to cloak, disguise.

Find your palliatives. Expose the harmful volition behind them. Then summoning your love of truth, find the right word and one-pointedly utter it.

Solace, a Much Better Practice

Solace, from the Latin *solacium*, is an easing of grief and loneliness; the verb to solace means to comfort and console. There is not cloak here, and therefore, no dagger. I can find solace for my pain with a friend, a mate or a teacher. I can be consoled and comforted only when I am truthful. I cannot be solaced for my palliatives because I have already dishonestly protected myself.

Find the real pain, the "good pain," the pain of self-rejection, self-denial, self-contempt. Then find solace in a friend's consolation, or a mate's tenderness, or a teacher's explanation or understanding.

"I Have No Say in This; I Have No Power"

On the contrary. **You** are saying this. You are saying what is happening. It is your word. It is not just that you have a say **in it. You are saying it.** Your saying it creates it, has the power to do so.

What you say goes, all the time. Believe it. You **are** having it your way, now. Only you don't want to know this. So, you complain. But you are still saying it, albeit silently!

Again, find out your say, expose it to your consciousness, and change it to your heart's content.

Proof of the Existence of Contrary Words

This proof is in the manifestation of anything consciously unwanted in your life. No matter how many affirmations, no matter how much you brainwash yourself, as long as unwanted manifestations exist for you, know that you are unconsciously speaking them, saying them.

If you confine yourself to affirmations, you are doomed to create ever increasing harmful life situations.

You are doing it. Yes. Find it and expose it. Feel the pain of it. Share it, thus healing yourself and others. **Any** situation in which ecstasy, bliss, serenity doesn't exist, must be the result of your say within. That's how wonderful the Universe really is!

****

Restore your faith in yourself by becoming conscious of your immense power to create. No self-love is possible without it. It comes with a price tag: the experience of pain for having harmfully created.

Pay the price of admittance into the world of power; benign, loving, truthful, joyous, blissful, blessed power; the power of God.

Be protected that way. Find solace in God.

Chapter 14
Giving Fuses With Receiving

Quotes from the Bible:
* *15 Moreover, as you Philippians know, in the early days of your acquaintance with the gospel, when I set out from Macedonia, not one church shared with me in the matter of **giving and receiving**, except you only;*
17 Not that I am looking for a gift, but I am looking for what may be credited to your account.
19 And my God will meet all your needs according to his glorious riches in Christ Jesus.
—Philippians 4

* *Give, and it will be given to you. A good measure, pressed down, shaken together and running over, will be poured into your lap. For with the measure you use, it will be measured to you.*
—Luke 6:38

Giving is at-one with receiving. They both are one and the same principle. Previous sermons have described this in greater detail. You can find proof of this when you examine how you feel in times when you defame yourself, when you utter or think or feel self-depreciating words. In that state, you firmly believe that happiness consists in being loved, being given to, not in loving and giving. Receiving and giving have been disconnected.

On the contrary, when you speak the one-pointed word, you experience as much facility in giving as you do in receiving. You can give and take at the same time. Being unified with the Cosmic Life Force, you are at-one with the ebb and flow of its movements. Both active and receptive, give and take are one. You are nourished by both. You experience grace in both. You tolerate both at the same time.

In a further test, ask yourself "if all of this love were given to me, could I take it in the state wherein I defame myself?" In that state, you cannot possibly be receptive to the very love that you say you need in order to feel better about yourself:

1) If it were given to you, you wouldn't be able to take it graciously; you wouldn't feel deserving of it for the very simple reason that self-defamation creates guilt; and guilt can only tolerate punishment, not love or pleasure, which it wards off.

2) Furthermore, you would be prone to push away, ward off, situations in which love would be given to you; even if it actually is there happening, you wouldn't recognize it as such; you would mistrust it and misinterpret it.

In the state of one-pointedness in which your word towards yourself is total acceptance, you attract love and appreciation without even seeking it. You also enjoy it to the fullest, taking full benefit from it without it interfering with your generous and on-going giving.

Can you take it? Are you big enough? Have you honestly cleansed yourself of self-defamation? Only if you do will you feel deserving of it and it will unquestioningly be yours.

****

What about giving? You cannot possibly give in the state of self-defamation because:

1) By defaming yourself, you are saying "I don't have it to give;" so how can you give?

2) Gi ving is pleasurable. If you defame yourself, your guilt for doing so will prevent you from the enjoyment of giving.

Therefore, speaking the word of self-love, feeling worthy, opens you to both giving and receiving.

Suppose you were to receive love when you crave it so intensely, i.e., in the midst of your self-defamation. As you receive this love, instead of healing you out of the state of self-defamation, it merely intensifies the pain of your self-rejection. "If I defame myself and you love me, it will intensify my self-hatred; the more love you give me, the more I will feel undeserving and hate myself."

Somewhere you know this. You sense in your state of self-defamation, that receiving love will be painful. So, you reject it with as much force as you desire it.

In Marcel Pagnol's *Manon De La Source,* a sequel to *Jean De Florette,* old man Soubeyran finds out that he actually was responsible for his son's death. All his life he had hated a young hunchback, precipitating the conditions of his death, only to find out that he actually was his son. His immense pain deeply drove him to wanting to die. He goes to his home announcing that he wasn't going to make it through the night. While doing this and requesting a priest for last rites, he talks about the fact that even the beauty of the trees was painful for him to take. In the midst of this great guilt, beauty became painful for him.

Hence:

1) Love is very pleasurable.

2) Therefore, in order to be able to give it, I must have developed the capacity to experience that pleasure which is a

function of having cleared myself of guilt—the guilt of self-defamation being one of them.

3) Furthermore, I will not be able to receive love if I defame myself, as we have seen.

4) But I also will not feel deserving of feeling love if I don't give it; and in the state of self-defamation, I do not want to give love, I only want to receive it.

So, unless I cleanse myself of self-defamation and of distortion, I will neither be able to love nor to be loved, which is death.

Therefore, cleansing is vital. Without it, no life is possible.

****

Let there no longer be any statements as follows:
- "I am unable to love and to give because I was not loved and not given to."
- "I must first be loved and be given to in order to want to love and to give."

****

As you can see, this exposes the dishonesty, the impotency and the capacity for unhappiness in the following doctrines:

1) Psychotherapy which blames others and outer circumstances for the conditions of an individual, encouraging and idealizing victimization.

2) Organized religion which presents salvation as only available through a Messiah who takes your sins away from you, and without effort on your part, restores your capacity to love and to be loved; you can see now how this would merely increase and intensify the pain of self-depreciation.

3) The wrong positive thinking which superimposes the conceited self-love of the deified self over self-defamation,

making the latter thrive and grow.

False One-Pointedness

An amazing number of people are stuck in a state of being incapable of giving and receiving. They superimpose this sorry state with forced giving—the type that implies that you owe them—and false receiving—the type that pumps itself through boasting, i.e., forced self-love. They have an insatiable thirst for praise in which they continuously indulge by aggrandizing anything that they can about themselves.

Catch yourself doing this. You do it all of the time. If you are not aware of it, your teacher certainly is and is thoroughly bored by it. If you don't have a teacher, get one and bore him so that he can honestly tell you how you do this. You will then finally come face to face with your false one-pointedness. You will also have the opportunity to finally liberate your self-defamation. You need this honest mirror. You need the thorough introspection that this faith offers you. You need a group of friends also to mirror this. Most of all, you need a teacher.

Most self-improvement activities offered in the yuppy world serve merely to pump up the false one-pointedness, i.e., the false life. As you know, you will reach the point where, consciously or unconsciously, you will want to destroy that false life and you will successfully do it.

Why are all self-improvement activities out there promoting the false life and how can I unilaterally make such a statement? Both questions can be answered very simply: no self-improvement activity out there involves cleansing. Show me one that does and that does not emanate from the teachings given here, and I will gladly change my statement. I will happily make contact with these people and kiss them lovingly. I will joyously cooperate with them in which ever way that I can.

One-Pointedness, the Only Climate
for Loving and Being Loved

As you dissolve the harmful word spoken towards yourself and towards what is outside of yourself, you cultivate one-pointedness as we have seen earlier in this series. This means that you are capable of expressing love with all of yourself. It also means that you feel deserving of receiving as much love as you can possibly tolerate. Only with the oneness of your word can this state be achieved. Here, not only is your word at-one and one-pointed, but so is loving and being love, giving and receiving. You are bathing in the luxury of the Universe and you are also entirely part of it, contributing to it.

This luxurious and abundant state is also impeccably precise, incisively sharp and harmoniously creative. It has ultimate discipline, total faith. It is at the same time capable of the ultimate pleasure and devoid of self-indulgence. It is as willing to experience pleasure as it is to experience pain, knowing that all pain is temporary and on its way to become pleasure.

Entrance to Our Faith
Giving and Taking the Word of God

Many people come to our Church only to be startled by the stark nakedness of the truth by the incisiveness of its word. Many literally **can't take it.** This is because they **don't give of themselves to it.** Those who can take it, give of themselves to it by taking it. Their open-mindedness and their willingness to give it a try is indeed a giving. It is a gift to us, for them to take what we have to offer of spiritual food.

This is true as long as it is done as a giving of oneself to this faith by applying its laws to one's life. However, many do not practice this type of taking. Their taking is dishonest.

Here, we encounter two types:

A) **Those who use their wealth to escape this spiritual training by buying it.** They steal the material, not applying it to their lives, but trying to take its power, dilute it and make it the servant of the false life and the false word. Notoriously, there was a rich woman who was introduced to this Church by a friend. She wanted our teachings because she recognized their great strength and beauty. However, she did not want to submit herself to the spiritual training as we practice it. She wanted her psychotherapist to read the books that I wrote and give psychotherapy in accordance to these teachings.

Now, we knew at the time that this was impossible. Still, there was such wanton dishonesty in this that I refused to sell her the books. This once again confirms how difficult it is for a rich person to give of himself or herself to this faith by taking from it. The misuse of their wealth makes them want to control these teachings by buying it, as they have controlled with their money, love, friendship, sex and all other contacts in their life. The pain that is experienced by these people is unimaginable. Indeed, all of this merely confirms their word of self-loathing. They continuously defame themselves by putting their value beneath their money's.

B) **Those who use their knowledge or position to escape this spiritual training by derailing it.** Others come here with conceit. They know better, having graduated from psychology or religious schools. They are hostile to this material which revolutionizes all they have learned. They use their knowledge against these teachings. They are not ready for this. Only if they question what they know and adopt an attitude of humility will they make themselves ready. To them we say, "Come with honest questions; we will detect and expose the dishonest ones. And remember: **we** teach and **you** learn here, not the other way round."

The more you sincerely enter this faith, the more you give

to it by taking big helpings of its food and yielding yourself to its nourishment. Those who do so can easily be distinguished by their expressions of gratitude for having found this. They exhibit a clear love for this, thus taking to it easily.

The price of entrance to this faith consists in leaving at the door your excess baggage. You must be willing to rethink and to rebuild. Don't worry, you won't lose any truth gained in the past. This will rediscover it for you and will renew it for you. Only you must let go and rethink everything.

So, to those who are new, to those who receive this material through the medium of television, or tapes, we say, "By all means, take it, it's for you. Take what you want and let go of the rest. Only, have an open mind to what you don't take."

By giving you this, we get a great deal. It is very much a pleasure to give to you under these honest circumstances.

So, here again, our giving and your receiving are one. Our giving is receiving and your receiving is a giving. In return, having received and benefitted by this spiritual food of ours, you will want to give it to others, thus becoming, yourself, a center and a source of light.

What Does it Take to Utter the Word of God?

1) It takes **strength and courage as well as faith and commitment.** Why is this a requirement? Because you still don't believe that the words—uttered or unuttered—create. You may know what the right word is, but since you do not realize the power of creation behind it, you may not be convinced about uttering it. Thus, you still utter the words of the false life, the false words of approval seeking. The palliatives.

Have faith. Commit yourself to only uttering the word of God. With faith, you will give it a try. Giving it a try, you will experientially demonstrate to yourself over and over again that it pays. However, you must still start with an act of faith, with an act of commitment.

2) Having uttered the false word for so long, having lived the false life, you have created commensurate obstructions which have undermined your faith in the word of God as well as the benefits available if you pronounce it. Again, courage is needed to utter God's truth in spite of your self-created obstructions. Even if you do not feel the benefits, even if you are still blinded by the false life, decide with your outer will to use the word of God and practice it. Decide to do the right thing and say the right words. You know what they are. Just do it. It will pierce through the walls of deadness you have created with your false words and your false life.

Once this is done, the Cosmic Life Force will find a way of flowing through you, energizing and increasing your consciousness. When you fray this passage, you make room for divine forces that are far greater than you. They will speak through you and you will identify with them. Their word will be your word. This is true one-pointedness in your speech.

****

Look at this place. It has never had more than 25 members. Yet, we are all amazed at its solidity, its strength, its ability to answer so many questions and solve so many problems! It is not perfect. However, by the continuous cultivation of cleansing of itself and with its members, the right word has prevailed over the wrong and has created solidity, abundance and expansion. We did not think that it was going to happen that way. We bow in humility and in awe to those great forces of creation that we have unleashed that have guided us in every step we have taken, that have protected us and that will carry us where we need to go. Obviously, it has been right to do what we have done. We pray to continue to do so and let the rest to God.

Chapter 15
Baptism by The Word

Cleansing by water was provided for humanity by the flood. The battle between the Forces of Light and the forces of darkness resulted in the ancient flood, which engulfed and ended the Atlantean civilization.

Cleansing by fire was provided by the combination of the two world wars of the twentieth century. As pointed out by the Tibetan, the great war lasted from 1914 to 1945 in a success—albeit partial from the Forces of Light.

Cleansing of and by the word, the one-pointed word is the new way. It destroyed the evil empire in the 1980's. It will destroy other evil empires that stand in the way of truth, of caring, of love and decency, no matter how big and established they appear to be. It combines the burning of fire and the cleansing of water into consciousness.

Baptism can, therefore, be effected through fire, water, or the word since it is in itself a practice which signifies cleansing.

When you use the one-pointed word, you baptize. You burn the distortion and you also wash it out, flood it with infinite goodness. Use the fire of your word to burn your way into your distortion and the distortion of others.

When using sharp and appropriate words, you cut into the distortion with truth, love and good will. Therefore, while burning evil through clearly denouncing it, you simultaneously enhance your goodness as well as the Universal Goodness.

For instance, meditate on the qualities required to call a coward a coward, a liar a liar, cheating, cheating, something inferior, inferior, a spade a spade. It takes courage, honesty, dignity, truthfulness, humility:

- It takes courage to reveal my cowardice and others'.
- It takes honesty to reveal my cheating and stealing, and to denounce others'.
- It takes dignity to reveal and confront inferiority.
- It takes humility to expose conceit in myself and in others.
- Exposing a lie makes me more truthful.
- Confronting cowardice makes me more courageous.
- Revealing dishonesty makes me more honest.
- Facing fear makes me courageous.

This is true about my lies, cowardice, dishonesty, fear, or about somebody else's. The facing of evil enhances the corresponding goodness in me.

By calling evil by its correct and precise name, I use the power of my word, the fire of my word, to cleanse, baptize, burn and flood. I cleanse with baptism, with faith in God.

Euphemistic Commitment

Sometimes, commitment to a relationship is made to escape an inferiority, a lack in the self. For instance, an inferiority in a career can result in taking refuge in a subsidizing marriage. The person will then make himself believe that he is in love, when he is not. Thus, he will make himself fall in love and marry, only to pay the price later in life for this marred integrity. We also have seen the reverse: buying a mate because of a deficiency in the romantic and sexual area.

But there are other possible scenarios for this rush to

commitment:

1) If I feel sexually inferior or immature or inexperienced, I will compensate by making myself fall madly in love. Also, knowing that loving is magnetic, I will overemphasize loving and committing in order to cover up for my sexual insecurity. I will take refuge in marriage.

2) If I feel emotionally inferior, I will use my overdeveloped sexuality to attract a suitable mate. Once this is accomplished, I will commit quickly and prematurely in order to protect myself from:

A) Having to learn how to love and open my heart; once married, committed, I erroneously believe that I no longer have to do it.

B) My sexual promiscuity; closing my loving heart resulted in an over energized sexuality with all of its dangerous consequences; so I retreat into the apparent safety of a commitment.

****

Do not be glamoured by false and premature commitment. It can be engaged in for the sake of self-protection and for covering up or compensating for a deficiency. Beware of sanctifying commitments for the sake of approval. Do not make your weddings into shows; into your opportunity to draw attention and approval to yourself.

All of this is marred integrity. It is a recipe for suffering, tearing and divorce which must happen later.

Cultivate total honesty with yourself and with your possible mate. Rather than taking refuge in a relationship, make it a way to filling the gaps, enhancing and improving yourself. If you are in a committed relationship, turn your commitment into a challenging vehicle for growth. It is supposed to be that. Using it as a refuge won't work. Whether you like it or not, you will have to deal with those lacks, even more so inside a relationship than outside of it.

Also, don't underestimate or denigrate exploration and learning prior to commitment. It is a necessary step, which, if skipped will create distortion.

Now, let's look at this distortion in Bible-based Christianity. From Paul:

- 1 *Now concerning the things whereof ye wrote unto me: It is good for a man not to touch a woman.*
- 2 *Nevertheless, to avoid fornication, let every man have his own wife, and let every woman have her own husband.*
  —I Corinthians 7

There, graphically, is marred integrity, false commitment, taking premature refuge in marriage, advocated by what those who call themselves Christians call the Word of God.

Need I say more?

Enter marriage with a full eye, having experienced life, experimented with your sexuality and well-anchored in an experienced heart. Then, and then only, can mutual love be experienced and can marriage be the way to God.

Part IV

Being and Pretense—Motivation

Chapter 16
General Principles

To be or not to be, that is the question. Either you are or you are not. If and when **you are,** you have a strong sense of yourself, you speak the one-pointed word, you do what you do for its own sake. Your worth is placed in the reality of existence, of nature.

Anything less than that, i.e., pretending to be, is a denial of being, and therefore:

A) A compensation for deficiency

B) An increasing of that same deficiency which must result in self-annihilation, i.e., **nothingness.**

Most of humanity is in a state of pretending, living the false life. Let's examine this closely.

Pretending Creates The Fall
I don't like or value myself, so I split myself in two:

1) My real self, my being, my needs, task, nature, which I repress, about which I feel shame.

2) My pretended self, that which I want to be, i.e., somebody else, artificial, made up, an exaggeration and an idealization of some aspects of myself which I favour.

As I emphasize my pretense, I devalue my real self, feeling worse and worse about it. Since the pretense is by definition false, it cannot bring me any true value. This makes me feel worse about myself. Now I try harder to be somebody else, and descend further into unworthiness and unhappiness.

That's how we fell, gradually creating this dualistic state. Thus, we create ...*the whips and scorns of time. The oppressor's wrong. The proud man's contumely. The pangs of despis'd love, the law's delay. The insolence of office...*[1] What attracts this to us is the underlying self-loathing, which is augmented by the pretense. We have thoroughly repressed our being and we have demeaned it to the point where:

A) It must attract commensurate distortion to justify itself.

B) It must attract punishment for the guilt created by rejecting our being.

Therefore, every unit of energy invested in pretense results in commensurate devaluation of your real sense of self. This is the fall. It has been going on and is still going on, despite the Plan of Salvation.

Duality Between Being And Pretense;
Immanuel Kant's Practical Imperative

Kant invites us to treat every person for his own sake. By extension, do everything for its own sake and for nobody else's, nor for anything else. This is the key to developing true value, genuine self-worth. True values enhance your true self. Pretense diminishes your value. Pretense values do too even though they seem not to.

Look for the areas of your life in which you cultivate your being as opposed to the ones where you cultivate your pretenses, having given up on yourself.

Anything thought, felt or done for its own sake will cultivate your sense of being, your sense of self.

Is this also true of distortions? Yes. This is continuously

---

[1] From William Shakespeare's *Hamlet.*

demonstrated in your spiritual training. Whenever a distortion is thought, felt, experienced for its own sake, it explodes. This, as we have seen elsewhere, gives you the chance to diffuse it of the goodness, power and intelligence invested in it. Then you can redirect these energies where they belong.

So, as you focus on the false self, you dissolve it and liberate the trapped real self in a particular area. Ultimately your whole being will be free and anchored in the one-pointed word, real values.

This is our faith, our way of cleansing and transformation.

Pretense Has its Center of Gravity Outside of Yourself

The point of pretense is to impress others. It is their reaction that counts, nothing else. The truth, love, good will do not really count. The **pretense** of truth, love and good will do. In pretense, you speak, think, believe and train yourself to even **feel** what **you are expected to feel, think, believe,** not what you actually feel, think or believe.

Even if what you are expected to be happens to correspond to who you really are, the volition to pretend will falsify you and dualize you. You would still not be thinking, feeling or willing for their own sake, but for the sake of approval. "What will they say, think or feel?"

Basically the pretense is a lie, a marring of your integrity. Yet, as obvious as it can sometimes be, the pretense goes deep, using an amazing quantity of energy and skill to conceal its false nature and pretend to be real.

You have trained yourself for incarnations to prop up the pretense. You are a master at your own pretense. You are the best. Therefore, unless you actively cooperate at denouncing and renouncing it, no one can, will or should help you. This includes all messiahs ever conceived by God. It must be your choice to do so, even if the pretense is detected and denounced by somebody else. You alone can and must be willing to remove it. **Then,** and only then, will you and should you get help.

Find out the extent to which you fear disapproval, rejection. You'll be amazed. You are anxious about it, as if you had continuous stage fright.

All of this nervousness translates into toxins that destroy you physically, emotionally and mentally. Since, by now, most of your pretense is unconscious, you literally have no idea of the damage that is constantly being done.

****

Being is centered within yourself. You do things for their own sake, for the good of the cause, for God. You are centered on the Good, the Beautiful and the True, as the Tibetan says.

Maslow talks about the high "being" ethics of the self-actualized person. There will be more on this later. No one needs to know what you do, or feel, or think. You are doing it for yourself, and for God. This doesn't mean that you must hide. It simply means that you are doing this for yourself. If it is appropriate, you would share it.

In being, you devote yourself 100% no matter how big or small the task is. That's what Seneca meant when he said that in virtue, there is no difference between an important or unimportant, big or small matter. All are treated equally.

In that state of being, you are constantly enriching yourself. Since giving is at-one with receiving, you receive what you give and give what you receive, always totally and openly.

Communications, Being And Pretense
A) Their perception of and their reactions to you.

When your center of gravity is your innermost self, you cannot be hurt. Indeed, suppose that you are in the opposite state, the pretense state of values. Since everything is focused on pleasing others, the slightest objection or displeasure on their part will be devastating to you. Since you have placed your value in their approval or disapproval of you, it feels as if your entire existence is depending on the slightest disapproval coming from them.

In this pretense, you will, therefore, fiercely defend against criticism, be it merely expressed in a mild suggestion. So, again you will have split yourself:

1) You seek approval by desperately trying to become what you think they want.

2) You are impermeable to any suggestion or criticism, however small, big, unimportant or not; so you defend, become paranoid and alienate precisely those whose approval you so desperately seek.

So, you will eventually lose the approval of those to whom you sell out. You are labouring against yourself.

Now think. If, by investing who you are in a pretense, you will reap disapproval anyway, you will have nothing left. If they disapprove of you after you have invested yourself in them, then there will be no reason for you to exist.

By contrast, in the state of being:

1) You may reap disapproval and rejection, and it will make you temporarily sad, but being anchored in your truth, that's the maximum pain you will incur. It cannot devastate you in your foundations. It can only do that if you have your roots into getting their approval.

2) You may even reap personal hatred of the most virulent kind. With your being values, you may shake **their** pretense, their foundations. Yet their attack will not hurt you. It can

only cleanse you, as we have seen in the communications series of sermons.

3) And, last, but not least, you will get the appreciation and respect of those few who count and are counted. Not that it even matters to you. But it helps—albeit a little.

Build within yourself an ethical being in which you are totally honest, totally sincere, doing for the sake of the task only. The result will be a deep sense of security, serenity and blessedness, a confidence that, in your utter nakedness, you are protected.

B) **Your perception of and reaction to them.** Pretense doesn't just blind them. It blinds you, too. You may believe that when you put on the disguise of pretense, you are just fooling them into approving of you. No. You fool yourself, too. You, too, get to believe that you are your pretense, what they expect of you.

You may have sold them a bill of goods but you too bought it. In fact, you bought it more than they did, since their disapproval affects you more than it does them.

But there is more. Blinded by your own pretense:

- You are blind about them, too, a) to their distortions, thus becoming victimized by them, and b) to their good, thus never appreciating it.
- You may not be entirely blind; just slightly distorted. Thus, you magnify one aspect and diminish another, warping reality and making hurtful mistakes.
- You are never sure of your convictions since you have adopted somebody else's. Thus, whether on small or big matters, you cannot take a stand, assert yourself, claim what's yours.
- You misperceive yourself, not being sure of what are your strengths and liabilities.
- You lose arguments, battles, competitions because you

don't know if you or others are in the right.

- So, you shuffle, wing it, try to bluff, lie or glide through life, euphemizing this as flexibility and lightness.
- But, inside, you are eroding yourself.
- You don't know what you want; you don't even know what **they** want of you, after a while.
- You don't want to know what you want because it may clash with what you are supposed to want. So, you force yourself to believe that you want what you don't really want.

Who Are You?

You will never know who you are until you stop pretending. Even if it temporarily means emptiness. Your real self must come in eventually with its real values of being. The deficiency is what creates loss of identity. Deficiency itself is, as we have seen, augmented by pretense.

When you are anchored in being, you know who you are, you know where you are going. Your volitionality and your motivation must eventually be cleansed. What does this mean? Your will is perpetually rejuvenated because it is at-one with the Will of God.

Chapter 17
Lower Needs

All needs are refractions of the need for at-onement with God, the Absolute. Having fallen, our need fell, refracting into myriad directions on the three-dimensional, relative plane. It created all the other needs, the more mundane ones.

Last week, we saw that pretense created the fall in removing value from being and investing it in others, i.e., denying the self and getting approval. The continuous and increased self-devaluation degenerated us into a primitive state.

The greater the pretense, the greater the greed and the egocentricity. It is an interesting contradiction to realize that the more I remove value from myself by seeking approval, the greedier I become for lower materialistic things. The more I focus on the value of appearance, the less I value my being and the more I crave for lower, decelerated aspects of creation.

Therefore, whenever you find yourself craving in a glamourous way for a car or for the shape of a body or for a million dollars, whenever you experience your life in a "me versus others" way, you are actively falling, devaluing yourself, disconnecting from God.

Thus, humanity fell. Thus, people fall. They create lack within, and therefore, without. Their intelligence drops, so does their awareness, perception, etc. They create poverty and primitive life conditions. **Greed creates poverty; then and only then does poverty create more greed.**

Lower Needs Become Genuine Needs

In this state, the more basic needs take preponderance over the higher ones. Thus, it becomes more important to satisfy food and shelter needs before one can satisfy the need for God. **Having made the material world into our God, we have condemned ourselves to worshiping it.** Gandhi understood this when he said, "Even God cannot talk to a hungry man except in terms of bread." Maslow understood this, too. According to him, basic needs must be satisfied **before** a person raises himself to a higher level of needs.

We can, therefore, conclude:

1) Appearance and pretense values lead to greed for the material which leads to inner and outer poverty, which leads to primary needs becoming Genuine Needs.

2) This means that you must drink the cup of karma to the fullest. Indeed, you must first satisfy your primary needs if you are at that level, **before you can raise yourself gradually to the higher needs.** Tell this to the swamis who wonder around with a bowl in their hands. In that state of discomfort how can they possibly meditate? **One needs a certain amount of luxury in order to cultivate spirituality.** Granted, in the old age, before Aquarius, it was necessary to remove oneself from three-dimensional reality.

This has brought to humanity the unfortunate distortion of idealizing and glamourizing poverty. Both Buddha with his middle path and Christ with His sayings have denounced this simplistic philosophy of life. When Magdalen anoints the Christ's feet with an ointment worth a year's wages, the

disciples angrily admonish her. However, the Christ protects
her and defends her motives as being valid. And what about
the rich getting richer and the poor poorer?

This leads us to:

Maslow's Hierarchy of Needs in a Spiritual Context

Maslow was a brilliant American psychologist who was
commissioned to work on a theory of motivation. He
concluded, having thought about it, that motivation must be
tied in to needs, which, of course, for us, involves the
instincts.

In his research, he found that needs can be classified into
the following levels, from lower to higher.

1) Need for food and shelter
2) Need for safety and security
3) Social needs
4) Ego needs
5) Needs of the self-actualized person

He named the first three needs **deficiency needs,** calling
them D needs for short. The last two he named **being needs,**
calling them B needs for short.

The basic difference between B and D needs, he said, is
that B is self-motivated and D needs to be motivated from the
outside. This, of course, brings back all that we have learned
about being and pretense, although the analogy does not hold
too far. Indeed, D needs are not always a pretense, and B
needs are not always real and ethical. But, we will study this
in greater detail later.

For the time being, let's continue studying Maslow and his
system.

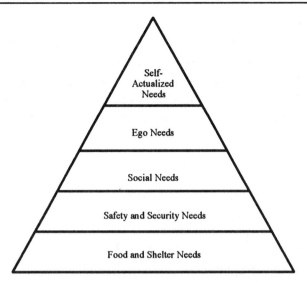

According to Maslow, the hierarchy of needs is based on the following principles:

1) There is a reason behind all human behaviour. Great! We certainly agree with that.

2) All human beings attempt to satisfy these five needs. This also is true since the self-actualized personality is the only one who can be characterized as being anchored in his own being.

3) These needs are hierarchical, from lower to higher.

4) When a person satisfies one level, he naturally rises to the next.

5) The degree of intensity of the desire to satisfy those needs is inversely proportional to their hierarchical rank. For example, the intensity for which I pursue my desire for food is greater than my desire for safety and security in intensity.

6) A person can reach a higher level of needs and fall back to lower levels under different circumstances.

7) The higher the need the more pleasure and happiness are experienced. Therefore, once someone has reached a

higher level of needs, he will always want to go back to it. **This of course reminds us of what we believe—that we remember when we were in the highest possible state of at-onement with God; that we always will want to get back to that; that nothing will ever satisfy us completely except the recovery of that state.** Let's remember that we have fallen and that we are trying to make it back.

****

Let's now take them one by one starting from the bottom.

1) **Physical Needs:** Primarily for air and food; secondarily for shelter, warmth and sleep.

Look at your life. You spend 40-50% of your time satisfying your physical needs. Yet, you are not motivated by them. Your level of needs is definitely higher than physical. In order to find people who are stuck in physical needs and are motivated by them, one has to go to a third world country. No one in this country is hungry, no matter what the liberals say.

However, to the truly hungry, God is an abstraction (see Gandhi's saying above). It would also be equally absurd to ask him what kind of car he would like to drive or which country club he would like to belong to.

There is a specific philosophy of life that applies to a hungry person. Utopia for him is having plenty of food. It is interesting here to remember that in Islam paradise is depicted as a lush green place with plenty of waterfalls and women constantly serving ice cold drinks. Of course, as you know, Islam was born in the Saudi Arabian desert.

What do we learn from this? Aside from the fact that this is a Genuine Need, albeit material, we see that **the pursuit of a Genuine Need always means the filling of a real gap. Religion, at that level, consists in glamourizing the filling of that gap.**

"If only I have food, I will desire nothing more for the rest of my life," seems to be the philosophy of people on this level of needs. Loftier pursuits really don't count, such as freedom, love, respect, etc.

One can say that man lives by bread alone . . . when there is no bread!

As we said before, this state is almost non-existent for us. We have forgotten the importance of this state. Yet, we are still involved in it to a considerable extent:

A) In big cities they talk about the rat race. Indeed, they do look like rats rushing into the subway tunnels or into traffic jams, always in a hurry, always fluctuating between anger/ frustration and numbness/boredom.

I was involved in the rat race. When you are in it you are not aware of it. Returning from vacations I would always be stunned by it and by the fact that I no longer notice it when I am part of it. An invisible cloak of greed envelops these people as they over pursue this level of needs. They are not motivated. They are slaves. Comparing them to rats is amazingly accurate. Indeed, what possible motivation can rats have other than becoming fat? No code of ethics binds them. There is no beauty nor decency about them.

B) When we say "I am hungry," we don't really mean it. Hunger is a far deeper state than we ever allow ourselves to experience. It is a state understood and experienced in the third world. Our hunger has been heightened to aesthetics. We no longer eat because we need to. We largely eat because it is time to, because it is fashionable to, or because we are addicted to it or to some sort of food. It reminds me of a line in Moliere's, "The Miser": *One must eat to live and not live to eat.*

Therefore, this Genuine Need has been pursued to such an extreme that it has become false. The truly hungry person is in a state of being, even thought he has arrived there through falling. The greedy yuppy is in a state of pretense. He is guaranteeing his future poverty.

How do you deal with a person who is really hungry? You give him food, or you invite him to places where he can get it for free. There are tons of them.

How do you deal with the person who is falsely hungry? You confront them. You attack and destroy their character. How do you deal with a rat?

Now, if I am satisfied in terms of food, I will raise my desire one notch higher, to

2) **Safety and Security Needs:** Here I am interested in conquering my insecurity. My whole organism is focused towards this. My entire philosophy of life is directed at it.

Let's think of some insecure entities. For example, the head of a multi-billion dollar concern can feel insecure if he is under attack from the government for dishonesty or racketeering or monopolizing the market. He will exhibit very specific behavioural patterns. The same can be said about the legal and medical professions as entities. They both are under sharp attack for their outrageous practices. Thus, doctors and lawyers will also exhibit those behavioural patterns. When you are insecure, you too exhibit particular behavioural patterns.

What are those behavioural patterns?

1) Avoiding to make decisions.

2) Hedging behind ceremonials; "how was it done in the past?"

3) Superstitious.

4) Over concern with order and discipline; compulsively neat and restrictive.

5) Fear of the unexpected which they avoid at all costs.

6) Convinced that the Universe is unjust, and therefore, obsessed with demands of being treated fairly, of being a fair shake.

7) Tries to go unnoticed; would rather screw up than ask questions.

8) Offensive in their defense, compensating for fear.

9) Amazingly quick at blaming others and enlisting in crusades.

10) Over reliance on the past, often referring to it as being a much better time than now.

11) Escape into a world of their own.

12) Cultivate unreasonably long silences.

How to Deal with a Person on the Safety And Security Level of Needs

- You reassure by demonstrating justice.
- You ground them in their beneficial aspects.
- You point out the problem at hand, making sure that you have separated them from that problem and that you and they are on the same side of resolving it.
- You finally deal with the problem.

But you also help them take responsibility for their own injustice, their own outrages, which are the real authors of their anxieties and insecurities. You invite them to sacrifice what has been dishonestly obtained, what has been used for harmful purposes, pointing out that a) the loss will be temporary and b) that which needs to be sacrificed will be destroyed anyway.

Additional Reflections and Connection with Genuine and Affected Needs

Maslow's connecting motivation to needs must lead us to connect it to genuine or affected needs.

1) Any motivation connected to a Genuine Need, which emanates from the genuine self, will have permanency, will perpetuate and regenerate itself.

2) Any motivation connected to a affected need which emanates from the affected self—the deified self, for instance, or the distorted self—will be temporary, short-lived, subject to burnout.

3) A motivation will acquire the features of its cause. If it is caused by a Genuine Need, it will be a light, flowing motivation, devoid of intensity, emanating confidence and lightness.

If it is caused by a deified self, it will be heavy and overbearing, even under the pretense of being good. If it is caused by the distorted self, it will be forceful and demanding, ruthless and cruel.

4) Burnout of a motivation, therefore, is an indication of a affected need at its root. One must find it and deal with it. Sometimes, the result is a dissolution of the motivation, and a resulting apathy. This is necessary in as much as the motivational impetus was created by falsehood, and therefore, was affected. It would have died anyway. It was doomed from the start. It was creating harmfulness and unhappiness.

Sometimes we can be healthily motivated by a Genuine Need, then, we make the need to become a demand. The motivation first intensifies and rigidifies, appearing to increase, then peters out and collapses into deflation and despair.

We must learn how to differentiate between all of these currents and guide our growth accordingly.

****

Hopefully, you have recognized yourself. With care, look at the different parts of yourself and detect at which level of need they happen to be stuck. Educate them and satisfy them of that level. They will organically raise themselves up the latter, raising you with them.

Next week we will look at the other levels of needs in Maslow's hierarchy. For now, see in it one more demonstration that ethics rule the Universe and the whole point of life is the pursuit of happiness. Thanks be to God.

Chapter 18
Belonging

We continue with Maslow's hierarchy of needs and deal with the next level, namely

3) **Social Needs:** This level is best characterized by an expression coined by Michael Ignatieff: *The McDonaldization of emotions.* Just as the other two levels, there is a legitimate point to this one as well. We all need a certain amount of recognition, particularly in the early years of our life.

We all need to **belong.** We belong to families, social clubs where we get support, approval, acceptance. We need friends. We need a mate. We need affectionate relationships. **This is perhaps the most frustrated of all needs in our society.**

Trouble starts when this need disconnects us from ourselves because it becomes too intense. Indeed, we stop being who we are and start being who they think we should be, which creates all of the damage that we have thoroughly discussed in part III of this series. Utopia on this level is to have everybody love us and approve of us. We sacrifice everything for that purpose.

We learn from Maslow three ways to recognize a person whose needs are arrested at this level:

A) **When someone asks for approval concerning something they know is right,** they belong in the social level of needs. They do this to get a sense of belonging, of being part of the team. It would be a good idea to indeed give them the approval that they seek. However, if they don't receive that approval, they

B) **Complain;** they will find cases for which they will whine in order to be the center of attention. If they do not get satisfaction, they will sink to the next typical manifestation of this level of needs which is

C) **Screwing up in a pattern form;** these are the uncharacteristic mistakes that people make in order to get attention. You find yourself saying to them, "This is not like you."

How do you deal with this? The problem is that, once you see this pattern occurring, it means that you already haven't made this person feel that they are part of the team, that they are acceptable as a human being. So, responding to these harmful manifestations is not enough. The problem has to be anticipated and dealt with **before** it manifests. This person needs to be occasionally taken to lunch, invited to parties, be regularly asked about the state of his family, etc.

If a person is satisfied on these levels, and still hasn't gone to the next higher level of needs, he will exhibit the following behaviour:

- He will be a good old boy.
- He will help old ladies cross streets and mothers with their baby carriages with perhaps too much intensity.
- There will be a good guy grin on his face with sickly sweetness about it.
- He will belong to accepted clubs and religious organizations.
- He will seem to have no enemies; everybody is his friend.
- He will find ways to convince everyone that he agrees with them no matter how contradictory his opinions will

seem.

- He will value approval getting a lot more than anything else—more than his job for instance, which may end up getting him fired in spite of how good he is. This will instantly propel him back to the safety and security level of needs and to antisocial behaviour.

In the social and belonging needs, the goal is to get approval and to be liked. In reality, as we learn in this Church, this need cannot be satisfied from the outside. One can never be satisfied through getting approval or through being liked. The intense seeking those always comes from self-loathing. The gap, therefore, must be healed inside of the self. Once you like yourself, the approval and the liking of others is not essential. It becomes a bonus which you can take or leave.

Examine the quality of your giving. Do you give for approval? If you do, you are augmenting your own deficiency. However, if you give for the sake of giving, you are giving to others and to yourself at the same time.

In order to satisfy your own need for approval, you must give to others—not approval, but the truth, whether pleasant or unpleasant. If you do, you will raise yourself to the next level of needs.

How to Deal with Someone on the Social Level of Needs

Make him feel as if he belongs. Ask him about his personal life. Do some appropriate sharing concerning yours.

If you are dealing with a group whose majority of members is on this level, organize social events. Satisfy their social needs **before** they become a problem by spending some time with them in the beginning of an activity or a work day. During that time, emotionally interact with them; talk about something exciting that happened to you the day before; tell an anecdote or two.

Difference Between Safety and Security and Social Level of Needs

Thus, there is a distinct difference between the safety and security level of needs and the social needs. The person in the former has passive behavioural manifestations; he wants to hide. In the latter, he wants to be noticed, and he pursues this actively. In safety and security, there is mistrust and in extreme cases, antisocial behaviour. In social level of needs, there is the exact opposite, an intense desire to be liked. This, of course, means that he hides a great deal of hostility and insecurity.

We can, therefore, conclude that the intense pursuit for social approval eventually regresses the person to the level of safety and security. With this regression is, of course, a diminution of efficiency and motivation which results, in its extreme, in regression to physical needs through poverty.

If a person is healthily satisfied on the level of belonging and social approval, he will no longer seek it. It will become a redundant and moot point for him. He will have raised himself to the being level of needs and values, the one in which he is self-motivated.

****

Dissolve your desire for approval and for belonging by anchoring yourself within yourself. In doing so, you will have taken a major step from having to be motivated on the outer level, to being self-motivated. You are closing in on the state of self-actualization, which is the state of at-onement with God.

Chapter 19
Being Needs;
Moi and Self-Actualization

---

4) *Moi.* That's the best way to describe this next level. They are the *moi* needs. Maslow calls them self-esteem, self-respect. From the point of view that they no longer rely on others' approval, protection or feeding, this is great progress. This person is motivated by the development his own abilities. In this and the next category, the person is self-motivated; he is well-anchored in being needs and values. He is involved with:

A) **On the beneficial level,** obtaining mastery, confidence, competence, independence and freedom. Shades of Ayn Rand are beginning to be felt here; the rest is to be found in the self-actualized person. Here, also, is to be found the beneficial side of positive thinking, of success type theories, of self-improvement, etc.

B) **On the harmful side,** A) becomes intensified into compulsive desire for recognition, importance, dominance, prestige, reputation. You can see here how the exaggeration of A) leads to B) and eventually regresses back to the deficiency of the social level.

Here we have the full fledged yuppy. Because he is self-motivated and because he puts a lot of good energy in his work, he is successful. However, his success is threatened by the intensification of A) which then becomes B). Unfortunately, he does not attribute his success to A). He would rather attribute it to B) because he is more in control of it. This is his demise. The more successful he has become and the more destructive and painful will be his fall.

The very self-esteem that was sought through the intensification of *moi* will be lost. This person will sell his soul out for a buck or a position or a car or the boss's daughter or the model wife, believing that the ownership of those things will get him even more self-esteem.

Obviously, we here at our Church recognize a very insecure person. Indeed, if, in A), this person has learned to master and achieve in all areas of his life, he would be totally satisfied and he would not have to intensify anything. Thus, when we look more closely to those who have switched from A) to yuppy scum, we find an incomplete person, someone out of balance, disconnected from part of himself. He is too successful or too handsome or too strong or too erudite. Alfred Adler's[1] theory of compensation comes to mind here.

****

Notice the similarity between the good old boy of the social needs and A) in moi. Notice also the differences between the two. In self-esteem, there is more integrity. The person achieves for himself rather than for others' approval.

How many times have you disguised your need for social approval under a pretense of giving? See how you give from a level of deficiency—for approval. If you do that, you are doing more damage than the selfish yuppy who admittedly wants all for himself. Look at it. Giving for approval is a

---

[1]Austrian psychoanalyst, disciple of Sigmund Freud, 1870-1937.

deficiency value. Giving to oneself is a being value, therefore, more ethical. **Giving to oneself brings you closer to God than giving to others for approval.**

To what extent are you giving out of deficiency? To what extent are you exaggerating your giving to yourself, missing out on the opportunity to genuinely and selflessly give to others? Your effort in answering these questions will be a good preparation for you to understand the next and last level of Maslow's hierarchy of needs, self-actualization.

****

Anchor yourself in your Genuine Needs and, in humility, accept your level in the hierarchy. Let those needs naturally raise you from level to level. Detect the parts of you that regress you. Raise yourself to God.

Self-Actualization And The Christ Example

The self-actualized person has his eye full, as the Arabs would say. He has gone through the lower levels of need. He has achieved success on the self-esteem/moi level. Yet, it is not enough. All of these achievements no longer motivate him.

What drives him now is serving a greater cause, a principle, an infinity.

1) **Sacrifice and yielding.**

Consider those in history who achieved self-actualization. Lincoln, who abhorred war, sacrificed his abhorrence because war had to be fought. He yielded all of himself to the task at hand. Nothing would stand in his way. The same can be said of Franklin D. Roosevelt who let Pearl Harbor happen in order to finally break down the country's fat cowardice and egocentricity. The same was true of Buddha who sacrificed his life as a prince in order to seek the truth. He then sacrificed his life as an ascetic Hindu when he obtained enlightenment and created his own religion.

Last, but not least, the same is true of the Christ, the highest incarnated being on earth. He sacrificed everything for the sake of the truth and for the sake of God.

This common denominator of sacrifice did not mean capitulation. On the contrary, all self-actualized people have contradicted, superseded existing knowledge or creeds. They **needed** to do so, to penetrate the existing and dying energy forms.

2) **Perceptiveness.**

This is another quality in the self-actualized person. He sees reality through the phoney, the pretense, the dishonesty and the spurious. This is true in all areas, even in the ones in which he may not be versed.

I just saw a documentary about the breaking of a money laundering operation by a female undercover agent. She was able to fool them for a long time. She attributes their poor intuition to the extent of their greed. Blinded by their greed, they did not want to believe that she was an undercover agent. Evil, harmful volition, kills intuition and clear perception. Perception and intuition are a function of inner cleanliness.

The Christ could perceive the traps set by evil people's questions. His answers and allegories would foil their volition. He accused so many of hypocrisy. Some didn't even know why or how they were being hypocritical.

When confronted by a self-actualized person, you will have a sense of nakedness, which will either feel wonderful if you are sincere, or awful if you want to hide.

How perceptive are you? Who around you is perceptive?

3) **Acceptance.**

He is totally accepting of himself and of others, of nature and of imperfections. Again this doesn't mean being a doormat. He also gets angry, sometimes violently expressing it, just as Christ did when He chased the money lenders at the temple.

4) Capable of flowing feelings.

Effusive and joyous love flows out of this person. His sexuality also flows. Christ would publicly demonstrate his sexual attraction to the Magdalen by kissing her in front of his disciples. His sexuality was expressed constructively, harmlessly. By contrast, Goethe spent practically all of his 80 years switching from one love to another—a little less harmless here, but then again, he wasn't the Christ!

5) Compassion.

Great understanding of human deficiencies are demonstrated. With that is to be found a way to help people bear them in a light manner.

6) Enquiring.

The more self-actualized, the more inquisitive is the person. He is uninhibited by the unknown, which fascinates him. He is willing to question all that he knows and has no problems admitting that he doesn't know something. On the other hand, if he knows, he will have no qualms in telling even at the risk of embarrassing people by contradicting them. When that happens, he will feel no false guilt towards others for their sense of shame and humiliation. However, he will have compassion for them, forgiving them "for they know not what they do."

7) Generosity.

They are willing to totally sacrifice themselves for the sake of what is right or for defending anyone who is oppressed. The Christ's generosity is quite well-known. However, consider Voltaire's[2] saying, *I disapprove of what you say, but I will defend to the death your right to say it.* Isn't that a lot

---

[2] French philosopher, historian, dramatist and poet, 1694-1778.

closer to the Christ than the inquisition or the excommunication of the Freemasons, which those who call themselves Christians were practicing in his day?

He actually devoted his later life to the defense of right causes and of the weak and poor. He purchased an estate in a French-Swiss place called Ferney and, from there, attacked injustice and defended the down trodden. In those days, people recognized him as a king. At the very end of his life, he returned to Paris, where he was received with so much popularity that they crowned his bust on stage. The King, Louis XVI, who was very upset by his return, did not have the guts to enforce the old warrant for Voltaire's arrest.

8) Spontaneity.

They are capable of being amazingly spontaneous, and they really don't care how you will take it. They are, of course, closer to the material released by their soul, and therefore, act, feel and think as souls.

9) Conventions and Mores.

They will respect those, only if they make sense. They will not if the existing conventions disagree with their own code of ethics.

They will drop formality when with those who don't require it. Christ is described in the Urantia Book as deliberately breaking bread without blessing it, once in a while, just to challenge superstition.

10) They are not well-adjusted.

They do not conform to what is expected of them. They make statements that rub people the wrong way with their truthfulness. They reject meaningless conventions, mores and rituals, often copiously and angrily ridiculing them. In short, they are not running a popularity contest.

So, when Maslow says that they are not well-adjusted, we ask "adjusted to what? To the conventions and mores? But they are very well-adjusted to their own code of ethics which they scrupulously obey. Since they do not conform to the expected mores and rituals, they seem strange, unpleasant, antisocial and undesirable to the majority of people. In effect, being truer to themselves, they are closer to God. Those who befriend them will have a deeper friendship with them than with those who reject them.

Christ was seen as a strange, far out rabble rouser. So are we.

11) **Problem focus.**

A) **They are capable of deep focus on a problem.** They will sometimes seem consumed by it, obsessing and despairing. This is because their personality still demands resolution now. The relaxed focus of their Divine Self becomes the intense demand of their distorted self. Jesus despaired on the cross. ("Why hast thou forsaken me?") He must have also despaired at other times. Of course, he didn't know that one of the conditions of the incarnation of the Christ in his personality was that there be no help from the World of God until death. So, the Christ did have a distorted self, a personality, named Jesus.

Nevertheless, in the self-actualized personality there is a stubborn grasping at a problem and not letting go until it is resolved; like a dog with a bone. And it is good and bad.

The focus, demand/despair and motivation for resolution is not, however, egocentric, but altruistic, concerned with principle, not individuals, not the self.

B) **Problem focus also means disengaging from personal cases.** For the self-actualized person, it is important to focus on the problem, not necessarily on the person. They are able to disengage the two and focus on the problem. This makes it possible for the person who has a problem to cooperate with them with a minimum of defense. It doesn't however exclude the cases wherein the defense is there in spite of that disengagement.

12) Philosophic.

They are constantly concerned with broader issues of universal import. They ponder on basic issues, on spiritual and natural law. Thus:

A) They are magnanimous, not petty, generous, not stingy.

B) However, when it comes to a matter of principle, they will treat the smallest subject as seriously as the biggest one, appearing to be petty and paranoid.

One thinks here of the rescuing of the lamb by the Christ.

13) Healthy detachment.

They need—and assert their need for—privacy. They collect themselves and draw deep from their inner self. This may frustrate those who are close to them. It challenges the places in them where they believe they own him. However, the self-actualized person has a daily need for intense concentration.

14) Autonomy.

They are free of the glamours that plague others, to the point where they seem not to belong to their environment or to their culture. Their tastes and penchants seem strange. Actually, they have

15) A greater capacity for pleasure.

Being free of defenses, they are more capable to appreciate and to enjoy. And, free of glamours, their enjoyment is deeper, more permanent, truer, less harmful and more long lasting.

16) Growth, motivation, mastery.

They continue to improve themselves in all the areas of their lives. They increasingly get better. For instance, if a job provides continuous growth, they will stay with it, regardless of remuneration (within reason, of course.)

17) **Resiliency.**

They do not disintegrate in crisis. They have bouts of despair which they quickly correct and recover the serenity required. Check here the Christ's dignity with those who were judging Him after His arrest. Although He knew that He was to be put to death, He still confronted these people in the sharpest manner.

18) **Awe.**

The self-actualized person is continuously in awe, surprised, delighted, capable of experiencing the same beauty again with renewed freshness and delight. Every sunset is a masterpiece, a wonder. Every moment is savoured to the maximum.

****

During this Christmas season, give yourself the luxury to ponder on self-actualization. Apply the 18 points I gave you to your life, asking yourself, "What is preventing me to, right now, be Christ-like?"

There will be more on self-actualization next year. Happy, serene, loving holidays to you. Be Christ, be peace, be God.

Chapter 20
Self-Actualization

The description of self-actualized people serves us in our own pursuit for self-actualization. Examine every area of your life and see if you can determine the extent that you are self-actualized in those areas. Whenever there is a difference between your behaviour and that of a self-actualized person, do the following:

1) Specify with as much qualitative and quantitative precision how you are different.

2) Seek and determine your volitionality in remaining inferior to self-actualization in those areas.

3) Experience and express this evil, taking full responsibility for the pain and the unhappiness that it brings.

4) This will create in you a motivation—an volitionality—to be self-actualized; with this urge

5) Set goals for self-actualization.

All of this will be very difficult unless you are guided by a teacher and by friends in spiritual training for self-actualization such as what we do.

Let us now continue with the description of self-actualized people.

Sex And Relationships
1) In describing their **orgasms,** they say that they

simultaneously find in them omnipotence and utter vulnerability. We recognize here that they have opened the door to the Divine Self, God within, feeling the power and the security of at-onement. That's the omnipotence. At the same time, the personality feels naked and exposed to the newly found immensity. That's the openness which seems vulnerable.

Generalization: The self-actualized person has developed this capacity for yielding, which, other than in sex, can also be experienced in art, or music, or in total immersion in solving a problem.

2) Desire for intimacy on all levels. Truth is cultivated; total transparency.

3) **Generosity:** Total giving and taking. They tend to do things for each other very often unsolicited.

4) A lot of time spent together.

5) A sense of deep friendship, not interfering with, but enhancing the passion.

6) A sense of mutuality is developed in which the roles are dropped. Thus, the battle of the sexes is no longer an issue. We can see here that Maslow is trying to describe what it is like to transcend the personality. This is what happens in a relationship and this is why it contains the deepest possible cleansing.

7) Physical appearance stops mattering; concerns about age, physical defects, etc. are dissolved.

8) Interest increases with time. Maslow compares this with the increasing appreciation of good art. By contrast, bad art tires us quickly.

9) Sex and love seem to be inextricably connected.

10) They are capable of varieties of sexual experiences, going from the casual to the more profound and passionate.

11) They are less interested in affairs with others, but more open to sharing with their mate, the sexual feelings that they

experience for others.

Mutuality

This word, by the way, is a legitimate English word, found in any complete and thorough English dictionary, such as *Webster's New Universal Unabridged Dictionary*. It is no one's sole property. Here, it is used to describe the self-actualized person's ability both to express his need and to respond to his partner's, both without reservations or defensiveness. The result is that each partner in this relationship experiences the other's need as if it were his own. Maslow calls this need identification. I prefer mutuality.

It is as if the two have become one entity. This phenomenon was well-known to Alfred Adler, who generalized this principle beyond the couple concept, into the social.

Check also Erich Fromm, in his work, *Man for Himself,* where he clarifies the following points concerning loving:

- The oneness between the loving person and the loved "object."
- The "productiveness," i.e., active giving of care and of respect in the act of love.
- The inherent sense of responsibility and consciousness; the acquisition of the necessary knowledge to rightly **effect,** implement this love.
- That love is **not** an attempt to **affect** anyone, i.e., to make them change for one's egocentric benefit.
- That love is actively endeavouring to help another, or others grow and be happy.

In that state, there is an enjoyment of another's happiness and a sorrow of another's pain, without distorted dependency.

And here is something that has not been clarified in

Maslow: there are times when a loving confrontation will elicit deep pain in the person confronted. The person who confronts will, to some extent participate in this pain, without being caught up in it to the same extent. He will do it for the benefit of the loved one, incurring, albeit temporarily, the displeasure—even the hatred—of the person confronted. Again, we find the principle of love in confrontation.

Distortion: Have you ever felt, about a loved one, that you would like to make their pain yours, that you would rather have it yourself than have them have it? Well, in that state, you are **not** self-actualized. The self-actualized person will lose himself in loving, in caring, in healing with complete abandon. However, he will not want to take away the pain created by the loved one's mistake.

Let's, for example, say that a strong man is ill. His manhood is idealized. His physical strength and health, also idealized are pillars for his manhood. All of this becomes deeply threatened to the point of despair. His mate will not want to take his pain and suffer it for him. She knows that it is his private pain, and that, furthermore, it is healthy. He will grow from it, becoming a real man, having acquired resiliency as he loses the idealization of manhood which, because of what he did, must now come through illness.

Conversely, suppose a woman, in her illness, loses her physical beauty and is despairing about it. Her husband will, to some limited extent be deeply sorry, but he will not want to take away her pain. He sees it as her own private pain. He understands that, through it, she will strengthen and become more real.

The **dissolution of the deified self**, in both cases, increases mutuality and love. So, crises such as these deepen the relationship, the love and the mutuality, rather than diminish or kill it.

Only if love is based on the superficial levels of the deified self will a relationship be threatened by an illness, a loss of a child, or another tragedy. The tragedy becomes unbearable because it threatens the disconnected and idealized identity of the participants.

Humour and Fun

The self-actualized individual and the self-actualized relationship, both will contain lightness, fun, laughter, a feeling of a constant party going on, a festivity, just because the two are together.

In sex, there will be room for laughter, humour, teasing, playful play acting, alongside passion and ecstasy. In no way does that diminish the responsibility, the respect and the caring. On the contrary, it enhances it. It respects and preserves each other's autonomy and integrity. It does not become sarcasm, hostility, or put down. It is not used as a dumping ground for cases. It has the purity, the childlike quality of children or young animals playing.

Generalization: Once again, this, generalized, becomes the feeling of fun and joy that we, at our Church, experience when we get together as a group. Having developed mutual intimacy in helping each other through our faith, we find fun and merriment to be naturally present whenever we get together.

The Two Will Become One

This is a saying from the Christ. He extends it to say that, when that happens, He is with us. The bliss, the joy, the ecstasy, the fun, the sense of eternal youth, found in self-actualized couples or self-actualized entities comprising many people, such as to be found in our Church, implies the presence of God.

In the last analysis, that's what it is all about. In mutual love and in group love are to be found the longing for and the presence of God.

Chapter 21

Self-Actualization Continued

Many of my friends have reacted harmfully to the material on self-actualization. They prefer continuing to dwell on the harmful aspects, in which they find comfort. They want me to continue to delight them in the intricacies of the distorted and the deified selves. They want me to also say "me, too," so that we can all commiserate in the same lukewarm cesspool, and get used to the smell.

This is as regressive as the pretense of the pseudo-good. It is just as dishonest because it denies the fact that we can and must meet the challenge presented by the role model of self-actualization. It is our natural destiny to self-actualize. We cannot escape it. It is our birthright, our natural state to which we must return.

The Path to God and self-actualization are one. Let's continue to study the characteristics of self-actualized individuals.

Gemeinschaftsgefuhl

This is a word coined by Alfred Adler to describe the feeling of identification with human beings found in the self-actualized person. They feel love and sympathy for human beings and for human family. This runs parallel to the feelings of contempt, irritation and anger that also exist for humans.

Consequently, there is here a great desire to help people,

as an older brother does, in spite of exasperation and impatience.

Friendships

1) They are deeper than on any other level. This is due to their greater capacity for love, greater integrity, good will, and ability to yield their ego. Thus, distorted dependency, as found in the social needs level, does not form deep friendships. Only the autonomy of self-actualization produces the deep friendships based on healthy needs and healthy dependency.

2) These friendships are formed with other close to self-actualizing individuals, healthy people.

3) Since those are few, there is a great deal of **discrimination** in the choice of friendships. Look at our community. The closeness that we have developed between us is a function of self-actualization and the preceding cleansing. Even inside the community, clusters of friends form, who, amongst each other, are not burdened by the distorted dependency of transference and counter transference. Within our community, close friendships are impossible when transference and counter transference exist.

4) The nature of the friendship being so close and committed, precludes the possibility of having a multitude of friends. The self-actualized person simply doesn't want to devote the time for more friendships. He has other things to do. This is unlike the distorted dependency existing in cults, where weakness and the debilitation of the individual are cultivated.

5) This discrimination concerning friendship has no problems co-existing with *gemeinschaftsgefuhl*. They still feel this great identification and compassion for humans.

6) Maslow says that, still, they will get angry and confront. He says that what particularly angers them are those who in

our terms are in their deified self, marring their integrity with hypocrisy and pretense.

Yet, the self-actualized person still sees the Divine Self potential in all of them. The anger is at the lost opportunities and the creation of unhappiness in those others. Thus, their anger is always beneficial to those who incur it.

Followers

Consequently, as you self-actualize, you will gather followers. They will:

A) Hound you with their constant demands, always wanting more than what you want to give.

B) Embarrass you; you will not like the intrusion; but you can always find a way to stop that, provided you dissolve the distorted and deified selves that actually enjoy this leeching.

Democracy

The self-actualized individual is capable of friendship with all classes, levels of education, race, colour or creed, or political affiliation.

In that connection, I remember some of the feelings that I registered and some of the observations that I had when, in the summer of 1981, I took a job as a driver for a limousine service in New York, using my car. This was a low time for me. I did not have confidence in the number of followers that my former wife, Judy, and I had. I was worried about what was going to happen. Fortunately, this episode only lasted a few weeks, less than two months anyway. In the fall, plenty of followers showed up and I no longer had to supplement my income in that way.

I was astonished at the extent and the depth of class structure. Suddenly, because I was a limousine driver, I was treated as an inferior by the clients. A surprising number of them spoke to me with an air of condescension and disrespect.

In one particular instance, I had decided that it was bad enough to stop and let the client out of my car, into the rain, rather than take him to the airport.

Don't be surprised if you find in yourself contempt for drivers, waiters, cleaning people, etc. Observe your attitude towards them. If there isn't the genuine quality of interest, caring and compassion described in the *gemeinschaftsgefuhl* part of this lecture, you are creating pain; you are into harmfulness, not harmlessness; you are not walking this faith of self-actualization.

As important as those differences may be for the lower levels of development, they have no importance at all for the self-actualized individual.

But it goes deeper. They learn from these others. They may know that they are more developed, yet, they are capable to, in humility, interact with everyone as equals.

Here we join the healthy leader, who, in spite of his position, still interacts with others as equals, applies all the rules for others even more deeply unto himself, is able to have fun with anyone. Yet, when it comes to asserting his authority, he has no trouble switching to a superior to subordinate modality.

The Path of God

Maslow extensively quotes Dr. David Levy who was his contemporary and who he seems to have known personally. According to Maslow, Levy told him that the description of these self-actualized people would have corresponded to what was thought of, in the old days as "men who walk in the path of God." This indeed, confirms once again that our faith of cleansing and self-actualization, using this material in this way is indeed the Path of God.

Maslow points out that not one of the self-actualizing people considered in his study belonged to any conventional religion. He even found an atheist amongst them. We recognize the swing of the pendulum once again in terms of the Path of God:

1) "In the old days," self-actualized people were religious people; even this statement has to be taken with a grain of salt.

2) Organized religion, having rigidified, became ossified and obsolescent, necessitating self-actualization to occur in spite of it; atheism, therefore, became a condition for self-actualization. Many are stuck in this late Nineteenth Century materialistic "positivism" as it used to be called. In fact, Auguste Comte,[1] the founder of "positivism" went through the trouble of creating a positivistic, materialistic religion, rewriting all Catholic rituals, including the mass, to suit atheists. The need for prayer thus still existed and will always exist.

3) We now experience a swing of the pendulum back to religion. This is what this church is all about—the restoration of the Path of God in the concept of church, i.e., giving church its good name back. Self-actualization—the Path of God—is very much our business **as a church.** It will increasingly become the business of churches as humanity evolves.

Ethics Dissolves Confusion

The self-actualized person is highly ethical. Therefore —and amazingly enough, Maslow also makes this connection— to the extent he is ethical, he is not burdened by confusion, by conflicts and by inconstant moods and behaviours. Thus, once again, we recognize that problems are created by lack of integrity. The self-actualized individual sticks to ethics, truth and harmlessness. The problems he once had become dissolved and he does not create new ones.

---

[1] French positivist philosopher, 1789-1857.

Means and Ends

1) The self-actualized individual has dissolved his Machiavellianism. He knows the difference between means and ends. He will not use harmful means to achieve his ends. He will conserve his ethics throughout achieving what he wants.

2) At the same time, he will use any possible means, albeit ethical, available to him to achieve his ends. His focus is on the end, the bottom line, the goal.

3) As focused as he is on the end and the goal, he thoroughly enjoys the steps involved in the means. The steps themselves—the means—become ends, in and by themselves. The traveling becomes as pleasurable as the destination. In doing so, they live the moment fully, enjoying the steps, inventing little games about each step in it, very much in a childlike fashion.

4) This does not mean that they collapse into the path of least resistance, wherein the means become everything and the goal is disregarded—an often committed mistake by the pseudo-spiritual pacifists who denigrate healthy competition out of cowardice. **There still is no A for effort. A only stands for accomplishment, achievement, the end result, and the self-actualized person knows it.**

5) While achieving, he is invigorated by the challenge of healthy competitiveness. It helps him **measure himself** both qualitatively and quantitatively. **This motivates him to surpass himself because he knows exactly what he has to do.**

Both ends and means are equally important. The self-actualized individual devotes himself 100% to both.

Creativity

All of this openness and freedom from the limitations and

misconceptions connects the self-actualized person with nature, "the involuntary," the infinite, the collective unconscious. As a result, they continuously create.

They are never really satisfied with imperfections, always striving for perfection which, as well, helps their creativity. (See the material on creativity.)

Duality Dissolves

All of the cleansing we do results in the dissolution of dualities. In the self-actualized person, these dualities no longer exist. Let's list some of them without necessarily delving into them since it has already been done in other contexts:

- God's will versus my own will is resolved into Augustine's saying: *Love God and do as you will.* This means that when I cleanse myself, I increasingly realize that God's will and my will are one.
- Selfishness versus altruism dissolves since giving and receiving are one.
- Spirituality versus pleasure and/or sexuality is resolved; the divine consummation of the sex Instinct of Procreation is religion.
- Maturity is childlike.
- Work and play are one when work becomes pleasurable.
- Esotericism and materialism unify in reality.
- The distorted self cooperates with the Divine Self.
- God is immanent as well as transcendent.

Again, measure yourself, look at yourself in this mirror. Establish the qualitative and the quantitative distance between you and the states that I have tried to describe to you. Then, establish goals for the removal of the obstacles that prevent you from being self-actualized. This then constitutes the cleansing at our Church, the cleansing of union with God.

Chapter 22
Pretense Results in Loss of Identity

When you pretend, you become somebody else. When you seek approval, you identify with what others think or feel about you.

The consequences of this are as follows:

1) You may be elated by their praise of you; however, this feeling is not grounded since in reality they are praising somebody else, not you. By contrast, when you are yourself, you may feel pleased about other people's approval; however, you know that what really counts is what you have found to be the truth.

2) As we have seen before, the slightest disapproval puts you off balance; you feel totally rejected as a person; having become one of their branches, any rejection of their part means death for you. By contrast, in the state of being, if they disapprove of you, you may feel temporarily sad; however, you are not deeply affected by it; you are not shaken up by it.

3) Your self-worth diminishes. Consider, for instance, that you cannot feel good in pretense about anything that you give since, deep down inside you, you know that your giving is a pretense and that it doesn't count. By contrast, in the state of being, even though your giving is done without an expectation of return, and even though it makes you feel better about yourself, it does count, having quite a few beneficial

consequences later.

4) In pretense, even if the giving is real and comes from a good place, you will not be so sure of that since you no longer know yourself, having become somebody else. So, you cannot even fully benefit from your real giving. By contrast, when you proceed from your genuine self, you know who you are, you know what you want, and you know what you give. Although you don't place too much importance on it, what you give nevertheless counts and is well-placed.

5) You will be devastated by any criticism whether constructive or destructive; you will not be capable of differentiating from the two. You will put up a fierce and comprehensive defense. By contrast, when you proceed from a state of being, you will welcome criticism, knowing how to differentiate between the constructive and the destructive, and knowing how to benefit from both. Since you are proceeding from your center, you are connected to the infinite, and therefore, you do not need any defense. You resist not evil.

6) Consequently, in pretense, you will be unable to learn anything. By contrast, your genuine self is continuously learning since it doesn't block itself through defensiveness and distortion.

7) Being so defensive, you will alienate even those from whom you seek approval and to whom you capitulate. This will make them disrespect you and denigrate you even more. By contrast, when you proceed from your state of being, you are relaxed which makes it easier for those who disagree with you or disapprove of you to see your point of view.

8) In pretense, when the defense will be broken, it will not be a healthy break. It will be a further exercise in despair and self-depreciation. By contrast, if a broken defense is able to liberate your genuine self, you will feel gratitude and relief, dignity in your humility, and a conviction that your are growing.

9) So, the very praise and approval sought through pretense will actually lead to disrespect and disapproval. You will have sacrificed your genuine self for nothing. By contrast, what emanates from the genuine self sooner or later will command respect from others even if there is disagreement. It may even get them to change their mind and see it your way. However, it may even change your mind to see it their way. In any case, there will be a climate of respect. Sometimes, expressing yourself from your state of being will get you worse than disapproval—deep hatred made personal by those whose depths you have reached and who resent you for it. In spite of that, you still will feel unaffected, albeit temporarily sad.

10) You will be unable to know whether someone is genuinely good, thus opening yourself to them, or genuinely harmful, thus justifying your confrontation of them. The total and unilateral focus on approval seeking and pretense renders you blind and dumb. On the contrary, the deep sense of security experienced in the state of being leaves you open since your focus is in knowing the truth; your defenselessness makes you sensitive to others and their volitions. You are not afraid to feel that they are harmful towards you or good for that matter.

11) You will never know whether you are right or wrong. You will never know when you are right that you are right and when you are wrong that you are wrong. By contrast, when you really are yourself, you commit yourself entirely to what you are doing and to what you believe. If you happen to be right, so much the better. If it turns out that you are wrong, then you are open to learning from your mistakes without being totally devastated. Being connected to yourself, you do not have to be defensive. You can afford to be totally open to reality. This makes you sharp, alive and savvy.

12) Not knowing who you are, you cannot know what you

want. Your Genuine Needs become voracious, false wants. You find yourself fluctuating between greedily wanting something, and then being disappointed once you have gotten it. You erroneously believe that what you have coveted with such greed, will give you the self-esteem and self-worth that you have long ago abandoned. "If I had this car, this dress, this hat, this relationship, then I will feel good about myself because I have made it, or at least I will appear to have made it."

The wrong conclusion here is to decide, as in old time religion, that the luxury car is bad, the sexy dress sinful, and the hat ostentatious.

By contrast, if I am myself, I will concentrate on the genuine value and the real beauty of a car or a dress or a hat. It will be an enhancement of my own value that I will find in these outer level objects, not a compensation for the lacks that I don't want to face.

13) In pretense, major decisions will be warped. You will make the wrong career and relationship choices. You will totally miss out on the real nature of your task. On the contrary, when anchored in being, decisions will naturally flow from well-balanced thinking and feelings. They will be obvious, devoid of conflict. Also, the self, having trained itself in decision making through small matters, is ready to recognize what constitutes a right decision. Of course, there will be cases when a decision cannot be made as yet in view of existing blocks. The genuine self will recognize that condition as well, humbly admitting not knowing and diligently engaging in the dissolution of the blocks so as to free the correct decision.

14) You will discover that pretense, in spite of the fact that it seeks approval, is bound to conflict with somebody else's pretense and to become its sworn, deadly enemy. Know that when it comes to being, you will never conflict with

another person's being. Your genuine self will never conflict with anybody else's genuine self. It will only conflict with pretenses, whether yours or other people's.

Unconscious Pretense

How do you know anymore whether the needs that you are feeling are true or pretense? You have been so frightened of the opinion of others that you have moulded yourself very thoroughly. Now, you are at a point where you are confused about the veracity and the originality of your needs:

- Do I really need a relationship or am I supposed to have one?
- Do I really need to get or be married or am I supposed to?
- Do I really need this piece of clothing or am I supposed to get it and wear it?
- Do I really need a house of this size or am I supposed to have one?
- Am I really attracted to this person or am I supposed to be?

As you can see, Genuine Needs themselves have subtly been distorted by pretense, which now has become second nature to you. Your pretense, having become unconscious, appears to be really you, your being. Nevertheless, it isn't. And since it isn't, you are still prey to everyone else's whim. You still sell your power out to others.

This damaging state has been gradually created by one simple everyday thought: "What will they think of me?" This repeated harmful mantra gradually builds up a clog to your genuine self, its needs and its values. It creates terror of your genuine self and terror of others. The effects of this terror are grossly under estimated because its cause—"What will they think of me?"—is equally underestimated. Besides, the connection isn't really made between that harmful mantra and its terrifying consequences.

Do not underestimate the insidious power of your harmfulness. Become conscious of the resulting poison in your system and the resulting chaos in your life.

How much easier, simpler, cleaner, more reassuring it is to be yourself, to claim your Genuine Needs and to live by your genuine values! No matter what happens on the outside as a result, you are at peace with yourself inside. You know who you are, what you need and what is really valuable.

How to Differentiate Between
Genuine And Pretense Needs And Values

1) It is not through your "feelings," gut or heart or other. By definition, the problem is that you have warped your feelings. You have bent them for approval. As real as they seem, if you are confused, there must be falsehood in them.

2) Nor is it through gauging the reaction it has on others, whether it be a beneficial or a harmful one. If you expect a beneficial one, obviously you still are vying for approval. If you expect a harmful one, you are trying to prove that you are not seeking approval, that you don't need their approval. Actually, you are still seeking that approval, approval for not seeking approval.

3) But, you may, on the inside, still be seeking approval and denying your real being. Indeed, approval within is sought from the deified self, the affected conscience. This part of yourself is none other than those whose approval you sought as a child. It has created glamours, illusions which lead you to Maya, distorted action, creating suffering and unhappiness.

So, the way out of this problem is through:

A) **Detection:**

1) Defining your deified selves, glamours, affected conscience, etc.

2) Whenever you have a need, ask yourself, "Is this influenced in any way by my deified self? What part of it is? What part isn't?

3) Finding out which part of your life is affected by these deified selves and which part is free of them.

B) **Dissolution:**

1) Looking at the false need and value, imagine life without it. What would actually be lost?

2) As a result of this removal, a void is created, an emptiness felt. Allow it. Allow yourself to long, need, even if you don't know what.

3) Sooner or later, nature will release the Genuine Need that corresponds to the pretense. Once found, cultivate it. Nurture it. Encourage it. Apologize to it for neglecting and betraying it.

4) Expect, once you found your Genuine Need, that the battle will continue. You are not free of what you have created as yet. The terror and the capitulation that creates it return. It will be up to you to continue the battle and dissolve the problem completely, albeit gradually.

5) The disapproval and the crucifixion that you will experience when you abandon your pretense will surprise you by its vehemence, its viciousness, its meanness. What do you expect? You can't very well sell out and cultivate approval for several decades—let alone incarnations—and expect those to whom you sold out to kiss you on both cheeks when you finally decide to be honest? It is what **you** created that is now crucifying you.

Actually, all that is being crucified is the deified self, the affected conscience and the glamours. So, let them do it. They actually are digging their own grave.

Your genuine self, with its values and needs is, and always will be, indestructible and immortal. Actually, by abandoning falsehood and embracing the state of being, the truth, you are safe, protected. No one can touch you. And what is built from this place is also safe. And the friends and relationships and loves emanating from this place are made in heaven and are blessed by its eternal quality.

****

By cultivating the state of being you become increasingly aware of the fact that your identity is merged with God.

Part V

Divine Faculties

Section I

The Faculties of God,
The Father

Chapter 23

God, The Father; Absolute Power I

- *Power tends to corrupt, and absolute power corrupts absolutely.*
  —Lord Baron Acton, 1834-1902, English historian.

- *Power corrupts, but lack of power corrupts absolutely.*
  —Adlai Stevenson, 1900-1965, American statesman.

- *... all power is a trust, that we are accountable for its exercise.*
  —Benjamin Disraeli, 1804-1881, English Prime Minister.

As we can see, Absolute Power or not having power at all are both causes for corruption. Indeed, you must have some form of power. If you don't, you will try to obtain it in a corrupt way. Also, if you are not clean enough, you will not be able to handle a great amount of power, and certainly not Absolute Power.

As in any aspect that belongs to the infinite, from the relative point of view, Absolute Power is perceived dualistically:

1) It belongs only to God, yet, it is our birthright.

2) The little child tyrant believes that he has it now; the adult knows that he doesn't and that, still, he must reach for

it.

3) Yet, the **acceptance** of temporary **powerlessness** in the adult often becomes despair and **collapse**, while the **demand** for instant omnipotence in the child tyrant is perceived as **vibrant and alive.**

There are many others. However, let's study these three dualisms:

I. Having the power of God.

Do you dare think and feel your longing for this? There is a false modesty here which prevents you from feeling this very legitimate desire. For instance, you find it acceptable to reach for perfection. You even find it acceptable to seek Eternal Life. **But, you hit a wall of taboo when it comes to omnipotence.** You freeze your natural movement towards it by associating it with a harmful wish, as if it were a sin, a desire to supplant God. There is a lot here:

A) Yes, part of you, the child tyrant does want to dethrone God and replace Him. More on this will come below.

B) But, throwing baby and bath water by, then, concluding that I am not entitled to omnipotence is a freeze. If part of my desire for Absolute Power is harmful, it doesn't mean that all of it must be. So why do I make it to be?

C) Because:

- **Fear of pain and effort:** On one end of the spectrum, i.e., at the entrance into this faith, I refuse to go through the necessary steps to achieving mastery. Life is a continuum of learning mastery of self and of the Universe. Every time I learn something, I acquire power, the power to use it, be it a concept or a computer. Omnipotence comes when I have mastered mastery. The dissolving of anything that stands in my way is no longer defended. It accelerates to the point of perpetual and infinite progress. This then is God, and is the ultimate good. (See the sermon "Mastery" in *From Crisis to Mastery and Ecstacy.*)

- **Fear of power and pleasure:** At the other end of the spectrum, in the second half of my cleansing, after reaching the highest point of the bridge, omnipotence becomes an achievable reality. **This frightens me.** I shirk away from the power of the infinite, from my own power. I don't know if I want it. I don't want the responsibility for it. I am afraid that it will turn against me. Well, don't worry:
  - If you have done your cleansing, you will not fear; you will have nothing to fear. Take the power that is yours. You cannot misuse it.
  - If you haven't sufficiently cleansed, you will be prevented by your Divine Self from having the power.
  - If you steal it before you are ready, it will harm you and you will lose it. You will want to, as thieves are known tto, waste the dirty money.

II. The tyrant.

A) **The offensive mode.** All tyrants are infants, shrieking in their demands. Hitler, Castro, Saddam Hussein, all are infants, demanding now an omnipotence that they don't have. They try to get it through egocentric attention seeking, through preying on people's weaknesses who collude with them.

Having seduced, they now use those who are seduced by them to do their bidding, to enforce their demands. This is familiar and obvious. Thus, it is less harmful than the less obvious style of tyranny:

B) **The tyranny of docility** in which you feign to yield in order to acquire power. You seduce by becoming a slave, so as to gain power and become master. How do you do it?

- By using your assets, your godly qualities of beauty,

intelligence, capacity to love and to have compassion on any level, mental, emotional or physical; the volition is to gain Absolute Power over others.

• By appearing to be a victim, feeling sorry for yourself; this too is tyranny, the tyranny of victimization. Its motive is the acquisition of Absolute Power.

• By obtaining approval, becoming anything they want you to be. Thus, all the achievements dedicated to this end, serve an evil purpose. If your degree that you are using in your profession has been obtained for approval purposes, it is now serving a tyrant, a Hitleric part of you out to conquer and subjugate the world. Here we meet the yuppy again. This is why, behind every achievement driven yuppy is a tyrant—and we sense it and are repelled by it if we, ourselves are free of this aspect.

C) **Escape,** which is nothing else but the demand for power in playing hard to get. All escape, withholding, indifference, etc., have a demand for instant omnipotence activating them. This takes the form of monasticism, asceticism, renouncement of life, or suicide. Thus, suicide is a power trip, the ultimate one, the one that makes the least sense, since it obviously results in utter powerlessness.

What does a suicidal person think about while contemplating ending his life? "They'll see; I'll pay them back; they'll be sorry for not acceding to my demands, I'll show them who's boss."

Well, what do you think about when you are bitter and withdrawn? Watch yourself think after a confrontation, or a defeat, or a reprimand against which you defend. You too say exactly the same suicidal things to yourself! You too, at that time, are committing suicide. Even your desire to be saved, which you call prayer and with which you cover up those despairing and suicidal thoughts, even that aids and abets suicide. It is a thought that has given up on you, that has condemned you to impotency. Consider also the demand for instant omnipotence acted out in playing hard to get, or in taking others for granted.

All of this constitutes a wrong way, the wrong way to omnipotence. It can be found in any and all of our distortions. All glamours and all underlying distorted self volitions are based on the demand for instant omnipotence.

III. Striving and acceptance distorted.

A) The contrived, forceful, rigid, tyrannical demand of the yuppy or the victim or the withholder are mistaken for striving, vigour and life. Nothing could be further from the truth. They are all death wishes, swan dances that peter out because they all are disconnected from goodness. Their volition, being harmful, they are doomed to die. They will want to die because they, by definition, have rejected themselves. Do you understand? You may not. If not, check "Needs III" in *The Path of Purpose and Pleasure,* or ask your teacher to explain.

The healthy way to strive is relaxed and unforced. It flows and will never burn out.

B) On the other hand, acceptance is seen as collapse, as giving up and as numbing. This too is idealized in the celibate monk and in the glorification of all docility and escape. It is none of that. Acceptance is alive. It is a movement. You move in your yielding, as much as you yield in your movement. And here we can see that, in the healthy and lawful pursuit of power, striving and acceptance are one. Vigour and action go hand in hand with yielding and learning. You want proof? You don't have to go too far to find it. Look at your breathing. There is yielding and receptivity in your inhaling. Yet it is active. There is relief and yielding in your exhaling, yet, it is a giving, a putting out.

Back to Nature

When you interfere with your breathing, you mess it up. You can only yield when you allow your breathing to be natural. You can only be vigourous and active in the same context. The harmonious striving for power must be accompanied by rest and by recharging.

As long as you maintain your tyrannies, your docility and your withholding, you will be forcing nature. You will never know when it is right to relax and to be active, to assert yourself or to let go. You will be confused as to what is right and wrong. Your loving will be warped, since used by your tyranny.

By contrast, the natural striving for power will illuminate all of these problems and solve them for you.

Reaching For Perfection And For Eternal Life Bring You Absolute Power

You cannot reach for perfection without acquiring power. It comes with the territory.

You cannot, as we have seen, reach for eternal life without reaching for perfection. They go hand in hand.

Well, the third element—actually the first—is power. Absolute Power comes with perfection. Eternal life comes with it. Dynamically expressed: the more you cleanse, gradually attaining perfection, the more you will have power, and the less you will need to be born and to die. The three must come together, being the Trinity. You cannot have one without the other. In order to have one, you must develop the other two.

If you want power, you must love, have faith, live harmoniously, and acquire knowledge.

If you want love, you must accept the responsibility of

power and the wisdom of knowledge.

If you want knowledge, you must accept the responsibility of the power that comes with it and the loving context required to acquire it.

If you want eternal life, you must develop infinite love and accept the omnipotence that comes with it.

All beneficial qualities are at-one in God. To possess one, you must possess them all.

Absolute Power

It does not, as the saying goes, corrupt absolutely. It only does so in the absence of spiritual cleansing. Then, it is stolen, not earned, and it must burn out. Thus, it is not Absolute.

The only Absolute Power is obtained through cleansing which liberates perfection and gives eternal life. That kind of Absolute Power neither is corrupt for corrupting. It can only be beneficial. It is, in Buddhist terms, harmless.

It is most unfortunate that harmlessness is so often erroneously associated with powerlessness. When we say "he is harmless," we mistakenly mean "he is powerless." This then facilitates another oft-mentioned freeze: "Power is harmful."

Both are distortions. Actually, harmlessness, which is goodness, engenders power. Harmfulness dulls and clogs the channels to power, to knowledge and to love. There are plenty of historical examples to illustrate this point.

Absolute Power when it becomes corrupting, has become corrupt, and therefore, cannot be Absolute.

Progress Mistaken for Absolute Power

You have mastered an area, or many, which, before, were thought to be insurmountable. This victory, this achievement corresponds to an open channel to the infinite, a place where you truly are contacted and are contacting your Divine Self. You have facility in this area. Having more power than you ever thought possible, you now believe to be omnipotent.

But wait. The worst is yet to come. You generalize this feeling by believing that you possess the same qualities everywhere else in your life! You use the mastery achieved in one area or several to block the others. You have decided no longer to struggle. You, therefore, clog yourself up, sewing a cocoon around you much like a worm, creating a shut energy system. You can no longer grow, since growth constitutes the continuous dissolution of distortions, of evil within.

The relative power found in the areas of growth is mistaken for Absolute Power. The child tyrant has gotten a hold of your progress and is now using it for his own benefit.

So many, having achieved some results through practicing this faith and having been astonished by the rewards, use this to stop labouring. They put an end to their spiritual training, sometimes quitting, leaving, sometimes staying a while and feigning effort.

Thus, those who have achieved, need to cleanse a lot more than those who have not. The danger of regression is commensurate to the amount of progress. Cleansing must continue, being an integral part of our progress.

****

The spiritual steps that lead to Absolute Power will always be there, leading us in our return to God.

Chapter 24
Absolute Power II

"Be God" is usually met with fear, resentment, anger, to mention a few reactions emanating from the Judeo-Christian anti-power freeze. We have spoken about this in the previous sermon. However, what is the volitionality inherent in that freeze? When a societal taboo exists or when a freeze persists, it means that the volitionality in it activates it, perpetuating it.

1) I don't want to be God because I don't want the responsibility that comes with omnipotence. However, this, in itself, is an excuse. It hides the unwillingness to take responsibility on the relative level as well. This leads us to the next element in that volitionality.

2) I don't want to be God because I want God to take care of me. I want Him to save me without my having to change. I want Him to make me change without effort. Actually, I also don't want Him to make me change. I want Him to give me what I can only obtain if I were to change.

Therefore, accepting a) the fact that I, in my Divine Self right now, am God, and b) the fact that the pursuit of Absolute Power is my right and my duty involve:

- The necessity to dissolve the harmful dependency on God to save me—or on Christ, or on any other saviour for that matter.
- The necessity to do it myself, i.e., to take full responsi-

bility for myself, for obtaining omnipotence through striving for perfection and for eternal life.

Abandon then those false beliefs. Remember that even the Christ said that we would achieve greater deeds than He. Open your brain, not just your mind, that Absolute Power already exists, waiting for you to integrate it. You know already that there is a place in you that always makes the right decisions.

By refusing to accept "I am God," you sacrifice your Divine Self for the illusion that someone will rescue you. Why should God rescue you from your mistakes? It is conceited to believe that He would. It implies that you are special. On the contrary, accepting my claim for Absolute Power—that "I am God"—requires humility, the humility necessary to accept the correcting of my mistakes and effecting my own salvation. You can see how conceit has wrongly been attributed to "I am God," instead of being attributed to the false humility of the miserable sinner. You can also see how humility has falsely been attributed to the miserable sinner, actually being more correctly attributable to the person who accepts and implements the way that leads to Eternal Life, the way of this faith.

Therefore, differentiate between genuine and affected humility.

The Absolute as an Experiential Reality

Scientists tell us that the Absolute is a mathematical abstraction. However, the Absolute is no abstraction to us. **It is an experiential reality.** In this spiritual training, we continuously anchor ourselves in it, and, from its vantage point, are able to look at our finite/relative world in reality, pointing out where it is beneficial and harmful.

If we were not able to anchor ourselves in the Absolute, if we did not have faith in its existence, we could not undergo the little daily deaths such as sleeping, meditating or having an orgasm. Nor could we tolerate the consciousness of being wrong, of the harmful aspects of the relative. Indeed, without faith in the Absolute, we could not even conceive of it, nor perceive it.

Without that, we would be convinced that our entire Universe consists of the limited air bubble of distortion that we have created. Challenging it by admitting that it is harmful would feel like total annihilation and would be resisted as if it were a matter of life and death.

Only when the Absolute is accepted and experienced can self-confrontation and cleansing become possible and can lead to self-actualization, omnipotence, eternal life and perfection. Also, only when the Absolute is accepted can the relative be corrected. This instantly invalidates any psychological, emotional, mental or physical healing that is not based on Spiritual Law.

All of this leads to a startling conclusion: that you can find proof of the existence of God and of the fact that you are God in all your capacities to yield—to die a little. Being wrong, being able to confront the self without fear of self-annihilation, capacity to sleep, to meditate or to orgasm, are all such proofs.

Revise Your Concept of God

Sometime ago, I gave some material concerning how you visualize God to be. The distortions of this concept run deep. You may intellectually have an evolved concept of God, while emotionally still harbouring a very childish one. It is the latter that must be detected and dissolved, the former being merely superficial. Don't let the former hide the latter. Once you have found these deeper concepts and freezes, transform them.

God is the eternal youth. His goal, among others, is very much to enjoy Himself. He doesn't grow old. He is in a continuous state of grace. He wants you to be He.

There would be nothing in your life that He wouldn't enjoy doing. This includes those chores that you find frustrating and beneath your dignity. Meditate on that. If God is willing to do it, you too can.

God does primarily what He does, first for Himself, then for us and the rest of His creation. **Being for Himself is what He practices at a hundred percent.** That's why He is constantly giving. He could not give if He did not have and He could not have if He did not give to Himself first, if He did not exist for Himself first.[1]

For whom do you exist? Do you practice being for yourself? When you sell out, you are being for somebody else. That's why you cannot give. It is those who sell out that cannot give, that withhold and that cheat. Those who are in a state of being for themselves are the only ones who are capable of being genuinely giving.

The same applies to the capacity of forgiving. If you are for yourself, you value yourself. Forgiving then becomes possible. As long as you do not value yourself, you will continue to want to hold "you owe me" cases, believing that you could thus add to your value. So, you will be unwilling to forgive, even unable to do so. Incapacity to forgive will then promote further self-depreciation through guilt. Once again, we find the merry-go-round of another vicious circle.

---

[1] "Being for oneself" interestingly enough is a fundamental concept in Satre's philosophy of existentialism, an atheistic one. However, unbeknownst to Satre and to the stuck up, bigoted Christianity of his father, it is also a fundamental quality of God and of being God.

The Primitive Self And Your Freeze of God

1) At birth, as we have seen elsewhere in my sermons, the little self is in despair. Having left the blissful oneness with God, where he too was God, he suddenly finds himself utterly powerless. Whereas before birth, his wishes were instantly fulfilled, now they are continuously frustrated.

2) So, the primitive self must find a quick and ready made God to replace the One God. He chooses the parent who seems to be the most powerful. It usually is the withholder or the irrational tyrant, since he has a greater effect than the rational and loving parent. So, God now is an irrational tyrant who withholds and who seems to be all powerful.

3) Having appointed that parent God and having given him omnipotence, that parent has become the paragon of power.

4) So, when it is time for the primitive self to exert his power, he will become, when first married for example, the bad parent with whom power is associated.

5) The manifestation of this tyranny will occur first against the loving and rational parent, both on the part of the bad parent and on the part of the primitive self emulating the bad parent.

6) This behaviour will be generalized to anyone else who is rational and loving, including on the rational and loving part of the self.

7) The primitive self has become the child tyrant.

8) Every time you let him get away with something, you confirm his illusion of omnipotence and encourage his desire for it.

Law: Absolute Power doesn't corrupt. The illusion of Absolute Power does. Distorted, the legitimate longing for power becomes the unquenchable addiction to the instant gratification of the feeling omnipotence. Incredible pain and suffering results from this. Consequently, a freeze, a taboo sets in whereby all power is seen as bad.

The Illusion of Omnipotence in The Child Tyrant

The child tyrant continuously and desperately intends to prove that he is omnipotent. Thus, he makes this into a life or death struggle, experiencing excruciating pain when, in the slightest way, things are not going his way.

The problem is that if you let him get away with something, i.e., if you let him get his way, he becomes worse. He is now encouraged to continue on his rampage of cruelty and demands, attempting to further prove his omnipotence. Having had his way, he feels rewarded for his harmful behaviour.

Therefore, do not mistake love with allowing a child tyrant to get away with something. Do not believe that someone who lets you get away with something really loves you.

The child tyrant will also misinterpret genuine love for allowing him to get away with something. He will wrongly conclude that he owns anyone who loves him or who shows him any inkling of kindness. The more you love the child tyrant, the more he will feel he is the master and you the slave. He will take advantage of the slightest show of love to manifest his desire for power and enslavement.

Commitment from another is seen by the child tyrant as permission to tyrannize. That's why it is foolish for someone in our faith to commit to a relationship to someone who is not, i.e., not in the practice of owning up to and neutralizing the child tyrant within themselves.

The Illusion of Omnipotence in The Tyranny of Docility

As you grow up, you learn that it is not wise to, at once, show your child tyrant in your desire to enslave. In order to have power, you must elicit in the other the love response that will enable your child tyrant to enslave. So, you make nice, you use a deified self of goodness and love. Since, in the first place, you have viewed love and goodness as weakness, your expression of love will be docile.

When you get the desired love response, you unleash the child tyrant who now feels once again that he owns you. Soon, you master the art of doing both simultaneously. **Thus, your docility itself becomes the tyranny; you use your capacity to love as a weapon of enslavement and tyranny.**

Here, we find the servants who are masters, the guilt trips of masochistic "Jewish mothers" or " Italian mothers" who have done so much for you that you are considered to be their slave for life. Of course, mothers are a prototype. The same can be done with mates, bosses, employees, countries, leaders, etc.

Look for the ways that you say "I will be whatever you want me to be." Look for the promises you make which you don't intend to keep, for the Jekyll/Hyde personality changes that you use for the purposes of seduction.

Another way to describe what happens to the thirst for omnipotence in a relationship can be expressed as follows:

"I don't feel that you love me or that you are committed to me. So, I am going to make you love me and commit to me by exciting your power over me. I will do so by being docile. Once you respond with some commitment to me, my tyranny over you will begin. I have made my docility a weapon to the service of my child tyrant. My docility itself, therefore, is my tyranny since it is making you do what you don't want to do and what I want you to."

The Illusion of Omnipotence in Withholding
Here we have a wide range of symptoms, from playing hard to get to committing suicide, through escape in

monasteries and abstinence. The basic philosophy here is expressed somewhat as follows, "I have tried to have my way directly, and it didn't work; I have tried it through docility and it didn't work; now I will try it through withholding and escaping."

Self-destructiveness and self-punishment belongs in this category. It is the last ditch of the stubborn child tyrant who has failed at enslavement.

In a relationship, this life position can be expressed as follows:

"I tried direct offensiveness and tyranny of docility. You saw through both and you put me in my place. Therefore, I will escape, pout, punish myself through destroying myself to make you feel guilty. Still however, I am acting out my desire to enslave you. My pouting or self-destruction is my tyrant manifest.

The point is here that I must have power over something. I failed to have power over you and over life. Now, I am going to exercise power over myself by escaping, making myself unhappy, hurting myself, or killing myself. Through this, I'll also have power over you. And you'll be sorry. I'll show you. I'll punish you."

This mode is the furthest removed from goodness, from the Divine Self. **Thus, as nakedly cruel as the blatant direct child tyrant appears to be, it is a lot better than self-destructiveness. The docility as tyranny is also better.**

Therefore, amazingly enough, no matter how cruel you can be, you are not as bad as when you punish yourself or when you kill yourself. Suicide is worse than genocide!

Guilt

We haven't even mentioned guilt here. We have demonstrated the fallacy of greed for power and its harmful consequences without even considering the guilt it creates. Let's do so for a moment:

Any power obtained outside of love and intelligence, i.e., of perfection and Eternal Life, creates guilt. There is enormous guilt in using others' love for the purpose of enslavement. The guilt is not generated only in case they fall into the trap. It exists whether you enslave them or not. It is created merely for intending to enslave.

Another guilt is added when you submit to tyrannize. It is the guilt of lying and of pretending. It is the guilt of making others responsible for your fate.

Yet, a third guilt is added when, having failed in the first two modes, you pout, withdraw or harm yourself.

Every single measure of guilt creates pain whether you are aware of it or not. Imagine all of the pain that you have created through all of your games! You must be in great pain! Isn't it time to stop?

Healing

In these three categories, you can recognize your own incredibly greedy desire for power.

Why this deep and intense need for it? **Because power has been tabooed in the first place.**

If you accept power as being legitimate, all of this will not need to exist. Thus, the remedy is to accept that you are God. How does that feel? I am God and I deserve omnipotence. I accept the fact that I don't have it now and that it will come in concert with, and as a function of, perfection and eternal life. I humbly reach out for all of that.

Omnipotence is your natural state. Seek it with elegance, with beauty, with kindness, with harmlessness.

Meditate on harmless omnipotence. See that obtaining

power results in healing. When you feel powerful, you don't need to cheat, to demand and to enslave.

You can experience power through walking the way to mastery. Master your problems one step at a time. Take them one by one. The little achievements will keep you continuously motivated. Before you know it, you will have achieved great results (consult the material on mastery, to be found in my book, *From Crisis to Mastery and Ecstasy*).

Power as Effortless Creation

That's what you really want, isn't it? Wouldn't it be wonderful if you could create all you want without effort? You see yourself endlessly struggling to remain above board, to "survive" as it were.

Actually, there is a part of you that is already effortlessly creating. **Look at the ease with which you create the harm!** You don't even have to strain to do it. **It comes by itself, apparently without effort!**

So, why couldn't it be as easy for your beneficial aspirations? Obviously, because there exists unconscious areas—perhaps harmful, perhaps not—that oppose it "effortlessly" because unconsciously. If those are removed or dissolved, the conscious aspirations would also become practically effortless.

By repressing the harmful, you have sent it closer to your source of power and creativity. The harmful has, because repressed, yielded more to the Cosmic Life Force and to the Cosmic Consciousness, immersing itself in them. These divine aspects are a lot more powerful in your unconscious.

By repressing distortions into your unconscious, you have allowed them to train that unconscious. You have created a machine which effortlessly manufactures the harmful.

You must now bring out to the light those harmful

mechanisms so as to correct the wrong thinking behind them.

Effortless creation exists with each one of us here and now. Only it is misappropriated. It is up to us to change this investment of power.

****

Reach out for power in the context of harmlessness and goodness. You have a real and divine need to have an impact on the Universe. Listen to and heed this need. Take the Kingdom of God by storm. In the words of the Christ, set the world on fire. Be God.

Chapter 25
Leadership and Authority

- *To pass a law and not have it enforced is to authorize the very thing you wish to prohibit.*
  —Armand Jean du Plessis de Richelieu, 1585-1642.

- *The rejection of authority can sometimes result paradoxically in an embrace of authoritarianism. Indeed, it can happen with insidious ease.*
  —Dinesh D'Souza, 1961- , Indian born American writer.

Growing into a leader constitutes your spiritual goal. Your cleansing is leading you to this position in organic and natural fashion. Those who follow this faith know this to be the manifest reality in any life area where Divine Law has been applied. Being a leader has nothing to do with diplomas, medals or crowns bestowed upon you. No title can give you what you grow into by yourself when you walk this faith.

Let us first consider the distortions concerning leadership. Since every distortion brings duality, let us consider the dualities also, the ones brought about by distortion.

First Distortion: Jealousy.

A) **You resent leaders and are hostile to them.** You compete with them. However, rather than admit your jealousy, you hide it and replace it by **cases.** You use those cases to obtain what you want from the leaders, i.e., their position and privileges.

For this purpose, **you revive early problems** with the first or past authorities of your life. Most of the time, **these problems have already been solved** and do not need to be brought back. However, because you look for **ammunition** against the present authorities, you unfortunately revive them, thus regressing, losing ground in this faith, wasting what you have already obtained and achieved.

Thus, you **antagonize anyone who is a leader.** Then, when you incur their angry response, you anchor yourself even deeper into your erroneous case, convincing yourself that you are being unjustly punished and cruelly deprived.

You have become hostile towards leadership.

B) **Your jealously also means that you want their position.** However, how can you want a position on which you have dumped so much hostility?

Furthermore, you do not want to grow as they did into it. You also do not take responsibility as they do. You want to lead what they are leading. You do not want to create your own leadership. You want to **parasite** on them. You do not want to take responsibility. You want their privileges and their freedom without the burden of their responsibility.

You want the leaders to give you the leadership that you don't deserve, that you haven't earned. **You do nothing to become a real and good leader, to obey the laws that govern it.**

It is your primitive self that is at work and that wants leadership in order to give license to its tyranny. You want to act out your tyranny rather than be a leader.

In short: A) I want to destroy leaders *versus*

B) I want to be one of them.

You have blocked the possibility to be a leader by a)

hating it and b) violating the laws and requirements that would lead you to it.

As long as you don't obey the Laws of Leadership and as long as you are not responsible, **you have no right to be jealous of leaders, nor to have anything they have.** In the sermon that will follow the Easter services, you will find the laws that govern leadership.

Second Distortion: Ownership of a genie, your leader.

A) **You want ownership and control over your leader.** You see him as Aladdin's genie. You invoke him when you wish something, no matter from where within you these wishes originate, your distorted self, or worse, your deified self.

He is supposed to make all of this possible as well as shield you from the consequences. You demand that he do all of this, and in addition:

- That you neither be required to love him nor be grateful to him.
- That once you have gotten what you want, you could order him to go back into his lamp and be forgotten about.
- That you don't have to tell the truth, be in truth, have ethics, and yet still get all you want.

Aladdin's lamp and genie is not a mere fable. It exists in everyone and it is acted out with every authority and every leader.

B) **You do not want to have his power. You only want to abuse his power. You want power over power, without having power.** You are afraid of power because you have made it into your slave. It has now become a habit, one that you have acquired early in your childhood. The couple of paragraphs that follow will explain to you how you have acquired this bad habit.

How would you like to be the genie, at the mercy of an Aladdin who uses and abuses you mercilessly and thanklessly? I have news for you. **If you have abused authority, if you were pampered in childhood, if you made one of your parents into this slave/genie,** I guarantee, for you, the following:

1) **You will be terrified of your children and your followers** because you will believe that they want to make **you** into the slave/genie, and that they have the power to do it by the mere fact that they are children or followers—underdogs—as you were when you bullied your parents.

Consequently, you will be unable to love your children and your followers in a real and adult fashion—the only true love. As a result, you will feel enormous guilt and

2) **Out of guilt for not loving them, you will become the slave/genie, believing that you thus compensate for your guilt.** Nothing could be further from the truth. In effect, by becoming a slave/genie as a parent, **you recreate, in your children and followers, the child tyrant/Aladdin** that was born in your childhood and that is still alive and well and destructive in a rampant way.

Thus, the permissive parent/leader who in effect hates his children/followers, makes to them an overall statement of cynicism: "Go ahead and enslave me; I'll make you into a child tyrant. You will suffer as I did, wanting everything and wanting nothing, being without a rudder, rebelling without a cause and creating the untold unhappiness that I have created for myself. I'll punish you in this way and you won't even know it."

So, I want the power of leadership and I don't want it. I want the genie's power and I don't want it. I want to use it but I don't want to be it.

Be a Follower to Be a Leader

If you don't decide for yourself, someone will decide for you. If you don't think for yourself, someone will think for you. That someone will be bad to the degree you want him to be a slave/genie. He is bound to be, even if he appears to be good.

However, this doesn't mean that you don't need leadership and direction. But, in order to choose the right kind of leader and leadership, you must yield to the necessity to hear what you don't want to hear. You must undergo the pain that you have avoided. You must yield to a leader that will not flatter you or cater to your distortions. To some extent, then, you must already know what your distortions are.

If you have wanted a slave/genie, you will attract a tyrannical and immature Aladdin, and vice versa. Your life will be filled with leaders who resemble both.

Nevertheless, you need guidance. Have enough inner authority to trust good leadership.

Reality

It is impossible for any entity to have power without autonomy, without freedom and without responsibility. When power is abused, it wanes. Examples abound. The most notable ones can be found in the history of the 20th Century which has abundantly demonstrated again and again that leaders who abuse their powers end up losing those powers and, either being destroyed, or self-destructing from within.

There is no such thing as a genie. The unfortunate parents who have played that role for their children created an atmosphere of mutual enslavement, ruining their own lives as well as their children's lives.

In this respect, it is also important to remember the master/slave relationship described in Hegelian dialectics. By being a slave, power is accumulated until it is time for the slave to topple the master and become master himself, starting the cycle all over again.

Make no mistake about the permissive parent's motives. They are worse than the tyrannical parent's.

If the genie had a modicum of self-respect, he would confront Aladdin on his distorted self motives. Aladdin's power to put the genie back in the bottle can at this point be acted out. Aladdin can choose to say "I don't want to hear the genie's confrontation; I don't want his wisdom and leadership; if he doesn't want to do or say what I want him to, I will disconnect from him."

This corresponds to your demands that your authorities be at your beck and call, doing what you want them to and saying what you want them to. When they don't accede to your demands, **you are the one who will be dismissed by them. Authority has the power to dismiss you, not you authority.** That is what should come to your mind when Aladdin puts the genie back in the bottle. You will be the one who will miss out on the benefits of being a follower and receiving guidance.

If the leader in authority would not dismiss you, you will instantly misinterpret his benevolence to be weakness. Thus, a leader cannot afford to be benevolent with you past a certain point. Past that point, you must be dismissed for the good of all concerned.

Govern Your Life

Life government; self-govern is the first prerequisite to leadership. **If you don't do it yourself, an authority will do it for you.** As much as you will desire to be autonomous, you will unconsciously seek to be led. You will attract bad leaders and specialists on the spirit level that will lead you astray.

**If you choose good leaders, they will show you the way
to autonomy.** If you refuse to take it, you will blame the good
leaders for your unhappiness, while at the same time
demanding that they save you from it. You can see here
another distortion and another duality creating yet another
conflict.

Turn this around. If you are here listening to this message
or reading these word you are bound to have the tools for
governing your life. Here are some steps which must be taken
slowly:

- First, take responsibility for your own life, for your
  creations, for your duties and for your support of yourself.
- Then take responsibility for your immediate environment,
  expanding your autonomy, loving and helping others in
  your immediate vicinity achieve theirs.
- Then find your task. If you followed the first two steps, it
  will unfold organically. You will recognize it in spite of
  your defense and you will follow it. Here you begin to
  teach what you were taught in this faith.
- Then take your global responsibility. To use the Tibetan's
  terminology, become a planetary citizen. Usher in the New
  Religion; be an ambassador of this faith.

Of course, these steps overlap. They don't necessarily
follow each other in a linear fashion. Life brings you daily
opportunities to walk these steps. Humbly take them as they
come.

The Sin of Stagnation

Many of your current problems have already been resolved
a long time ago. Yet, you persist in maintaining yourself in
repeated old patterns, acting them out over and over again.

The price to pay for such stagnation in a distortion is

far greater than the price you pay when you first encounter that distortion. This is particularly true if you are honestly engaged in resolving it. Then, you neutralize its damage. But, the longer you persist in reviving old issues, issues that have been studied in all their facets, considered, pampered and dealt with ad nauseam, the greater the price to pay.

The guilt is now greater because you knowingly continue to be harmful. You simply don't want to step into the position of leadership which awaits you. You find safety in the increasingly noxious old issues and you are poisoning yourself. You thus escape leadership.

Here, we encounter a Spiritual Law:

- The rate of growth expected for an individual is commensurate to his spiritual development. The greater is his development, the more diligently is he expected to solve his problems and move on to leadership.
- Consequently, the degree of damage, guilt, pain and suffering, created by stagnation—by the volition to remain harmful—is also proportional to his spiritual development.

How long will you veterans of this Church continue to recreate your distortions? How long should we allow you to continue to pretend that you are cleansing them?

This must stop. Inhabit your progress. Take this spiritual training seriously. Don't ruminate on old issues. You are getting sicker that way than you were when you started.

Growth must be continuous to find leadership and to find God.

Chapter 26
Requirements of Leadership I

- *The manner of giving is worth more than the gift.*
  —Pierre Corneille, 1606-1684, *The Liar*, I, i.

- *Behold, I do not give lectures or a little charity.*
  When I give, I give myself.
  —Walt Whitman, 1819-1892, *Song of Myself.*

I. Selfless Giving

It is the first and foremost requirement. The degree of leadership is commensurate to it. Yet, it is violated by the very people who **covet** it with so much intensity. The coveting of leadership, therefore, precludes it by definition. He who covets leadership doesn't deserve it, shouldn't have it.

The fundamental motive for wanting leadership must be selfless giving. When you covet leadership, you believe:

1) That the leaders are taking away from you what you believe is rightfully yours.

2) That they are unjustly forcing you to accept something. Therefore, you blame them for your own lack of leadership and power.

The selfless giving of a leader must go beyond the mouthing of it, the words. It must manifest everywhere, from the great to the small issues, acts, thoughts and feelings.

Observe the quality of your giving. Do you detect bitterness, hostility, regret about having to give, lack of good will? If any of this is present, it annuls your giving. Your giving won't count. It is more honest not to give. Therefore, your giving should be:

1) Free and loving, coming without conditions, no strings attached.

2) It is—pardon the expression—**obeying a command.** Yes, if you want leadership, you must obey the **command to give,** and selflessly at that.

If you don't like it, stay in your mediocrity and don't have the audacity to covet the position of leader.

If you want leadership, pay the price of entrance. Learn to give. Cleanse the covetousness and the volitionality to abuse leadership and power.

Leadership, therefore, is only possible when **obedience** has been willingly learned, embraced and practiced. Obedience to what? To the perfection of Spiritual Law, which is utmost justice. Do not then behave as if this required obedience were unjust. Find your rebelliousness, your resentment and your dishonest whitewashing and rationalizing of it.

Once again, find, in your giving, the caveats as follows:

- I regret, on second thought, having given selflessly, without expecting anything in return. (This also exists if I have gotten something in return, such as in a purchase, creating the oft-mentioned but misnamed buyer's remorse.)
- I give with the volition to get something, but I pretend not to have that volition.
- My giving is measured to what I will get back; here is a mercenary attitude which, albeit cleaner than the previous hidden volition, cannot pretend to be real giving.
- Unspoken haggling: "If I give so much, God, or some

authority will notice me and reward me with this and that." Consider Salieri's haggling with God, according to, of course, the film *Amadeus*. It was not an uncommon type of haggling at the time, nor is it uncommon today. Every single person today haggles in the same manner. Salieri promised chastity to God. In exchange, he expected God to give him genius and creativity. Of course, he was shooting himself in the foot, since there is no creativity outside of sexuality. Creativity is a sexual act and sexuality is a creative act.

- Safety valves and caveats. I will commit **but.** I will commit up to a certain point. **But** I will pretend to be committed all the way. And when I am called to my word, I will lie, cheat, steal, betray and denigrate.
- I will hold grudges when confronted with the Law of Giving and with my non-giving.

All of this negates your giving. It can neither satisfy you nor anyone else. **It creates the lack of return.** All of this, negating your giving, also negates the expected returns. This then justifies not giving to begin with. Now you have proven the original secret premise: that giving doesn't work, that commitment is against you. In reality you never gave. So, it is only just that you never got.

Giving Is Nature
Originally, giving is effortless and simple. It comes naturally. It includes:
- The thinking, the Third Ray, Mother.
- The love, the Second Ray, Son.
- The volition and act, the First Ray, Father.
  Say the following:

Evocation for Selfless Giving
I place myself in the service of God's Law,
Becoming its tool and its usher,
Giving it bountifully and boundlessly.

I relinquish my little selfishness,
And my glamourous self-idealizations,
My hidden motives and my haggling.

I place all I have, inner and outer
To the service of my God self,
Expecting nothing in return,
Rejoicing in my contribution
To making this a better and richer world.

The Fruits of Selfless Giving
1) **The sense of self-worth and self-love** which makes self-assertion possible. Anything less is guilt ridden and cannot enlist the full power of the Cosmic Life Force and the Cosmic Consciousness. In it you feel you deserve the best and you claim it.

2) Covetousness, envy are moot. You cannot want anything else than what you are getting. You cannot want to be anyone else than who you are.

Pseudo-giving makes you unable to receive. You find yourself constantly missing out on opportunities, on life.

Pseudo-giving also guarantees your envy for those who do give, and therefore, do receive.

Consequently, consider your jealousy and frustration as a yardstick with which to measure your lack of giving. The more sincerely you give, the more abundantly you receive.

3) **Self-protection:** This selfless giving leads to leadership in your life. You will make the right decisions, resolve all

conflicts and dualities because you will have unified yourself.

II. Fairness, an Essential Leadership Trait

You claim to be fair by rationalizing your little distorted wishes, your ego trips and your distortions.

In order to be a leader, you must:

1) Be honest enough to detect your harmful contribution to a situation, and to admit it.

2) Be wise enough to be positive that this contribution will not deter from what is Good, Beautiful and True.

3) **Disqualify yourself**, in humility in case of any doubt about it.

This faith constitutes training in fairness through the ability to know yourself and to be honest about revealing it. You cannot qualify as fair in areas where you are still full of jumbled emotions, envy, cruelty, fear, demands and despair, or guilt. Yet, watch yourself pretend to be impartial in your judgment in the midst of this confusion.

You would truly be a leader if you had the honesty to disqualify yourself in these situations.

By maintaining the lie in a defensive mode, you make yourself truly weak and open to attacks from others. As vicious as they will be, these attacks, directed at your one or few faults, help you to overcome them.

As a leader, be prepared to have every weakness attacked. As a leader, you have an infinitely greater responsibility to cleanse than do your followers. This is true of all your faults, whether or not they pertain to your area of leadership.

Today, in this country, once again, we have a prime example of this in our president, Bill Clinton. By now, everybody knows that he has had—and possibly still has—a sexual addiction. He compounded the damage to himself by most probably coaching his mistresses into lying, directly or indirectly.

Unfortunately, if he is impeached it will be for the latter offense, not for the former. He cannot be impeached for having affairs. But, he can be for obstructing justice.

Hiding his addiction led to even greater harm. Let's remember that as an example for ourselves.

Now, if he honestly came out and admitted his affairs, he would demonstrate true leadership, loving leadership in a free country. He would gain so much self-respect that, in his position, he would have the courage and honesty to lead all of us to even greater happiness and prosperity. His self-assertion would solve a lot of world problems. Besides, he would save himself and Hillary immense legal expenses, incurred. Because the vultures in the legal profession would not have his liver to pick on. Besides, he would be unchained, having both hands at his disposal.[1]

****

More requirements will be given about leadership in subsequent sermons.

****

Adopt, as a motto, the following:
Freely give true love
Freely love true giving
and leadership will gradually blossom into your life, as you grow closer to God.

---

[1] Those are two allusions to the myth of Prometheus, who, having stolen fire from the Gods and given it to humanity, was chained to Mount Atlas and had a vulture picking on his perpetually regenerating liver. He was rescued by Hercules—according to the Tibetan—on his way to finding the golden apples of Hesperides.

Chapter 27
Requirements of Leadership II

- *Men at sometime are masters of their fates:*
  The fault, dear Brutus, lies not in our stars
  But in ourselves, that we are underlings.
  —Shakespeare, *Julius Caesar*, I, ii.

- *The abuse of greatness is when it disjoins*
  Remorse from power.
  —Ibid., II, i.

Before studying the next two requirements, let's study the consequences of violating the first one:

Consequences of Non-Giving
1) When you don't give, you develop selfishness and egocentricity, resulting in alienation, separation, disconnection.

2) In that alienated state, first you are unwilling, then unable to communicate and share experiences.

3) You feel alone and unique in this problem, thus inferior to the entire world.

4) You believe that you are the only one experiencing something in a particular way.

5) This secrecy creates guilt. Guilt creates pain and self-depreciation.

6) Self-depreciation creates shame.

7) Shame propels the cover up of super-sharing and pseudo-altruism, of the ego of egolessness, or of super-goodness and super-success.

8) The loneliness and inability to share is dishonestly turned around and becomes a glamourized and glorified sense of uniqueness. **True uniqueness comes through the humility of sharing and identifying with others, a mark of true leadership.**

9) So, non-giving which was supposed to bring you happiness and abundance, instead brings you poverty, unhappiness, deceleration and death.

10) The alienated aspects incarnate alone, no longer able to hide behind substitutes, having to find God within themselves.

Stagnation

When someone is ready to take the next step in leadership and doesn't, stagnation sets in. When someone is ready to take any forward step and doesn't, it is the same thing. All that is said here about stagnation applies to all reluctance to action and to progress.

This stagnation seems harmless, but it always hides active harmfulness. Long periods of stagnation mean that something harmful is active and hidden. *Qui n'avance pas, recule*—he who doesn't go forward, goes backwards—contains more truth than you may think. He who doesn't go forward is secretly involved in active harmfulness, hostility, deceit, betrayal and so much more ugliness. Make no mistake about it. Those of you who are in that state are seriously urged to put this in practice.

Stagnation means that the person who stagnates is untrustworthy. He is hiding something. And that hiding is more often conscious than unconscious. It is at least preconscious.

Stagnation must be dissolved if leadership is to be pursued.

****

We now continue to study leadership and its requirements. Remember that they are all important. One of these requirements cannot exist without the other.

III. Openness to Confrontation

This is truer for the leader than it is for the follower. **Accepting constructive criticism** is an essential condition for leadership. Whoever wants to use the power of leadership for the purpose of defending against or forbidding criticism:

- Negates his position as a leader and becomes lower than his followers.
- Substitutes tyranny for leadership.
- Stifles and kills the life of his and of his follower's task.
- Begins an inner conflict between what he is doing and what is the right thing to do—accepting and dealing with criticism.

What about destructive criticism, or dumping? Should that too be accepted? Resist not evil said the Christ; turn the other cheek. What he meant by that is abundantly explained in our code of conduct, namely, that any confrontation or criticism should be graciously received, regardless of the manner in which it is given.

Dumping: Of course, a leader should not incur dumping of anyone's distortion without an appropriate response.

What is dumping? It is the discharging of distortions which have been created in a different place or issue. For instance, I may have resentment—justified or not—for someone, boss, mate, etc. I may be reluctant to express this resentment to this person or situation. I displace it onto someone or something else who, I believe, is more likely to eat it without repercussions for me. Usually, the person who incurs the dumping is a leader, a fair and caring one.

****

If you want to be a leader, you have to accept:
- That you will be criticized constructively and destructively; you must learn how to accept and deal with both.
- That you will be misinterpreted and misunderstood; that too must be accepted and dealt with.

Listen to yourself in your covetousness towards leaders. Watch yourself rebelling. Have you exposed yourself as much as your leader has? If you haven't, you have no right to covet, rebel or resent.

First be as responsible and open as your leaders, **then** see if you want to rebel, resent, or criticize.

IV. Transforming Frustration

The primitive self believes that leadership means, at last, never having to deal with frustration; i.e., to always have it his way. Unless this belief is dissolved within you, your leadership will become tyranny and will fail.

The first step is to accept and reveal your frustration, and not deny the accompanying rage, but rather expose it.

When exposed, this state will reveal a duality, a dialectic between fulfillment on one side and frustration on the other. My fulfillment is against my frustration in that state.

I intensely demand and pursue fulfillment. I, with equal

intensity, reject and refuse to accept my frustration. I am thus painfully torn apart between the two demands. I would like to force reality to obey my command and fulfill my demand.

Steps to Transforming Frustration Into a Gift

1) **If I am frustrated, it means that I must be.** What I want cannot happen under the present circumstances. Something is marring my fulfillment, and there is a good reason for it.

The cultivation of this attitude is a *sine qua none* condition for the transformation of frustration. It is respect for the Law of Cause and Effect. What's more, it relaxes me and makes it possible for me to deal with the problem.

2) I will go ahead and **yield to the pain of frustration** in spite of the little self in me that has decided such a long time ago not to do it. I will muster the courage necessary. I will invoke the faculties at my disposal to do it.

3) **I will not exaggerate its importance**. I will have faith in the fact that goodness is infinite and distortion finite. I will not play the game of inflating what frustrates me in order to give myself the excuse of sinking into the path of least resistance, saying it is impossible.

4) I will trust that the frustration must be teaching me something, must be the consequence of a lack within myself and therefore an opportunity to better myself. In every frustration is a gift of learning and growing.

5) This attitude will **dissolve my anxiety.** Anxiety consists of the uncertainty about something, the demand that it only be my way and the refusal to accept anything else. It will align me with reality rather than with my desire to force that reality into going my way.

6) Doing this will **reveal the irrational and childish nature of my demands** that it be my way, which is at the

bottom of the creation of the frustration and the non-acceptance of it.

7) I will thus yield to causality rather than be disconnected from it.

8) If I do all of this, I will demonstrate to myself that I have the power and the wisdom to handle something that contradicts my wishes. **This alone will increase my sense of self-worth and my autonomy, my freedom from the old capitulation to the little willfulness.**

All of this prepares me for

9) **Looking for the inner deficiency behind the frustration.** What exactly have I neglected within myself which in turn has attracted this frustration on the outer level? As mentioned above, this then becomes an opportunity and a gift.

10) The continuous practice of these points creates deep within myself a sense of **welcome** to frustration, a **healthy curiosity** towards it rather than an enmity. Frustration now becomes a guide, a teacher, not an enemy. **It refreshes my Instinct of Enquiry.**

11) The cultivation of all of this reveals the inner deficiency. What the frustration means to tell me is finally clear to me. There is always here a sense of pleasant surprise at the depth of this realization. Instead of being deprived, we find that we are given something, something deep and wise, something necessary for our growth, something that was bound to happen.

12) Rather than seeing the world harmfully, I now see its goodness. I trust life. Consciousness inhabiting everything becomes a living reality for me. I get a sense of unity that replaces the previous duality.

Eventually, you will get to the point where you will be able to focus on the frustration itself and see the presence of God in it. Indeed, you wanted something but you were stopped, not by a harmful devilish entity, but by God who is trying to teach you something.

Frustration is the only way to God. Here we meet a concept which in spite of the fact that it is oft repeated, is even more often forgotten: **it is through the dissolution of our distortions that we find God, not through the escape from them into the positive, i.e., that which has already been achieved.**

Frustration, being the consequence of the existing distorted self, becomes the road to it. If you did not have a distorted self, you would experience no frustration. Since you have frustration, a distorted self in you has created it. The frustration itself is an exquisitely precise—if that word can be used in this situation—reproduction and consequence of your distorted self. Therefore, it must be a guide to it.

Look at what it is that frustrates you as precisely as you can. There, in front of you, you will be looking at your own distorted self, and therefore, at an opportunity to grow.

In meditation, zero in on the nucleus of the frustration. God resides right there, waiting for you to reach Him.

****

Leadership as anything else must start with baby steps. The beginning is always the most difficult. Eventually, the way accelerates and yields wonderful results. So, practice the four requirements: selfless giving, fairness, openness to confrontation, accepting and transforming frustration. Each one of these steps present you with an opportunity to find and follow the ultimate leader, God.

Chapter 28
Obey the Laws of God I

- Rebellion to tyrants is obedience to God.
  —John Bradshaw, 1602-1659, President at the trial of Charles I.

- *It is always easy to obey if one dreams to command.*
  —Jean-Paul Sartre, 1905-1980, French philosopher.

- *The thing that impresses me most about America is the way parents obey their children.*
  —Edmond VIII

Freeze:
Pursuing Freedom=Being Rebellious
The pursuit of freedom happens to be a privilege and a duty in the search for God. Unfortunately, it is often associated with rebellion against an authority, or against any authority.

Let's extend that to the freeze: *freedom = no frustration.* The refusal to deal with frustration, a requirement of leadership, is the same type of rebellion. The frustration itself is erroneously seen as the doing of an unidentifiable authority who deprives you of what you demand.

Soon, you find someone who personifies this authority.

Right or wrong, you now can blame, which is always wrong.

Rebellion Against Limitations

From the above, we need only to take a short step to our resentment of any limitations, and our rebellion against them. Let's mention and study a few:

A) **Limitations that we have created for ourselves:** That's bottom line. In effect, whether we are conscious of it or not, we have created **all** of our limitations, all of our rings-pass-not, including the group one, such as gravity, for instance. We create them, then we rebel against them. Thus, we are making them into authorities, hating them, fearing them, then placating them, deifying them as immutable, insurmountable. The following limitations merely are consequences of this one, attracted and maintained by it.

B) **Limits set by parental and other authority figures:** They are necessary to protect us from our rampant primitive self. Without them, we would not grow up. Civilization depends on it. As you know, it is out of love that these limits are set. Good, purposeful limits actually motivate and generate gratitude, even though there is often denial of these benefits by the recipient. Limits are essential for everything in life.

Structure

Another word for limits is structure. Nothing exists without structure. The whole order of the Universe is exquisitely structured. How do we join it? By first structuring our own chaos. This must first be deliberately wanted, lovingly pursued. Often, the intellect and the will must be summoned on the outer level. An outer level structure—a scaffolding—must be erected to allow the inner level structure to be formed. The outer level structure—the outer will intelligently applied—is temporary. It becomes unnecessary when the permanent structure is built. Then, one can effortlessly enjoy the permanency of the inner and greater structure.

It is the same with us. The scaffolding corresponds to the effort needed to funnel the permanent forces of nature. Without it, there is chaos.

Yielding without a scaffolding is dangerous and deadly. Yielding without having built the inner structure leads to insanity. Yielding after the structure is built brings happiness on a permanent basis. The structure creates good habits, which can then be enjoyed with freedom. Freedom to pursue bad habits is an euphemism for slavery to these bad habits. "I want to be free to get drunk every night" actually hides "I am a slave to alcohol." This person must erect a scaffolding limits, laws to obey within which to build permanent strength. Then and only then can he truly enjoy his freedom with alcohol.

The same is true of a pianist, painter, teacher, driver. The outer level effort to painstakingly learn the keys must be sustained, with love and good will. Then, one day, it links up with the involuntary and makes yielding possible.

Once the permanent structure is built, he must not forget to destroy the scaffolding. So many build permanent strength but still live in the scaffolding, unnecessarily relying on its strength and forgetting that they built a beautiful inner structure, and therefore, deserve greater freedom.

Don't forget to remove the scaffolding, or else you will never enjoy the freedom, the beauty and the power that you have earned. This means:

- You don't have to continue to go to Alcoholics Anonymous once you have conquered your addiction; you can resume normal life; if you can't, what's the point of having gone there in first place.
- You must go beyond the skills that you have developed into yielding, allowing creativity to flow out of you; don't

escape in the facility of your virtuosity.

If you don't do this, the scaffolding will become your next addiction. The same problem of freedom versus law will be repeated towards the scaffolding. This is unnecessary and unfortunate.

We arrest growth by refusing to realize the freedom we already possess. We do this by narrowing our vision to the progress that we have already achieved, refusing to move on to or to move into the far greater task that awaits us. It is indeed akin to living in the scaffolding when the house is already built. It is continuing to rely on the little ego, when it is time to yield to and liberate the Greater Ego, the Divine Self.

The shortsighted path of least resistance says, "I've done enough, now I can rest." So, we waste ourselves in perpetual repetition of what we already know.

Been There, Done That; The Point of Renunciation

Time to let go of your achievements and move on. Get used to the idea that the only stable thing in life is change and growth. Time to find a greater and more permanent structure, to find and obey greater laws, to claim greater freedoms, as well as greater responsibilities.

Veterans of Alcoholic Anonymous who are now addicted to that method are afraid of success, of inhabiting the house that they built. The personal responsibility that they used to structure and solve their problem has become victimization thus reversing the healing, sending them back to addiction.

Their addiction, as bad as it was, was a misguided attempt for pleasure. As long as they haven't replaced their pleasure in their lives, they will always be tempted to recreate other addictions. It is conquering pleasure and lawfully integrating it into life that dissolves addiction.

C) **Universal Law and order:** Nature obeys laws. The entire Universe does. Every facet of creation obeys. Disobedience leads to chaos and creates chaos. The harmony of our body, of the solar system, of the galaxy, depends on obedience to law. They obey limits that prevent them from clashing into each other. Each planet, star, sun, planetary system has a deliberate autonomous consciousness, as does your body. Within these laws, freedom is found, the only true freedom. Each of these entities **freely chooses** to obey.

By extension, all civilization, community of humans or ants, big multinational concerns or unicellular amoeba, all obey law. To the degree they do, they thrive. To the degree they don't, they degenerate into chaos and die.

Freeze: Law Imprisons And Diminishes

Not true. Law enhances, liberates. Therefore, if you want to be free and grow:

- Detect your distortion towards law and order, the disobedience in you.
- Reveal your rebellion against authority. Realize that **authorities** merely remind you of the existence of a Universal Law. They did not create these laws. They merely interpret them for you. And in **childhood,** they prevented you from harmfulness to yourself and to others by—yes—**making you obey.** Remember, childhood can be extended in an adult body. If you don't make your "inner child" obey, someone else will do it for you and that's good, good for you more than for anyone else.

Anatomy of Rebellion

Let's do some psychic surgery on a rebel. We find the following layers.

1) On the outer level, a violent resentment against

authority, who appears restrictive, blame of authority.

2) A little deeper a demand that the rules of the Universe not apply to him; an unreasonable expectation, i.e., a **tyranny** imposed on the Universe.

Examples: "I want to get drunk without hangover; get laid without AIDS; get stoned without insanity; get rich without working; get famous and recognized without giving anything; be immortal without cleansing my distorted self."

The rebel is a tyrant. He is acting out the child tyrant through the blames. He wants to find fault with authority so as to escape his own monster. He actually is the slave to this monster which he obeys. He would rather obey the little monster within than obey God and His laws. Because he knows that he can always be forgiven by God but not by the devil. He fears and worships the devil. He is to himself the worst possible authority. He nurtures, protects, aids and abets this bad authority being at the same time afraid and ashamed of it.

It is out of that fear and shame that he then deviates his resentment onto another authority, a good one, attributing to it all of its own harmful traits.

Freeze: Indulgence = Love

"If you indulge me, you love me."

"If I indulge you, I love you."

"Unless you indulge me, I will hate and resent you. I will withdraw my love from you. I will find fault with you and punish you."

"Unless I indulge you, I will not love you and you will not love me. I want your love, so I'll indulge you. Actually, although I want you to love me I have contempt for you. That contempt used to be valid limits which, if I truly loved you, I would have given to you.

All of this is illusion. The reality is that there is no love in indulgence, whether it is self-directed or directed at others. It is out of self-hatred that we indulge. Self-indulgence is an escape from ourselves out of desperation, having given up on ourselves. So, a) we give up on ourselves, which is bad, b) we indulge to feel good, which is bad. So, we add badness to badness in an attempt to feel good.

Indulging others isn't any better. It is because we have given up on their distortion that we indulge them. We appease them. Thus, not only are they the slaves of their distortion, but we too become, with them, slaves to their distortion. Appeasing and pampering, compromising and placating are all insults, first to others and second to ourselves. It essentially says that there is no hope for betterment, so might as well appease.

Antifreeze: Limits = Frustration = Hatred
The other side also becomes true: "If you set limits, you don't love me You hate me. If I discipline myself, I don't love myself, I hate myself." The same applies here as for the previous freeze.

It started early. Retrace all of this to your childhood. Find, again, the pampering that you idealized, the false laws which you obeyed, the tyrannical rebellions that made genies of your parents, making you little "lord of the world Aladdin."

Choice
Choose to obey. Choose freely. Choose to discriminate between Divine Law and human law. Obey Divine Law. Obey human law if it conforms to Divine Law. If it doesn't, choose to disobey human law which actually is a choice to obey Divine Law.

You fail to remember to exercise this choice, that you have

this power. You fail to remember yow choice to change your condition to the better. You instead insist demand that others change the condition that you are creating by violating Spiritual Law. You want to continue to violate the law and have others change the consequences of your violation.

No one but you can change what you have created. And it can only be done by finally obeying the Laws that you chose to violate.

Freeze: "I must Rebel"
Do You Have To?

You act as if you are required to rebel. You don't have to. You really don't. You can finally obey and enjoy, come home and partake.

You are not required to rebel against authority all the time. You act as if it is honourable to rebel, just for the principle of it. See how foolish this is. Start accepting a universal principle: Obedience.

You actually desire to free yourself from the tyranny of the little primitive self. **He** is the tyrant, but you fear him so much that you displace your outrage on to authority figures. You thus create more trouble for yourself.

Self-Imprisonment And Self-Acceptance

You created the limitations, the straitjacket. The first steps of liberation must, therefore be.

A) Acceptance of the self-imposed prison.

B) Recognize that it is self-imposed. That will yield instant freedom, a sense of liberation.

"I accept my present poverty. I limit myself to what I earn and I work within my capacity, within my means."

Limitations Accepted

Choose to accept your limitations, don't collapse in despair. This acceptance is required before you can deal with it.

Choose then to do something about them in an adult, mature way, not with rebellion.

Your limitations come from your violation of Spiritual Law. Make that personal connection and start obeying the law that you have violated. Your acceptance of your limitations does not mean the following dichotomy:

A) Capitulation and giving up in a docile weakness or depending on a reseller.

B) Irrationally rebelling and blaming.

Here in A) and B) you are still the slave of your child tyrant. The acceptance comes from good will, from the pursuit of true causes of my limitations, from love and faith.

****

Obey and accept, lovingly willingly. Discriminate and decide. Free yourself of the tyrannical yoke of your child. Replace your resentment where it belongs—towards that child tyrant and thus restore your welcome and embrace toward the laws and rules of God.

Chapter 29
Obey the Laws of God II

- *If hopes were dupes, fears may be liars.*
  —Arthur Hugh, 1819-1861, English poet.

- *Perfect love casts out fear.*
  —I John 4:18

- *Curiosity will conquer fear even more than bravery will.*
  —James Stephens, 1882-1950, Irish poet, novelist.

- *How many pessimist minds end up desiring that which they fear in order to be right!*
  —Robert Mallet, 1915- , French poet.

- *Fear and Loathing in Las Vegas.*
  —Hunter S. Thompson, 1939- , American Journalist, Rolling Stone, 1971.

- *Fear follows crime and is its punishment.*
  —Voltaire, 1694-1778, French philosopher, historian, dramatist and poet.

- *Fear is the parent of cruelty.*
  —James Anthony, 1818-1894, English historian.

- *Fear of death is worse than death itself.*
  —Proverbs 116

- *Courage, or shall I say lack of fear, is a result of discipline.*
  —Richard Nixon

Healthy Discrimination

Only when accepted will your limits yield their nature, their origin and their purpose. You will then be able to discriminate between the healthy and unhealthy limits, laws, rules. You will also be able to healthily decide which should be obeyed and which challenged or even disobeyed. You will clearly see their origin, their purpose and volition.

Healthy limitations, restrictions exist for the sake of harmlessness, or, to put it differently, for the Good, the Beautiful and the True. Here are some examples:

I put a limit on:
- My arrogance, my desire to dominate, to own and to use;
- My self-indulgence and on my path of least resistance;
- My laziness, which always hides an active hostility, a harmful volition;
- My perfectionism and my judgements;
- My demands and my despair;
... and so I should.

Unhealthy limitations are harmful even when they appear harmless and good. For example:
- Defense against pleasure.
- Limiting my self-assertion for the sake of approval.
- Limiting my claim to infinite happiness and bliss to conform to wrong teachings and wrong creeds.
- Limiting my claim to my rights.
- Limiting my freedom by giving limitless power to others

over me.
- Limiting my rights by obeying bad laws.
- Limiting my faith in this Universe by overprotecting myself.
- Limiting myself by not taking risks, not committing myself to goodness, not squandering myself with generosity.

Liberation in This Faith

Gradually, but surely, this faith will lead you to the dissolution of all your limitations. You will do it with open eyes, open arms and an open heart, not with the insanity of tantrums and the shortsightedness of rebellion. As seen above, this is the acting out of your own child tyrant. He owns and manipulates you. Your resentment against authority is a deviation of your resentment against him.

When you realign this deviation, you can start the real dissolving of your rings-pass-not, your limitations. You can cleanse for your liberation.

This liberation involves love. You will choose to **obey** good laws and **accept** right limits **with love,** with care and concern. You will feel towards these laws and limits the **tenderness** that a mother feels for her new born child.

You will accept the temporary discomfort involved in this obedience and acceptance. You will do so with **love.**

You can accelerate this liberation to the point where the meaningless restrictions will dissolve from your life by themselves. You will stop creating them with your unconscious.

And so, this will free you, with good will and love, to welcome the good laws and limits, obeying and accepting them.

The Most Damaging Slavery

It is the indulgence to the child tyrant's whims. It is mistaken for the greatest freedom. It is sought through the dishonest and manipulative means of double standards—wanting more than one is willing to give, bargaining and bartering. Or worse, it wants all and gives nothing, opting for the path of least resistance.

It hides behind the legal deals of adulthood. Yet that's the way you are still enslaved by your child tyrant's illusion, becoming its soldier in its battle against reality, a battle that you both are bound to lose. Reality always wins.

Love as a Yardstick

We, in our faith, often talk about being in zones. See if you can define your **rebellious zones** when you are stuck in them. See if you can recognize in them **blind rage**; the state in which you narrowly only admit rage as an experienced feeling, nothing else but rebellious and blind rage; road rage is a good example of this state. In it, I don't think about something else and I don't want to. No other solution is admitted into my consciousness but murderous vengeance.

You certainly are not in a **loving zone**. If you were:

1) You would be able to tolerate another solution, or even another suggestion of a solution to the problem at hand.

2) You would not capitulate, even though the rebellious zone would like to think you would.

Rebellion Wants You to Capitulate

You see, your rebellious zone, in its blind rage:

A) Has only one conscious goal: to make the other capitulate; to humiliate him. In order to insure its determination, it makes loving appear weak and cowardly. It also sees any contradiction or frustration of its demands as self-annihilation and self-humiliation

B) **One unconscious desire:** to capitulate to a good and forgiving authority, **seducing** them into letting you be infinitely self-indulgent. "Under the protection of this all powerful person, or God—who loves me because I submitted to Him—and with their blessings, I will have unlimited license in my life."

Of course, this is impossible. Look at what's wrong here:

- **You sold out your integrity** by capitulating under false pretenses. You really didn't want to submit. You did it for protection, so as to continue to act out, this time under the protection of authority. You are still enraged and harmful; you are creating unhappiness and pain; **it doesn't work.**

- You sold out your freedom, which intensifies your rebellious rage; here again you create unhappiness and pain; **it doesn't work.**

- Because it doesn't work, you blame the authority to which you capitulated and the whole world, if need be.

In short, you sell out, you capitulate for license. You adapt to glamours, you conform, you cope, you appear good for the purpose of obtaining license for your murderous rage. Here, we have reversed the order of things. **Conscious is the desire to capitulate and unconscious the desire to rebel.**

Choice

In all of this, loving is absent. When loving is present, **free choice** can be effected. Without love, in the dichotomy of capitulation and rebellion, there is no free choice. The person is under the constant pressure of two tyrants:

1) Either blinding capitulating to a straitjacket

2) Or violently and blindly rebelling against it.

In that state, the person is doubly blind and wants to be. In a state of loving, the person is open, free and intelligent. He sees the truth and chooses to follow it deliberately. He does not create a dialectic of submission and rebellion because there is only one truth.

Inner Authority Through Love

Can you visualize yourself **freely and lovingly choosing limits, because you need them, because it is right?**

Conversely, can you see yourself lovingly choosing **not** to have a particular limit, to claim your freedom from it without destructive rebelliousness?

This is not capitulation, nor rampant rebelliousness. This would be personal responsibility. Exerting this choice, you accept its consequences which are no one's fault but yours. Exerting this choice, you also claim the benefits which, too, are yours and only yours.

This then is true resilient strength. It is built through loving See the road thus, built: through love to intelligence and strength.

Self-Love Versus Fear

The continuous erosion of the old distorted self becomes, through this faith, a greater reality than you allow yourself to realize. Progress achieved through this faith is deeper and greater than you want to admit. This is particularly true for the veterans of this faith. It is too early yet for others to experience this. Therefore, what I am about to say is mostly for the veterans, not for those in the beginning of their spiritual training. Consider then, brother and sister veterans of this faith, the following:

1) You have achieved progress in our faith. You have eroded your distorted self to the point where now, the Universe is opening up to you. **Pleasure, blessings,**

abundance are coming to you; they are at hand.

2) You still dislike yourself; partly because you haven't quite let go of your old ways, albeit mentally and or emotionally. Thus, you don't make room for your blessings.

3) You experience existential fear, paranoia, fear of death, obsessions about health, etc. This fear, as terrifying, as terrorizing as it appears to be, is never the less **false.** It really is there because your self-loathing makes the yield—to the pleasure and blessings that you deserve—a frightening fall into an abyss. Let go. Let God invade you. You are ready.

4) Because you don't recognize the falsehood of this fear, it precipitates into physical problems. The old self-destructive patterns will be resuscitated. You will find yourself being self-destructive. Those are the residues of distortion that you are still hiding. With this oncoming and liberating blessings, they must be looked at and dissolved.

5) Thus, you may at this point regress back into more familiar greyness of exhausting mediocrity (see the last sermon). Some quit this faith, unable to sustain all the goodness that has come to them.

****

In what specific ways do you still rebel? Hate yourself? How do you deny this? How do you then deviate your self-hatred towards others? Does that create guilt? Does that make you dislike yourself even more?

Are you afraid? Do you manufacture false, existential fears? How do you resist the oncoming goodness and bliss? Do you love this incarnation of yours? Why not? Why do you have to escape it into illusions, into the past?

****

Love the present. Love the now. Love your limitations.

Love your freedom and your responsibility. Love your present incarnation. Let love guide you to wisdom, the wisdom to know and dissolve the walls of your prison and to find, all around you, the ecstasy of being at-one with God.

Section II

The Faculties of God,
The Mother

Chapter 30
Eternal Life I

• *We feel and know by experience that we are eternal.*
—Baruch Spinosa, 1632-1677, Dutch philosopher, *Ethics.*

Your Divine Self knows that you have it, that there is no death. But, in your bubble, your fear distorts this knowledge of eternal life into becoming fear of dying. Nevertheless, in that fear is to be found the expression of desire for eternal life. In that fear, you also have lost faith in the infinite. You do not experience the infinite because you are caught in the bubble of your limitations.

So, you commit a tour-de-force on yourself, as do the positive thinkers: "I'll will myself, with my willfulness, to believe in Eternal Life; I will take on and brainwash myself with spiritual teachings that talk about my eternal life; this way, I will cover up for my very personal fear of dying, wishing never to experience it."

This is dishonest. Yet, it is encouraged by most so-called spiritual disciplines or religious practices. This hypocrisy extends itself into the dishonest declarations of "taking Christ as my personal saviour," or of "I believe in God," without really experiencing any such thing on a real and deep level.

Making oneself superimpose a spiritual belief over the fear of its opposite further alienates a person from the truth. It is a lot better to stop pretending and start revealing the truth that lurks behind all of these false beliefs.

Stop condemning yourself by mouthing, driveling that you believe in something when you actually don't:

- Experience your deep and personal fear of death, yes, on its primitive, childish level; it exists behind your intellectual belief in eternal life.
- Face your own problems responsibly rather than "giving them to God," which is a truth, but which you use in order not to do the cleansing. "Salvation" without cleansing is impossible. Wishing it is a violation of Spiritual Law.

So, since mortality constitutes your experiential reality now, accept it. Let go of your desire for Eternal Life for the time being until you can feel it as your true reality. It will happen gradually. First, you will feel it when you make deep connections. Accepting mortality itself may be the type of connection that will give you a glimpse of Eternal Life.

Fear of Death as a Way to Eternal Life

The greatest fear, the fear of dying, becomes, for a person who evolves by practicing faith, **desire for eternal life**; for a person who is not evolving, it becomes lack of faith.

Many pretend not to be afraid of death. Actually, very few are not. I recently heard someone say that she discovered, in a recent crisis, that she was unafraid of death. I didn't believe her. I felt she was numb to her pain and her fear, afraid of fear, petrified in rigidity.

If she yielded to the experience of the fear of death, she would discover the reality of immorality. The experience of the fear of death yields the reality of Eternal Life. That's why wise people, philosophers and thinkers are so often represented as having a skeletal head on their desk. They often meditate on death, and their personal experience of that fear yields, for them, the deepest and wisest thoughts. Experiencing fear of death requires the shedding of both willfulness and conceit. Thus, the three distortions of the Trinity are dealt with at once:

- The distortion of the Greater Will, willfulness.
- The distortion of Love/Wisdom, fear.
- The distortion of Active Intelligence, conceit.

Don't be glamoured by your own lofty thoughts. Don't believe your own beliefs. Remember, Eternal Life is available through honest doubt.

Fear of Death Found Every Day

You die every day several times. When some jerk passes you in an arrogant manner on the road, and you let go of your desire to punish and humiliate him, you die.

When you make a mistake and you punish yourself for it by giving yourself undue emotional pain, you die. When your conceit is broken you die. When you can't have your little will way, you die.

If you take each and every opportunity of death and fully live it, without pretense or cover-up, you would train yourself in the conquest of the fear of death. Then, when a bigger death—a bigger crisis—comes, you will be much better prepared to deal with it. And when the biggest one—the end of this life—comes, it will not be painful. You will feel it as liberating.

Considering the little bubble in which you live (see the last sermon), that's how you can allow it to burst, joining in at-onement, the rest of the Universe. In our work in this faith, we die so many times! Each of these deaths connects us to Eternal Life.

Positive Thinking as a Source of Dishonesty

If I believe that I have to cover up my distortions with the pseudo-good, I believe that I must be dishonest to be a good person. This harmful, evil thinking is supported both by positive thinking institutions and by many who call themselves Christians.

Actually, it is un-Christian, as well as un-beneficial to be dishonest. It also happens to be un-Moslem, un-Buddhist, un-anything, any self-respecting philosophy or religion.

If I firmly believe this way, then why not cover up for the acting out of my distorted self? When Clinton covers up his sexual escapades, he is merely following so-called positive thinking, as well as the faulty morality that he was taught. He is actually moralizing in the worst way, i.e., against himself. Think about it.

Nevertheless, he is convinced that covering up is the way to go, the right way. And he is wrong. It is the evil way. **Acquire the habit of pretense and you will commit the evil of lying, covering up and perjuring yourself.**[1] After all, your parents taught you to do it, didn't they?

Pretense of Faith as a Barrier to The Experience of God And of The nfinite

The lie of pretending to believe in God, the mouthing of belief of Christ without truly experiencing Him or believing in Him contains a self-condemnation.

Indeed, we pretend to believe because we are intolerant—we condemn—the place within that doesn't believe, that fears, doubts, and that becomes cynical.

Thus, the cynicism and the self-condemnation become

---

[1] For the sake of good order, let me say that this was written in the month of January of 1997, well before Clinton's demise of August 1998.

more real than the pretense. And the longer we pretend, the stronger becomes the disbelief.

Now, it is this very disbelief that blocks the true experience of God, that at last will make pretenders into true believers.

You cannot experience God or Christ as long as you deny and condemn the place in you that rejects Them.

You cannot experience God or Christ as long as you put yourself down by pretending to experience Them. The longer you do that, the more you will have to inevitably create a crisis, exploding your pretense, revealing your cynicism so as to cleanse it.

Experiencing God

You cannot experience, and therefore, believe in god, unless you experience your own Eternal Life.

Pretending to believe in God alienates you from truly believing in Him. Pretending to believe in your own Eternal Life alienates you from truly believing in it.

Experiencing your own Eternal Life is a precondition to believing in God. No true belief in God can exist without that experience.

That's why the atheist is closer to believing in God than is the bigoted religionist who pretends.

Yet, it was necessary, for a while, to believe in God as an idea and an ideal. For primitive humanity, a concept of the Absolute was needed. That was the task of so many teachers of humanity—to come in and give us concepts of the Absolute which made sense. Akhenaton, Moses, Socrates, Plato, the Christ, Mohammed are all such teachers, to name a few. Christ was, and is, the greatest of them.

Outside of them, humanity constructed their own gods, through projecting their own little selves on greater beings.

The idols, thus formed by humanity's deified selves, had distorted selves, often crasser than the lowest humans.

These idols are not as yet quite dead. They crept into Christianity, falsifying and distorting it beyond recognition. As an individual, you still worship idols created by your deified self.

Example: You deify money, houses, idealized people who you imitate, golden ages which you haven't abandoned. All of these make you an idolater, addicted to your god, but disconnected from the one true God, and therefore, from life.

So, an intellectual concept of the Absolute had to be taught first. It was then used as a cover up for lack of faith, and still is by humanity to an amazingly large extent. For early humanity, only God without could be understood, God transcendent, the God of the Bible, particularly of the old testament. It was a punishing and vengeful God. He became a loving God through Christ who personalized Him and brought Him closer to us.

Now, we are ready to re-experience what we once knew. God is within and that's the only way to find Him. But in order to do that, we may have to destroy the subtle way in which we have falsified Him by believing in Him. We have to let go of any superimposition of belief, rethink everything in order to rediscover Him in reality this time.

God is within and without, immanent and transcendent. The experience of this reality is available when fear of death is undergone and dissolved. That's the barrier that prevents the building of the bridge between God within and God without.

And the experience and conquest of the fear of death is none other than the focus on the dissolution of, our private problems! It is not any better or worse than that!

The Experience of Death as Seen
From The Point of View of Eternal Life

If I know that life is eternal and that it cannot be non-life, I will accept physical death in an entirely different way:

- I will see it as a liberation from the limitations of three-dimensional reality.
- I will prepare for it by focusing on and accomplishing my task.
- I will accept it as an initiation, not as a calamity.
- I will realize that disconnecting from the physical point of view does not mean disconnecting from the point of view of the soul and the spirit.
- I will know that I will continue to do my task which doesn't stop just because I have to change bodies; you can change cars without changing your job.
- The foolishness of lying, hiding, cheating, in short of dishonesty, will be much more easily given up since I will know that nothing can be hidden from the light which is met at the time of death.
- It will increase my courage in facing my life right now.
- It will help me conquer the fear of death.
- It will help me face, without defense, all of my faults and it will motivate me to dissolve them.

Eternal Life And Cleansing

Cleansing leads to Eternal Life. Eternal Life is inconceivable unless the person undergoing it has purified. Consider in that respect the formation of your various bodies—mental, emotional and physical. They all constitute levels of deceleration which, itself, results from violation of Spiritual Law, error, evil. Thus, if, on the mental level, a freeze is formed through error of judgement, through marring of integrity, or through misguided volitionality, the soul energy decelerates creating a body. The next descent creates emotions, and the next the physical.

Cleansing consists in reversing this harmful deceleration. The revelation of evil, the taking of responsibility for its consequences, the re-adjustment of thinking from wrong to right, and the realignment of volitionality from the little will to the Greater Will, all of this cleanses these bodies, filling them with light. Eternal Life is merely the faculty of getting in and out of these bodies, by choice. Thus, each human being will get to the point where he will be able to continuously renew and rejuvenate his vehicles, shaping them at will in order to serve his purpose.

Eternal Life is not something that will be bestowed upon you. No messiah and no God in His right mind will want to do this to you. Imagine being bestowed Eternal Life without undergoing cleansing. What will live forever? Your distorted body which is becoming increasingly distorted through the permanent damage that you have inflicted on it? How would you feel if, instead of only living 80 years in this condition, you lived 200 years, or permanently? You would merely increase the suffering and the distortion. This is an impossibility because distortion, pain, wrong thinking and suffering are finite. There comes a point where they must explode and re-arrange themselves. That's called crisis or death.

Apply the same reasoning to your emotional and your mental bodies. How long would you like those recurring nightmares that you have created and that you now refuse to cleanse, expose or be responsible for?

At this point, you have committed some errors which you cannot redress. You have repeated those errors so many times that they have become an addiction and have created a terminal illness. That's why you have to die. This habit has not started during this lifetime. You started these distortions a long time ago. All you can do now is to accept this fact and totally yield to cleansing.

Therefore, Eternal Life is achieved through this faith. This is the way to Eternal Life. You cannot be immortal unless you are squeaky clean, free of all violations and dishonesties. This is one of the requirements for Eternal Life. Let's list a few more:

- Total dedication to service.
- Total self-knowledge and self-mastery.
- Total order in your life.
- Total faith in the goodness of the Universe.
- Total sense of harmony and resolution of conflicts.
- And to repeat, total honesty.

Anything short of that would make Eternal Life a very unhappy burden, indeed.

****

Thus, as seen with perfection, eternal life can only be obtained when you let it go. Let go, let God.

Chapter 31

Eternal Life II;
Fear of Dying Results From
Concealing The Dark Side

I condemn myself deeply, severely and totally by concealing my darkest side. By being ashamed to reveal it, I have condemned it to death. I want it annihilated.

Yet, it is an integral part of me. Hence, I have condemned to death an integral part of myself, a part without which I cannot live.

Thus, I have instilled within myself the fear of dying. I am afraid of death because I refuse to look at my darkest side. By condemning it to death, I have condemned myself to the same fate. No wonder I am so afraid of dying.

Forgiveness
The way out is to forgive myself and accept my darkest side, cleanse it, give it a chance to grow. Since forgiveness will eradicate my death sentence to this dark side of me, it will also eradicate my fear of dying. Therefore, forgiveness dissolves fear of dying. Therefore, also, unwillingness to forgive creates and maintains fear of dying.

Point-by-Point Recap

1) I don't accept part of myself. I condemn it, hide it from others and from myself. I pronounce and try to carry out a death sentence for it.

2) Since that part of myself is integral, the death sentence will threaten me. I am now afraid of dying. Fear of dying comes from self-condemnation, albeit partial.

3) The way out is to **forgive** myself, accepting, revealing and helping that dark side of myself.

4)This will dissolve the death sentence to it and its execution.

5) Thus, it will also dissolve my fear of death. Forgiveness dissolves the fear of death.

Forgiveness Without Palliatives

Forgiveness doesn't mean forgetting that the dark side is indeed harmful and needs to be cleansed. Only by cleansing it, restoring it to its original goodness, will we dissolved our fear of it, as well as our tendency to condemn ourselves for it.

Freezes

Do not confuse revelation of your darkness with condemnation of yourself. Reveal yourself with acceptance.

Also, do not confuse forgiveness with forgetting, as explained in the previous paragraph. Thus, forgiveness must be practiced outside of these two confusions and freezes.

Revelation, forgiveness and cleansing must be practiced in a unified manner. They are really one.

Fear of Self-Revelation Linked to Lack of Faith

The other side of this is that as long as you don't have faith in your eternal life, it will be exceedingly difficult to reveal your darkness. It will be felt as death, the ultimate humiliation and disintegration.

On the contrary, from the point of light, eternal life, revelation of darkness will be a liberation, a consummation devoutly to be wished.

When hiding darkness, faith is impossible because you believe that darkness is your innermost self.

Yet, in order to reveal that darkness, you need to have some faith, albeit intellectual, enough to give this faith a chance to cleanse you.

Disease And Fear of Dying

What do you expect will be the effect of your unattended darkness on your body? If you think that you can perpetuate the harbouring of the harmful without physical consequences, you are very much mistaken.

Every cell in your physical body, every atom of it, are precipitates of spiritual atoms arranged in your mental and emotional bodies. Every particle of your body, therefore, contains all of your thoughts and feelings, just as surely as your DNA contains complete information about yourself.

Every thought or feeling, conscious or not, affects these DNA's, these physical cells. Any thought or feeling contrary to nature—to the Good, the Beautiful and the True—creates a conflict, friction which, aggravated and spread, gives you disease of all kinds.

Condemn any part of yourself and you are setting up the growth of two areas of darkness:

1) The part that is being condemned.

2) The part that condemns.

Both, intertwined, accelerate diseases which must result in death.

You believe that perhaps you can live with only part of you, having condemned or condoned the other part. You are wrong. All of you is a whole. Distortion and darkness contain potential which has as much the right to live and thrive as the parts of you that you like the most.

When you die, you will not be any different than now. Only your physical vehicle will be shed. Every single thought and feeling will remain what they are at the time of death. They still must be changed, "dead" or alive. That which is alive cannot be dead. _A_ cannot be non-_A_.

The "dead" vehicle, in turn, having been activated by your consciousness, has, itself, been raised to a considerable extent. Yet, it contains the disease that you have left in it. Through nature, it will create other vehicles to be cleansed by other forms of life, who will also benefit by the raising of consciousness that you brought to the matter.

That then is another way for us to contribute to the growth of our planet. So, settle down. There is no escape from cleansing. Sooner or later, "dead" or alive, as it were, you will have to face and transform the places that you have condemned. Commit yourself, then to total honesty with yourself without condemnation, total caring for yourself without palliatives and condoning, and total good will without forcing. You have nowhere else to go.

Auras, Radiations And Emissions

The more subtle bodies emit precisely what they contain. The darkness—distorted self and deified self—in you, that which you condemn and protect at the same time, emits a scent which is unpleasant, a disharmonious sound and a repelling feeling. It looks, in your aura, murky, sometimes shooting lightning and fire of anger, cruelty and rage.

The good side of you, your Divine Self, on the contrary, emits goodness, radiates bright and well-defined colours, representing your rays. It smells pleasant and its auric essence is attractive.

Experience it and believe it. Open your mind to your and

to other's emissions and radiations.

Now how long can your body tolerate the harmful emissions before it gives in? Consider these two points:

1) You are most intimate with yourself. You are more intimate with yourself than with anyone else, past, present and future. You are, therefore, the one to suffer the most by your unpleasant emissions, and to enjoy/benefit the most by your pleasant ones.

2) Imagine stepping out of your dwelling place in the fresh morning air. You fill your lungs. You are cleansed by the goodness of the air. You go back inside and realize that it actually smells bad, or stuffy. You weren't aware of that badness before you stepped out into the goodness. Thus, you numbed yourself to your own bad smells. Only now will you want to clean it up. Unless, of course, you procrastinate and forget about it once again by getting used to the badness in which you dwell. Your house is yourself, your bodies, on all levels. What are the smells which you have numbed? Step out into the newness and freshness, and then step back in to cleanse. Keep going in and out, until it smells inside as fresh as it smells outside. You must do both. If you just stay inside and are so glad for the warmth that you don't mind the smell, you will never cleanse, perpetually creating unhappiness and pain. If you just stay outside, you cannot enjoy your achievements, your comforts. You cannot accomplish your task which requires the tools and possessions that you have inside the house. Nor can you cleanse what you have created, the bad smells which you have left behind.

Your life circumstances, your bodies are your house. Only by stepping out and stepping back in will you cleanse those and create happiness.

You can change this by cleansing thoughts and feelings, by living an ethical life, by total commitment to total revelation of yourself. The more you cleanse, the more obvious will your emissions be to you, and the more urgently will you want to cleanse. The more I am aware of how badly I smell, the more urgently I want to bathe.

Also, as you grow, you will be able to detect others' harmful emissions, no matter how well they are covered up. So, you will increasingly ward off harm. You will see, sense, smell and hear it long before it affects you.

Law of Attraction

A harmful emanation will attract harmful entities, incarnate or disincarnate, whose energies are similar. Thus, our distortions and darkness will be reinforced and deepened. This syndrome will, at some point, feel as if it has a life of its own. The ultimate of this feeling is to be found in the stunned horror of being told that you have a terminal illness. But, what do you expect?

- You have condemned part of yourself to death, while protecting it at the same time.
- This creates torture which you repress.
- It acquires a life of it own and gets reinforced by colluding entities.
- It must have a result on your body.
- Even these results are at first not heeded; so they become terminal; the only way to stop is to terminate this incarnation of yours.

By contrast, goodness, beauty and truthfulness attracts entities that will enhance these qualities. They will reinforce the sense of ecstasy and serenity which can be perceived through human senses and beyond. A glimpse of superhuman senses begins to be felt and to be developed.

This state heals. It also makes the other state intolerable, reinforcing the sense of urgency in cleansing. This, too, is healing, perhaps the most effective and dramatic.

Reach out for the bliss and ecstasy of your Divine Self. Then, let it illuminate and cleanse the rest of you. Whenever you are in a harmful and unpleasant place, go to its source. Find the volitionality behind it—why you want it to be so. You will find instant relief.

But that's not enough. Refer all of this to your Divine Self. Invoke its magnificent, pleasurable presence. Penetrate with it the darkness that you have just exposed.

Agnus Dei Qui Tollis Peccata Mundi

There is a recurring theme in our faith. It is repeatedly expressed in sermons through different words. Today we express it in the following way, hoping that it will, once and for all, penetrate our problems.

The problem is the denigration of love, the betrayal of it, the taking it for granted, by the child tyrant, the primitive self. I dump most on whoever loves me the most. I exert my power on them, which becomes vicious cruelty. My worst comes out against those who love me the most.

Consequently, I create matter, my character type, my personality, my distorted self, my harmful emissions that smell bad. I mistake commitment with license to dump. So, I place, on the shoulders of love, all of my distortions. *Agnus Dei, qui tollis peccata mundi.* Lamb of God who carries all the sins of the world.

Now we understand what that means. The lamb of God is the principle of love, Christ. We dump on it all of our sins. That's our worst sin; the original sin; the most outrageous act of betrayal; the one that produces the most guilt; the one of which we are the most ashamed; the one, therefore, which we condemn the most, numb the most, rationalize the most.

It is also the one which, therefore, is the most connected with the fear of death, since it is the most difficult to forgive. We can only reverse this by dissolving the child tyrant, take responsibility for our own personal outrageous behaviour and for our own cleansing.

Thus, the original teaching was not that the Christ—love—will take care of all our sins. If it were, it would be an encouragement to the outrageous behaviour of the child tyrant. The original teaching is to stop this dumping—exactly the opposite to what it has become in organized Christianity.

The original teaching is to love one another and to remove the beam in our own eye. Christ never said that He would remove it for us. Those who have claimed He did have lied. They have engendered a massive collusion with the child tyrant of the world. *Tyrannicus mundi, don't dumpus on me* is what Christ actually said. He came to stop this, not to perpetuate it. He came to do battle with the child tyrant, not to perpetually clean his diapers. He came to make it at last possible for good spiritual training to bear fruit.

Help Him out. Stop dumping on Him by dumping on love. Stop forming the dead crystals of your character type.

****

Meet love with love. Anchor yourself in the constant renewal of love, to cleanse the harmful. Anchor yourself in self-forgiveness with the purpose and the determination to cleanse.

Make room for God.

Section III

The Faculties of God,
The Son

Chapter 32
Perfection Through Yielding to God

- *Faultily faultless, icily regular, splendidly null,*
  Dead perfection no more.
  —Lord Alfred Tennyson, 1809-1892, English poet laureate.

- *The pursuit of perfection, then, is the pursuit of sweetness and light. He who works for sweetness and light, works to make reason and the Will of God prevail.*
  —Matthew Arnold, 1822-1888, English poet, critic, *Culture and Anarchy.*

- *Culture being a pursuit of our total perfection by means of getting to know, on all the matters which most concern us, the best which has been thought and said in the world.*
  —Ibid.

The Universe consists of infinite energy and consciousness capable of goodness, beauty and truth far surpassing our limited imagination. We are part of that Universe. Yet, our consciousness has separated itself from it, forming its own cocoon, one might say a bubble. Within this cocooned bubble, it seems to the limited consciousness that nothing else exists. In the bubble, the rest of the ocean is negated. This is the state in which we find ourselves in our limited consciousness and with our little ego.

Meanwhile, we are still being kept alive by consciousness and energy which nevertheless seep through and penetrate the cocooned bubble. Unfortunately, these penetrations become somehow distorted by the limited consciousness which wants to maintain its isolation inside the cocoon that it has built.

What does this mean? It means that no matter how much inspiration is allowed in your sphere of consciousness, you will distort it, bending it to your limitations and it will lose its original purity.

About 2400 years ago, Plato spoke to us in these same terms, only he used other allegories. He spoke about the nature of reality beyond this three-dimensional world, on a higher plane. In this plane existed all that is manifested in our plane, only in perfection. The creation of this world in which we live is a cocoon living in an ocean of eternal perfection.

Yet, within this bubble, we remember what it was like to be in the Absolute state. We are reminded of it through the ever present messages coming from our Divine Selves. So, we demand that our level of reality acquire the Absoluteness found in the higher level. We want perfection. We remember it. We aspire to it. We are reminded of it whenever the Cosmic Life Force and Consciousness seep through their messages into our bubble.

The messages coming from the infinite ocean of force and consciousness surrounding the bubble become distorted by the time it reaches the limited consciousness of the bubble. For instance, the Christ showed us the way to perfection. He invited us to follow it. However, the little bubble interpreted this invitation as a demand for perfectionism. Indeed, as early as Origen, misguided Christianity confused the seeking of perfection to be rigid perfectionism. This mistake was maintained in the Roman Catholic religion and in many

Protestant sects.[1]

Thus, it is important for us to differentiate the longing for perfection—which is legitimate and non-threatening—and the error of perfectionistic thinking found in organized religion.

From the point of view of the cocooned bubble, perfection appears to be static. This is the error committed by both Plato[2] and Xenophanes.[3] God for them was unchanging. In effect, we, in our faith, understand, as Hegel[4] did, that in our relative world, we must accept that we have a dualistic view of the Absolute. Thus, perfection changes and doesn't change at the same time. It changes because it is in continuous flux as is the ocean. It doesn't change in that it has already attained perfection. See if you can meditate on this and synthesize the two seemingly opposite points of view. In doing so, you would be synthesizing, thus following Hegel's inner Path to God.

See how it is actually the little cocooned bubble of ego that is afraid of annihilation if it were to be flooded by the seemingly impersonal ocean of consciousness and energy. In its fear, the little bubble dualizes, separates itself from the whole and increasingly rigidifies. **It is that rigidity that distorts the invitation to perfection presented by the surrounding Life Force, making it a rigid demand and a threat.**

The invitation to perfection is thus an invitation to yield

---

[1] See *Dictionary of Philosophy and Religion*, William L. Reese, under "perfection" pg. 565.

[2] Greek philosopher of the 5th Century B.C.

[3] Greek philosopher of the 6th Century B.C.

[4] German philosopher of the 14th Century.

and to sacrifice.

Do you identify with any of this? Do you long for and at the same time fear the Absolute and its perfection? Where is it that you have dualized yourself, rigidifying yourself?

Perhaps you need to relax and let go of your longing for perfection for a little while. Appreciate what you have as imperfect as it is. Live totally in the now of your imperfection. Yield. That will revive, in a very healthy way, your longing for perfection. This longing will change from rigid to resilient, from harsh to open and loving, from mistrustful to trusting and full of faith.

Remember the Spiritual Law whereby one must give up that which one wants the most in order perhaps to have it. Remember also, the Chinese proverb whereby men (people, in modern parlance) reach for the stars while trampling on the little flowers at their feet.

The Tibetan would call for the little ego personality to yield to the Greater Ego, the Divine Self.

Immutable Perfectionism And The Golden Age

The existence of a freeze of immutability in a person leads to attributing Absolute qualities to many aspects of their relative live. Take, for instance, your Golden Ages. They are the times of your life that you have idealized. You have trained yourself to see them as perfect and as immutable. Many of these are to be found in adolescence. However, there may be others in childhood or adulthood.

If you look at them, you will recognize the unreality of stasis, the immutability that you attribute to them. You have made them fixed in all ways—time, space, etc. This is bound to bring you unhappiness because:

A) Nothing in reality can match this illusionary perfection.

B) You can never recreate the past in its entirety.

C) Even if you did, you will find out that it wasn't as great and perfect as you made it to be.

Volitionality And Perfection

What is contained in your striving for perfection? To the degree it is caring, you are on the right track. If your volitionality is of this beneficial nature, then it is natural. It is of the same essence as nature. It is primary as Avicenna[5] would have said. Volitionality grounded in love and commitment blends with and invites the help of the Cosmic Life Force and Consciousness.

However, if you have disconnected from your natural urge to love and give, then your volitionality will be egocentric. Your volitionality in reaching for perfection will lead to the distortion of perfectionism, the error committed by organized Christianity. You will find yourself rigid and static. Your bubble will burst and you will finally, kicking and screaming, allow God to penetrate you.

Thus, as you can see, harmful volitionality, i.e., secondary, can only be short lived and can only lead back to primary and beneficial volitionality.

We can relate here to Maslow's ego/moi level of need in contradistinction to his self-actualized level. Indeed, the self-actualized level of need is the more natural and the more direct. **Thus, the lower ego/moi—and therefore, the other levels—are a descent from the self-actualized. Yet, the self-actualized is the natural original level.** Once again, we see here a proof of the Fall. At the end of this sermon, I will give a brief version of the view of the Fall, seen from considering Maslow's needs in reverse.

The self-actualized person's volitionality is loving and giving. The ego/moi's is selfish and self-serving, leading to

---

[5] Arab philosopher of the 10th Century A.D.

burn-out and to rigidity. Yet, only through the self-actualized mode will the little ego find what it really wants—perfection and reunion with God.

Many other philosophers have enriched us with their concepts of intentionality; among them are to be found Husserl, who was educated in Vienna and who lived in Germany late in the last century and early during this one.

We never want to die. We want Absolute Power, Absolute pleasure and no pain. We do not want to go through the steps of once again finding this infinite level. This would involve the bursting of our little bubble and the immersion in the ocean. We do not want that. We resist it. We convince ourselves that we are not ready for it.

This means that we have to learn, i.e., accept the fact that we live in a relative world in which we have to die and be reborn, which means that we have to experience pain alongside with pleasure. We have to admit our powerlessness in order to find our serenity. Here I am reminded of the prayer of serenity from Alcoholics Anonymous:

God, grant me the
Serenity to accept the things I cannot change;
Courage to change the things I can; and
Wisdom to know the difference.

Those who are fighting addictions are familiar with this prayer. The addiction itself is an attempt at instantly finding the Absolute while refusing to deal with the relative. The addicted person is in his own bubble, limited to what his addiction can give him.

Therefore, in our limited bubble, we must learn that we have to temporarily give up perfection if we are to strive towards it. We must accept our powerlessness if we are to gradually recover Absolute Power. We must accept pain and abandon the demand for total pleasure if we are to create happiness in our lives.

We must give up that which we want most in order to have it.

Where we depart from Plato in the concept of perfection is as follows:

- Plato seems to present perfection as immutable.
- In reality, perfection is continuously flowing and changing.

The little ego seems to favour the concept of an unchanging perfection. It seems easier this way, more controllable and more accessible to demands while at the same time not requiring effort.

However, if for instance we consider perfect love as being unchanging, it will have to exclude other forms of love, and therefore, create duality, i.e., imperfection. If I want perfect love now, I have a limited and limiting concept of how it is going to happen. In my demand for perfection now, I limit my capacity for loving and for being loved. "I want to love you in this way only."

The crystalization of this can be found in the limited habits in a couple's sexual life. They get into a routine because of their demand for perfection and because they see perfection as static.

So, we have two freezes here creating crystalization and limiting the capacity for pleasure:

1) **Perfection is static,** immutable, unchanging. Therefore, there is only one way.

2) **I must have perfection now** without going through pain and change. This precludes growth since it denies imperfections.

Therefore, it may be necessary for the little ego—us, in most cases—to temporarily abandon the pursuit of perfect love, accepting love as being imperfect. This is the most loving attitude to have and the closest to perfection on our level of existence. What's more is that through this acceptance of imperfect love, we gradually gain access to the experience of true love in its perfection.

The same is true of all other aspects and attributes for which perfection is sought.

Relaxing and accepting the relative reality of our imperfection will make room for the spontaneous experience of the state of perfection.

Perfection as a State

The state of perfection can indeed be experienced in our dimension. In it, we exude our Divine Self and its qualities:

1) We manifest good will, strong and beneficial aggression without self-righteous rigidity. We are **willing** to risk and sacrifice for the sake of the truth, without fanaticism.

2) We express love and create, without the emotionality of its opposite: fear. It is the lion-hearted love, unafraid of confrontation.

3) We can apply right softness or right firmness when needed; we can tell the difference and the different circumstances requiring it.

4) Yes, we are totally open to revealing our faults as well, and that too is part of the state of perfection; we do not defend or boast or justify or rationalize.

5) We are as we are and we respect ourselves that way.

6) We pursue, the Good, the Beautiful and the True.

7) We have intuition without abusing it, i.e., in a grounded way.

8) We have knowledge without boasting it, with wisdom.

9) We have faith but we are still searching, valuing our doubts.

10) We have order through natural self-regulated forces.

The Fall Through Maslow's Needs in Reverse
This concept will be expanded in my future book called *The Ethical Yuppy*. However, it is valuable here. So, I'll give you a shorter version:

5) **Self-Actualization,** the ultimate need, the summit of all Maslovian needs is actually the natural, primary state. Here, volition, personal and Divine are blended. The descent from this comes through egocentricity, from lack of trust or lack of self-worth, from the well-known despair of the self-actualized person behind which, of course, is a demand for perfection. This descends the individual to:

4) *Moi*, the self-centered, egocentric, egotistical, success driven person, who, of course, is desperately trying to compensate for a deep self-loathing, leading to:

3) Need for approval from others, converting him into craving a sense of **belonging;** he has reached the **social level of needs.** His insecurity is increased. In the previous stage, at least he relied on himself for self-satisfaction. Now, he relies on others. His self-loathing has augmented, leading him to:

2) Seeking **safety and security**, out of great and increasing insecurity. In this state, self-effacement sets in, productivity diminishes; the person becomes dull and poor in spirit, mind and emotions. This in turn creates:

1) Poverty; poverty of the self becomes poverty on the outer level engendering great need for **food and shelter.**

****

The state of perfection is your nature. You are bound to get back to it. It is your birthright and your destiny. All you have to do is adjust your misconceptions. That will make it easier for you to gradually yield to your Maker. Be at-one with Him, God.

Chapter 33
The Life of Christ

The life of Christ establishes for us a pattern which we all follow. His task consists of several steps which are common to us all. When He was born, He did not know what His task was. He went through a normal childhood, learning His father's trade, learning to make a living.

This is something that we must all go through. Some don't even make it past this first stage, opting for a parasitical life under all kinds of banners and excuses.

By age 12, He teaches at the temple. Rabbis listen to Him and learn from Him. He is considered a genius. He has not as yet antagonized them as He does later. He even has glimpses of the "hatred of parents" step but He expresses it in non-threatening ways. He expresses this with disarming humour: when His father admonishes Him about being late, He astutely responds that He was about His father's business, His father being God, of course. Thus, He dissolved His earthly father's wrath. It is not yet, "My mother, who is my mother?".

Before we enter this faith of cleansing when we are still in the self-improvement era of our life, we still conform. We do not innovate, nor antagonize. This is a necessary stage without which innovation is impossible. A painter must learn the basics before he becomes creative. Pablo Picasso[1] is a good example of this. His early works conform to neo-classicism. Only later does he explode into cubist creativity. Even then, he reproduces the works of the masters, Diego Rodríguez de Silva y Velázquez[2] and others.

We can generalize this principle to say that there never really is an original except in God. Human creativity must start by conforming to the past, mastering it before creating, on top of it as it were, the "new."

Christ's father Joseph died when He was 15. He takes over the task of providing for His mother and younger siblings.

****

So, He reaches adulthood. He provides for His family and, in His early 20's He leaves them enough to live on and travels. It makes sense. That's how He spent His "lost years." The Urantia Book makes a lot more sense than the Bible.

During His travels, He learns, but He also teaches. He realizes that very little of the existing knowledge makes sense or is true. The rest is garbage. We, too, at our Church, get to this point of realizing how little maturity, integrity, common sense, exists in the world.

So, He teaches as He learns and as He travels. He teaches by reacting to the existing needs and misconceptions. He carries the light with Him. He enlightens. The light does not have to be educated in order to reveal the truth. It simply sheds itself on something and reveals its shape and its shadow effortlessly. You too find yourself knowing so much when you

---

[1] Spanish painter and sculptor, 1881-1973.

[2] Spanish painter, 1599-1660.

are free of acquired misconceptions, freezes.

****

He reaches His mid-twenties and meets John the Baptist. His baptism marks the beginning of a more difficult phase of His task, His spiritual cleansing. Here, the cleansing becomes harder. He has reached a point that is very familiar to all of us at this Church, a point distinguished by the following characteristics:

1) That it is no longer enough to merely follow your predecessors; He must bring innovations.

2) That in order to liberate those innovations from within Himself, He must cleanse Himself of all misconceptions.

3) He must rethink, and therefore, doubt everything that was taught Him. This involves the relinquishing of many pet ideas to which He may have been attached.

4) He must, therefore, challenge what heretofore has been seen as sacred, within Himself first, then outside of Himself. This usually happens in the late twenties. We can find parallels in the life of Buddha who at the age of 29 left his princehood behind embarking on an independent path of search.

This period of self-examination and self-exploration leads to self-reconstruction, i.e., a **transfiguration.** After a long and arduous cleansing, this transfiguration, at first experienced in glimpses, becomes relatively permanent.

His time comes when He is well-anchored in the new self. He can inhabit His new self at will, most of the time. He has brought to at-onement His soul and His personality. He now can teach and does.

Before He does so, He goes through a time of false shame during which He does not dare reveal and teach His new discoveries. This shame of the new self makes Him a reluctant messiah, albeit temporarily.

Many of you are caught at this juncture. You believe in the teachings that are given to you here, but you are ashamed of them. You still don't want to fully inhabit your already existing transfigured self. You still don't want to risk revealing this new self. You hide behind your old self in grey comfort.

You even go so far as to want to discredit the source of your transfiguration rather than do what you are supposed to do, which is to challenge what is expected of you and usher in who you really are. Thus, you delay your opportunity. You deprive those who are waiting to receive your help. You retard salvation.

Since you have grown and transformed, you also bring on outer level success, even before your transfiguration. You arrest your growth upon obtaining that outer success. You then use the outer success itself as a weapon against your total transfiguration, against the total identification with your new self.

You crystallize yourself, ossify yourself in those achievements, never making it to full transfiguration. You have sold your spiritual training out to the forces of darkness.

This point of your cleansing is thoroughly described in our *Catechism for a New Millennium.* You are on the verge of the first real initiation on earth—the third. You are fighting the fiercest of all battles in your career as a human. You are being tested as you never have before.

Having achieved this progress also makes you a target of the forces of darkness. Indeed, your distorted self is still there, alive and kicking, being charged and pumped by the dark forces. Your parents, inner and outer, are on the side of those dark forces in spite of the fact that they appear to advise you for your own good. They are telling you to go back to the old ways. Even your own personal success is telling you to do the same. These combined forces are none other than your own personal distorted self, the sum total of all your problems, appearing to you in an angel's clothing. This is your **dweller on the threshold**.

On the threshold of what? Of initiation. This simply means that you are on the threshold of inhabiting your real self and of finally accomplishing your true task.

You cannot escape those tests. Escaping them means failing. Failing means that you have to take them all over again. You cannot escape transfiguration. An apple tree cannot escape producing apples.

The Christ passed the test, confronted, taught, revolutionized, set in motion a force that will eventually destroy the seemingly indestructible Roman system. Buddha also succeeded at his end of the world. You too will unleash forces that have incredible powers, powers that you haven't even dreamed about, that are beyond your capacity to conceive at this point. He said so Himself when He predicted that we would do greater deeds than He.

This is the focal point of your spiritual training. This is the task of this Church—to help you through the training for transfiguration. A person who is transfigured is reborn. It is difficult for his parents and for his old connections to recognize him in his new state. Thus, we understand Christ's saying, "My mother? Who is my mother?", as well as His utterances concerning the oft-mentioned hatred of parents.

The rest of His story can be read in the *Catechism for a New Millennium*. Read it and identify with it. Nevertheless, all of you are still fighting the same battle at the same juncture.

Let's briefly revise the above:

* From **birth** to early manhood Christ reproduces for us the life of the conformist who must learn his world before he can transform it. This phase is necessary. It corresponds to the positive thinking teachings, to the twelve step programs and to other similar endeavours that do not as

yet take into consideration the distorted self. When a person is ready to take the next step, he must take it or degenerate into the false life, the yuppy life, the life of cults.

• From **baptism** by John the Baptist to "my time has come" the Christ reproduces for us the most difficult period in human existence. It is then that He is tempted. It is then that He struggles with the devil. He passes. Many falter. It is during that period that He hesitates to fully use His powers, knowing the dangers of sensationalism and self-idealization. He refuses to crystallize Himself into yuppidom. He challenges His false shame and increasingly becomes His real self. It is at this point, just before transfiguration that the dweller's temptation for selling out is the most dangerous. Indeed, it is, as we have explained above, aided by the very outer level progress that has been attained through the individual's good cleansing. Many of our friends who were once part of this church have faltered at this point of their faith. Many of you will also falter unless you get off dead center and finally resolve your recurring issues.

• **Transfiguration** is stabilized. He teaches the powerful lessons that will transform the world.

****

The following may help you:

The Hall of Ignorance

Much is usually said about the Hall of Knowledge and the Hall of Wisdom. Not enough, if anything at all, is ever said about the Hall of Ignorance. Before we can qualify to enter the Hall of Wisdom, we know that we have to master the Hall of Knowledge. Before we can qualify for the Hall of

Knowledge, we have to master the Hall of Ignorance.

What is the Hall of Ignorance and how do we know that we are in it? Of course, we must realize that only our distorted self and our deified self are there, weighing down the higher parts of us which are already in the other two halls. **What generally characterizes this hall is the willfulness to remain ignorant and numb to Spiritual Law; the statement which is made here is:** *I want not to know.* However, there are specific indications that reveal the belonging to the Hall of Ignorance. They are:

- Hatred or non-acceptance of our condition.
- Fierce defense against doing our job.
- Harmful volition in all of its forms.
- Wanting not to learn, finding it too difficult.
- Pretending to know by covering up what we don't know with what we know.
- Pretending to love for egocentric purposes, glory or emotional satisfaction or material possession.
- Expediency and compromise which show the ignorance of the fact that truth rules the Universe; dishonesty.
- Demands that our condition magically improve without us doing anything to change ourselves, to change the causes of our unhappiness within ourselves.

I can go on like this for a long time. However, you get the point. But let's go further. When are we in this halls? Is there a time or a state wherein we no longer dwell in the Hall of Ignorance? Can we progress enough so as to eliminate the possibility of sinking back into the Hall of Ignorance?

As long as you still carry any harmfulness, any distorted self, or any deified self, you run the danger of regressing into the Hall of Ignorance.

Indeed, a person who is resisting the fact that he is ready

to take the next step dwells in the Hall of Ignorance, no matter how much progress he has achieved. For example, a person who resists transfiguration after having gone through considerable cleansing is in the Hall of Ignorance. Any defense, any refusal to yield, instantly puts you in the Hall of Ignorance. In it you are blind, you follow the blind, or you lead them.

The way out is to seek the two other halls as follows:

- You first must seek the Hall of Knowledge by entertaining a dialogue with your defenses and with your distorted self. You raise yourself to the Hall of Knowledge with the parts of you that are already at-one with your Divine Self. If you are incapable of doing so, you use your intellect and will to help you. You also yield to this cleansing. Having done that, you are able to govern yourself. You have made it into the Hall of Knowledge.

- The continuous exercise of raising yourself from ignorance to knowledge will eventually become a habit. Your emotions will gradually follow you there. There comes a point when reason, emotions and will are at-one in the Hall of Knowledge. You no longer have to raise yourself. You are there and you have discovered that it actually is your nature.

- Without knowing it, you have made it into the Hall of Wisdom. This hall is characterized by the harmonious and spontaneous blending of the three Rays of Aspect—will, emotion and reason. In that state, you can trust your reactions, trust your feelings, trust your unconscious and your spontaneity, not before.

With this sermon, we close our spiritual training year. God bless you, my dearest friends for the wonderful cleansing that you do. By practicing this faith, you are the pillars on which this Church is resting. Beware of the path of least resistance during this time of vacation. Continue your spiritual training every day. Be protected by it. Find your way to God.

Part VI

Other Sermons

Chapter 34
Labour Day

Our work is the most important activity in our life. Indeed, it is a result of the activation of the Instinct of Self-Preservation. Only when we are well-grounded in our work can we then make a commitment to a mate from a place of autonomy and independence. Anything short of that creates distorted dependency; not having found ourselves professionally, we are bound to rely on our partner to do it for us. The relationship then becomes a parental one, not an adult to adult one.

There is also the reverse distortion. Many have let their work give them sexual value, thus depending on their mate to take care of their sex instinct. No matter how much they think they are grounded in their work, burdening it with sexual duties will create discomfort, tightness, anxiety, and ultimately, destruction.

What is your position in terms of work? Do you under emphasize it, seeing it as a necessary evil, while waiting to be rescued from it by a good catch? Do you over emphasize it, thus becoming as good catch yourself, vulnerable to sexual seduction and entrapment—the tender trap?

Remember that your work is an entity. It has a soul, a life, and many bodies, just as you do. It has a growth pattern, going through childhood, adolescence, adulthood and old age.

If abused, it will resent. If over protected, it will become self-indulgent. If over flattered or put down, it will disconnect from reality.

Conversely, if loved, cared for, confronted, supported, given the truth and encouraged with good will, it will thrive and accelerate itself. You will grow through it and you will benefit by it on all levels.

Thank God for this work. It is food in so many different ways. It is my window on the world. It is my way of contributing to how the world works. What's more, I get paid for it.

I pray to feel the brotherhood that comes through it. I would like to become aware of the joy of participation with so many other courageous people who yield to the ritual of being at their best and giving of their best day after day. I pray to find pleasure in my work. I pray to give pleasure through it. I pray to find, through it, my at-onement with God.

Addendum

Now, let's talk about **this** work, the ultimate work which activates and enlivens all of your life. It is the most difficult and yet the most rewarding. It is accessible to anyone who has the courage and the honesty to undertake it, and yet, very few can find those qualities within themselves to practice it. It is our religion—*laborare est orare*—and yet as blessed as it is, as many blessings as it brings, you find ways to be ashamed of it, to put it down, to insult it by daring to call it a cult or to even think about it as such.

Sometimes you know that such thoughts are outrageous. So, you dishonestly say, "that's what others think of it." The truth is that **you** project that image out there because **you** want them to think that way. **You** want to denigrate this faith, particularly in public because it destroys the false values that your vanity flaunts there.

You actually are asking ordinary humanity to help you deny and betray this faith which gives you everything. And yet, in spite of this insulting, outrageously dishonest and ingrate attitude, you know the precious value of this faith. You jealously guard it as you would a secret, not letting others benefit from it. You draw from it. You draw from it and quench your thirst, yet, instead of inviting others to drink from its infinite well, you say to them "Don't drink; I am ashamed of this well; it is poisoned; it is a cult."

Thus, not only do you clog up your own growth but you prevent others from theirs, and you prevent this divine essence to be shared by people in your sphere of influence. You then present the material in watered down, mediocre fashion. You do this in an attempt to build your own empire out there. But, since you clog and divert the source, your empire is harmful. You then will be incurring the consequences of your own distortions, as well as the consequences of those out there to whom you lie about this faith, and who you control by the watered down versions of it. And yet, all of this duplicity, this dualizing, this betrayal, demonstrates the power of this work. It is so thoroughly transforming your life, that the devil is violently reacting against it. It wants to create two empires which it controls; one here where the wisdom is found, the other out there, where it is abused for selfish purposes while its source is denied.

When you actively participate in this, you are the agent of the devil. Yet, the activation of this evil proves that the work is penetrating you. There is the beneficial aspect of your denial of this work and of your shame of it. When is all of this most likely to happen?

- When you are reaping the fruits of your labour in this faith;
- When, through your work here, you have achieved status

there;
• When you are number one.

Regression then sets in, and "You are number one," sadly diminishes to "You are numb."

Chapter 35
Creativity

Artistic creation is the most selfless and, therefore, the most beautiful, the most spiritual form of creation. It is to be found in some measure in all we do, all our accomplishments. It is the act of love between the soul, that perceives the beauty, and matter, on which this beauty is recreated. No matter which creation we consider, we will always find this act of love, a longing that finds fulfillment, a tension brought to conclusion. Thus, creativity, the ability to create, involves the union of two opposites. It resolves duality to bring unity, and this unity continues beyond the artistic creation itself. When we listen to Johann Sebastian Bach,[1] or when we admire a bronze Poseidon in the Athens museum, and, when in doing so, we experience something very deep, we are fusing with the artist, and, therefore, with the creator.

In order to get the original idea, inspiration, the artist must fulfill three requirements. The first is technical ability. He must become an excellent instrument. The second is a special kind of receptivity, as if to invoke the idea, the pictures, the notes, which already exist on a higher level. It is a form of a prayer,

---

[1] German composer, 1685-1750.

an act of yielding to a greater power, a relinquishing of all he perceives, all he has learned, in a sense. And, here we see an apparent contradiction, as we always find when trying to squeeze, in human language, truths that are divine. On one hand, the artist must master his craft to the point where he can practice it effectively and effortlessly, to the point where even his unconscious can respond with virtuosity. On the other hand, he must yield this acquired knowledge so as to make room for the new. But, only if the first requirement has been fulfilled can the second one occur. For the idea must penetrate the instrument, and to the degree the instrument has quality, the original, divine purity of the idea will come through and will deeply touch people.

Since we have just defined instrumentality and invocation, let's define evocation. It is the capacity to express, to penetrate the world with the creation. It is the ability of the creator to present his creation, to steadfastly believe in it and assert it. It is the publication of the manuscript, the showing of the art, the performance of the music or choreography, or the finding of the appropriate vehicle to do the same, such as an agent. It is the capacity to deal with the outer level reality. So, instrumentality, then invocation, then evocation are all essential in the act of creation.

Whenever an artist under emphasizes or overemphasizes one of these, something goes wrong. And, it then depends upon the artist to want to correct it. Let's take each separately and examine what happens when they are out of balance.

When instrumentality is overemphasized, we get a super virtuosity that negates new ideas. Performance takes precedence over inspiration. New ideas don't matter. Only the old must again, and again be repeated. The classicists are an excellent example of this. All has been said, according to them, and we come too late, merely repeating, copying the truths of the past. The rigidity of that position excludes renewal, invocation. It becomes an ego trip. All schools of thought or art have gone through this phase and have, thus, petrified and died.

When instrumentality is overemphasized, performance also takes precedence over evocation. The artist loses touch with outer reality. It no longer matters to him whether he is being heard or seen; only how well he plays or paints matters. Of course, there is a need for this type of attitude for art to maintain its purity. But, the overemphasis of it alienates the artist from the reality of his audience. It is true that it is very difficult for new ideas to become accepted. It is also true that having given himself this excuse, the artist often loses himself in absurdity.

As an artist, try to recognize yourself here. See if you can honestly determine whether this applies to you. It is through this honest self-examination that you will be able to recapture the spark.

When inspiration or invocation is overemphasized at the expense of instrumentality or skill, we have the lazy artist who finally produces absurd material. Some artists, lately, have pushed this point to extraordinary heights. The more outrageous, the wilder their material, the more creative they believe themselves to be, and, to some extent, they will find an audience of shallow people who will buy this misconception as well as its product. What is being avoided here is, very simply, the desire to do the tedious step-by-step learning of technique which they believe is beneath them or unpleasurable. And, here again, we have another ego trip, another lack of yielding to the greater power, another form of rigidity, but this time it is cloaked under the banner of extreme openness, ultimate egolessness, the ego trip of egolessness.

It is the same when inspiration overshadows expression. Then, the artist becomes a bottomless pit of ideas. He never has enough. He lives only to be fed and over fed by inspiration, without ever sharing or giving. He becomes the habitual and perpetual student, another form of rigidity and pride, the pride of saying, "There is always something new to learn," which, of course, is true, and once again becomes a banner, a cloak disguising an ego trip.

Here, again, if you can recognize yourself, honestly check and see if you are falling into this distortion.

Finally, when expression overshadows instrumentality, we have the cheap artist who produces only to sell. He has no talent, but he doesn't care. Only performance counts. His profuse inspiration is like a perpetual wave, hopelessly throwing its abundance on the rock of his ineptness, unable to penetrate it, except, perhaps, in trickles.

And, when expression overshadows inspiration, we again have the shallow virtuoso that was described earlier. We have come full circle.

An artist burns out when he favors one of the three principles, which then burns him out. His art, at that point, is sometimes given up, possibly, for a while, possibly, for the rest of his lifetime. Only through self-examination can he begin to re-establish the balance without which nothing can be accomplished. If the balance is re-established, inspiration will flow unimpeded into the instrument and out through the power of expression, and Divine Reality will, thus, be expressed.

What is usually going wrong in an artist's life? What are the artist's usual complaints? Let's see if we can determine some of these problems and look at them from this point of view, so that art, itself, becomes the medicine and the cure.

We've often heard, "I have no money," or "No one recognizes my art," or "The public is dumb," or "I can't make a living as an artist." In examining this attitude, we find that it presumes something. It presumes that there is nothing wrong with the artist, himself or herself, and that everything is wrong with everyone else. It says, "There is no question about the fantastic creativity that I have and the fantastic skill and performance that I am capable of. I am the best. I am better than any of these others who don't appreciate me." Of course, no progress can be achieved with this type of attitude. To have, one must become, and there is no room for becoming if the blame is thrown elsewhere before honest and courageous self-examination. Usually, if an artist holds this type of attitude, he or she will be very defensive when it comes to being told that they don't have very good inspiration, that they need to improve their skills, or that the way they produce or present their art, evoke it, if you like, has something wrong with it.

Test yourselves. When confronted with the notion of not knowing your art very well or not being open to inspiration or of not taking into consideration the way in which you perform, what is your attitude? Some artists will be much more open to criticism on any other level. They will be able to discuss, openly, any area of their lives, sometimes the most intimate, such as sex or money. At the same time, they will be very defensive about their craft. They will be unable to sustain any type of criticism in that respect. Being called mediocre or second rate in this or that aspect of their art is the worst possible insult for them. Outrage will be expressed at the slightest criticism, as if it is a given fact that they are the best at what they do.

Most people are more willing to share their deep dark sexual secrets than to admit that they are mediocre in their professions, that they have faults in them, and that they can vastly improve.

Let's, for example, take the classicist. He denies inspiration. He relies on what has already been done and repeats it ad nauseam. His complaint, often, is that nothing of any value is produced now. In some cases, he will see humanity as regressing, not progressing in his field. He may have less trouble with finances, since he continually dwells upon and gives the public that which is accepted. But, invariably, he burns out, and not only stops creating, but sometimes stops performing as well. He is focusing on activity and has forgotten about receptivity. He needs to develop it. There are many ways of doing it. The best, and perhaps the easiest, is to consider two sets of people and decide that he has something to learn from them. The first set of people are the ones that he particularly dislikes, the ones he judges as too loose, too airy fairy, too emotional, although emotion is not necessarily a trait attributable to receptivity. His dislike, contempt, and distrust for them needs to be transformed into recognition of their ability to be less rigid, more accepting, more trusting, less concerned with form and more with content. The second set of people are the ones he falls in love with. They, invariably, will fall into the same category. They will be capable of receptivity, inspiration, trust, fatalism to the point of irresponsibility. The irresistible attraction and revulsion that he will feel for them constitutes the very cure to his problem. That irresistible movement, itself, is an attempt to integrate within himself what he is missing. So, it is an act of creation. The attraction and the revulsion, if pursued constructively, become creation themselves, and therefore, engender creation and creativity.

Let's now look at an artist whose instrumentality and inspiration are well-developed, but whose delivery or expression or evocation is lacking. He doesn't care whether his creation is accepted. As a result, he has money problems, adjustment problems. "The public is dumb," he says, "I am not recognized. I refuse to deal with the realities of everyday living." Those are the Franz Schuberts and the Paul Gauguins.

However, for every Schubert[2] and every Gauguin[3] there have been millions of untalented and forgotten about artists who deluded themselves.

Do not confuse being misunderstood with being talented. You are probably glamourizing a deficiency.

Are you talented? Is your inspiration valid? Are you open enough to consider the possibility that you do not have talent, brilliance, inspiration? If you will ever get it, you must first consider that you may not have it, or that you may need to improve it. At this point, what I usually get is the artist's temptation to say that no innovative creator of art has ever been concerned with evocation. That's wrong, wrong, wrong. The examples are plenty. Bach was always concerned with his audience, and yet, was eminently creative. He, and many others, had the humility to consider those who would be exposed to their art, without losing, for that matter, the integrity of the inspiration, and without giving up anything of the virtuosity, of the instrumentality.

If you fall into this category, you must ask yourself whether you want to continue living this way, denying the existence of the real world with its pleasures and beauty. How long can misery sustain the creative urge? An example of someone whose creations were not understood (he didn't even try to make them understood, for that matter) and yet lived a happy and abundant life is Charles Ives.[4] Successful in insurance, he still managed to create and perform in a very unique way and have a happy and full life. Why not you? Why can't that be possible for you?

---

[2] Austrian composer, 1797-1823.

[3] French painter, 1848-1903.

[4] American composer, 1874-1954.

Let us, now, go back to the case where inspiration over-shadows instrumentality. These artists have inspiration; they have invocation, but lack instrumentality, lack talent. This is the artist who produces absurd material in abundance, never taking the trouble to learn his craft. The super surrealists, who spit on a canvas, spread it, and give it a name at random are a good examples of this. Many of them can be found in music and other arts. They are full of ideas, all right. Their so-called inspiration is without limits; so is their productivity. They will produce thousands of big round-eyed people in different absurdly melodramatic situations and will sell them. Another example, here, is Judson Dance Theatre in New York in the sixties, which was very popular and made some contributions to modern dance choreography. However, many of them were not really artists. Standing on the stage and not moving at all, or jumping off a chair on the stage cannot and will not ever be art. Nevertheless, some of these choreographers who were responsible for such absurdities went down in history. Invocation was there, evocation was, also. Instrumentality was not. These people have contempt for the public, as well as for their art. Their laziness is the problem, their lack of good will. If they only took the trouble of developing themselves as good instruments, they would so very much improve. Unfortunately, their own success is sometimes their greatest enemy. For, once they have been accepted, it is very difficult to argue with them about their laziness. Nothing is more convincing and more destructive than success, because a cheap idea will die, and they will burn out.

If you belong in this category, can you muster the courage to let go of evocation and invocation and focus on yourself as an instrument? Pablo Picasso, himself, had to learn how to paint reality before he could paint surrealism. The public isn't dumb, in the long run. Courage, here, is needed more than any other attitude. Let go of your conceit and bow to the masters.

Learn from the past.

Once you have honestly and courageously recognized where you need to improve the best is yet to come. Claim all, for after a temporary time of hardship, in which you will overcome your path of least resistance, you will be able to create beautifully, brilliantly, and effortlessly. Your art not only will nourish you, but will enhance all aspects of your life. You will be able to draw others to you and teach them that art. You will also show that art is not just a skill. It is a way of life, a wisdom that continually teaches you, gives to you while you give to it.

Chapter 36
The Real Self on Valentine's Day

- *Young men make great mistakes in life; for one thing,*
  they idealize love too much.
  —Benjamin Jowett, 1817-1893, English scholar and
  theologian.

- *A room with a view—and you*
  And no one to worry us
  No one to hurry us.
  —Noel Coward, 1899-1973, English dramatist, *Song.*

- *I was not in love yet, yet I loved to be in love...*
  I was looking for something to love,
  in love with love itself.
  —St. Augustine, 354-430.

- *Absence is to love what wind is to fire;*
  It extinguishes the small, but exalts the great.
  —Translated and adapted by me from a maxim
  by La Rochefoucauld.

In the past few weeks, we have examined aspects of the
Divine Self and how they become distorted in our little
consciousness. Put in other terminology, we have seen how

the Absolute and its message becomes distorted into the relative.

Specifically, and as known in philosophy, the longing for Absolute perfection degenerates into perfectionism. The longing for eternal life becomes fear of dying. The longing for Absolute Power becomes the tyranny of instant omnipotence.

We have drawn the conclusion that yielding to and acceptance of the fact that we don't possess these qualities was an essential step towards obtaining them. The state of being in which we find ourselves cannot experience this Absolute. We are on the way to reaching a deeper state in which this is increasingly possible.

Meanwhile, in our impatience and in our demands, **the ideal becomes idealized.** The Divine Self is straitjacketed into the deified self. In the midst of all this, the real self is denied. What are the consequences for romance?

Consequences For Romance

In your approach to a prospective mate, you want to be at your best. The problem is that you confuse being at your best with being in your deified self. Thus, your deified self gets emphasized and magnetized at the expense of your real self, which gets diminished.

As things get more intimate, having made believe to yourself and to the significant other, that you are your deified self, you will only show the false needs coming from it. You will only allow yourself the pleasure coming from the deified self, convincing yourself that's all there is.

So, you have invested your capacity for pleasure into a false self. Now, it appears as if the greatest possible pleasure can only be experienced through that false and deified self.

However, the deified self in its illusion denies the existence of the real self, and therefore, cannot tolerate the expression of Genuine Needs. **Genuine Needs have become unacceptable, lowly, unworthy and guilt producing.**

The deified self has become the enemy of the Genuine Needs. So, in order for the Genuine Needs to be expressed, the deified self must be dissolved, i.e., die. Since the real self is real, it is stronger than the deified self, in spite of the emphasis that you have put on the latter. The battle will be won by the real self one way or another. How does that happen in manifestation?

Let us suppose that the relationship envisaged above deepens to a committed relationship. The real self will manifest in an attraction to somebody else, culminating in an affair and the possible destruction of a committed relationship.

Another manifestation occurs when a person becomes disenchanted with their partner whose real self finally shows up in a relationship. With this lack of interest, hostility, conflict, dumping, constant battles occur, making the committed relationship a nightmare.

Yet another manifestation can be found in the very well-known syndrome of becoming disenchanted and sometimes disgusted by the partner immediately after sex.

The deified self is a lie, a pretense of reality. Being disconnected from reality, its life is diminishing. Even if it were not overrun by the real self, the deified self would shrivel up and die on its own.

Genuine Needs Polluted

If I can't express my Genuine Needs, I can't experience my real pleasure. Therefore, the pleasure experienced through the deified self is very limited indeed. Yet, I keep it alive by secretly indulging in false fulfillment of my Genuine Needs through fantasy. Since I am ashamed of my Genuine Needs, the fantasies must be experienced in shameful and guilt producing context. Now, my Genuine Needs have become polluted.

So, while pretending to be my deified self, I secretly indulge in the experience of my real self. Strangely enough, this prolongs the life of my idealize self since I partially fulfill my Genuine Needs in a secret manner. Thus, I make it very difficult to dissolve the deified self.

For example, I may pretend, with my partner, to be dominant and strong while secretly indulging in my need to be receptive. This need for receptivity has degenerated into docility. However, experiencing the two together creates a pseudo-balance and perpetuates the distortion and the insincerity of the situation.

That's why and how the deified self is kept alive. In spite of itself, the Genuine Needs come through for a while, albeit partially.

Diminished Capacity for Pleasure

Not experiencing my real pleasure, I will never feel fully satisfied, intensifying even more my deified self with my expectation of fulfillment, and diminishing my Genuine Needs and my real self. So, we have two vicious circles, two growing addictions, one in the deified self, boasting and inflating itself, the other around the real self, increasingly expressing contempt and putting the self down. This leads to all real and imagined unhappiness: greed, obsession, compulsion, self-punishment, cruelty, masochism, misogynism, hatred of men. In the extreme, this leads to sociopathy and to all crises.

Increasingly, the Genuine Needs will become associated with unacceptability, shame and guilt. Thus, their fulfillment will only be allowed in unacceptable, dirty, shameful and guilt producing context. This, too, diminishes pleasure and capacity for it. It propels you to yet even more reinforcement of the deified self.

Healing

Suppose we reverse all of this and start off on a truthful foot as it were. Decide to be truthful from the beginning. "This is truthfully who I am, and therefore, what I have to offer; what you see is what you get." If this is done, the entire problem becomes eliminated. Without the pretense, Genuine Needs will be expressed, real satisfaction will be experienced, no guilt will be manufactured, and no distortions will become necessary.

A benign circle of continuous acceleration of love and pleasure will be established. Intimacy will become a greater and greater reality. Mutual confidence will promote self-confidence which will spill over in the other areas of life. "If the truth works in my sexual and intimate life, I'm going to try it in my professional life, my hobbies, and so forth."

What to Watch Out For

1) Beware of confusing "I am my real self, what you see is what you get" with the path of least resistance of not caring for myself enough to be at my best.

2) Beware also of confusing being at my best with pretending to be somebody else, i.e., my deified self.

I can be at my best and be myself. I can be at my best and show you, in a responsible manner, my worst. In fact, being at my best depends on the degree to which I can be totally honest and open.

Strangely enough, being myself, I become a lot more attractive than being somebody else. I radiate magnetic forces that are infinitely more powerful than my little self. I create an atmosphere in which the other feels equally comfortable to being him/herself.

I also ward off those who are still magnetized in their deified self. They will feel uncomfortable in my presence and will go look for someone their own size to manipulate. Good riddance.

****

If you haven't attracted someone who is as truthful as you are, it is because you still believe in your deified self. You still want to attract another deified self. You still are repelled by and are repelling other people's real selves. You are setting yourself up for unhappiness. You still need to do some deep cleansing.

Some Rules

On this Valentine's Day, let us remember the three main rules governing relationships:

- The cultivation of complete transparency, avoiding the lies of the deified self and the myth that you must, by concealing and withholding, create an aura of mystery around you or play hard to get.
- Mutual and total acceptance of self and of the other in a context of a continuous cleansing and actualization. "I reveal all of myself to you and I accept all of you; we both commit ourselves to changing for the better."
- The cultivation of good will and commitment where all sexual energies, romantic love feelings are all devoted to the partner and where his well-being becomes first priority. It is understood here that what is good for you must also be good for me. If it isn't that way, then we are on the wrong track and need to get back on the right one.

Salvage and Repair

Every relationship has to some degree been started from the point of view of the deified self. Some have even been started clearly from the distorted self. Indeed, as mentioned elsewhere in my sermons, the grossly mercenary marriages of convenience of the past have become:

1) **The yuppy unions of the present**: women look for "most likely to succeed" men as mates. Men, in turn, look for "most likely to adorn" women, i.e., those who would look good at a dinner party with the boss's wife.

2) **Prostitution disguised as finding and capturing a "good catch":** parents thoroughly train their children—particularly girls—to sell themselves to men who have good and stable positions so as to live in the style to which they **should have been** accustomed—the parents most often not being able to do that themselves.

3) **The fixation on body types**: union here depends on body measurements, disregarding soul and personality compatibility.

4) **The climbing on the social ladder:** what used to be marrying into nobility has become marrying the boss's daughter or son, i.e., marrying someone who is highly placed in society. Not that marrying into nobility has, mind you, disappeared, what with Di and Dodie, Jackie and Ari, etc.

This is not just idealization of self. It is a direct and naked manifestation of distorted self motives such as blatant greed, conceit, social climbing and sexual addiction.

In spite of all of these distortions, a relationship can be salvaged if both parties decide together to sacrifice their deified and distorted self reasons for getting together, make soul contact and commit themselves to cleansing such as done in this faith. In the majority of cases, **if the deified and distorted selves were compatible, their souls will also be.** Indeed, we can deduce the nature of somebody's soul from their deified self as we have seen in our earlier training (see *Know Thyself*).

Therefore, in no way do we suggest that a relationship should be abandoned merely because it has begun—or even survived—for the wrong reasons. On the contrary, we encourage those who started a relationship to respect the depth of the Law of Attraction which has gotten them together in the first place. Who knows what is contained in it? Who knows how deep it goes?

At the same time, in no way do we suggest that divorce is a sin and that there doesn't exist cases wherein a relationship should not be scrapped, having been corrupted beyond repair, just as a body or an incarnation before physical death. It is up to the individuals involved to make that decision and to live with the guilt of having made the wrong one, the rewards and liberation for having made the right one, and/or both!

****

Create with your relationships mutuality in which no stone is left unturned. This is what the Christ wanted us to do. It is not only possible, but an integral part of a romantic relationship. Happy Valentine's Day. Your capacity to love is blessed by God

Chapter 37
Love and Respect of Self

Love and respect of myself should be a natural and easy feeling to have. It is my natural state of being.

So, why is it that I find it so difficult to maintain it, to sustain it without forcing and pretense? I often lose myself into the negation of its opposite—loathing and disrespect of myself. Or, I find myself condemning myself to perpetual damnation for my faults.

The first difficulty, i.e., the first hurdle, i.e., the first goal is to:

- **Confront myself without condemning myself:**
  A) Face the dishonesty, greed, rationalizations, bad will, bad faith, unwillingness to experience any pain, cruelty, inertia, conceit, stubbornness.
  B) At the same time, respect myself, love myself.
- **Accept myself without condoning:**
  A) Practice self-clemency without
  B) Self-indulgence or whitewashing or rationalizing.

****

Some are still in total denial of any harmful trait within them. I sometimes say "of course I love and respect myself; so what's the big deal? Why all this fuss about learning self-respect?"

Obviously, I am defending against experiencing my worst. This also occurs when I receive a confrontation. I "moi?" it, deny it.

At that time of defense, or with those who defend, the detection of distortion must be **indirect.**

Here are some telltale signs which will lead to the fault and to the dislike of self, if they are pursued:

- Timidity.
- Indecision.
- Anxiety; stage fright.
- Insecurity; fear.
- Fear of rejection.
- Fear of confrontation.
- Fear of disapproval.
- Fear of criticism.
- Fear of feeling inferior.

Accompanying these, you may experience an irrational sense of guilt, as if to say "why do I have to be so shy? Why do I feel guilty about speaking up? Why do I feel guilty about decisions? Why is it that whenever I am about to claim what is mine, I feel that I don't deserve it, or that I'll be punished for it?"

Obviously, I dislike myself, am incapable of giving to myself. I have contempt for myself. I certainly don't have self-esteem. Yet, I still am incapable of defining why and what causes it.

****

However, now, I **want to** find the root of this. I refuse to rationalize and pseudo-good fake self-love and confidence. I pray to honestly find it and face it. I assert my determination to be honest with myself. I want to find what is harmful within me.

****

I find something harmful within me—a thief, a liar, a cruel and unfeeling person, a greedy and self-indulgent entity within me.

Now, I am afraid that if I admit this, I totally must reject myself. So, I start defending again:

- I rationalize, giving myself excuses.
- I minimize and whitewash.
- I deny and cover up.
- I embellish my fault, glamourize it, although it is very harmful.

I am now back to the dilemma with which I started: I defend against confronting by condoning; I defend against forgiving by condemning. I condemn and condone at once. I could not condone if I didn't condemn and I could not condemn if I didn't condone.

False And Unnecessary Modesty

Instead of claiming what is rightfully mine, I convince myself that I can manage with very little and I glorify this. I minimize my need and I idealize this, as well as my poverty. That's called false modesty or poverty consciousness.

- Rather than looking at the fact that I feel too guilty to claim more, I idealize by lack of power, dishonestly making it appear as if it is my choice.
- Looking at the guilt will uproot the distortion that is creating it. Both are the cause of my diminishing myself.
- As long as I remain poor, denying my need and my frustration, I will never liberate myself from the prison of distortion and from the poison of the guilt it creates.

- I will never be satisfied in spite of my pretense of spiritual simplicity.

False modesty hides greed. That greed is the Genuine Need for fulfillment wich has been repressed, thus intensified and magnetized.

False modesty creates greed. It transforms Genuine Needs into demands, cruelty, greed.

****

Now we can construct a solution.

1) **Believe** that I am infinite in my resources and potentials. I can grow infinitely. I can transform myself completely and at will. Whoever I am and however wretched I feel I have become, I still have available to myself the infinity of life, just because I am alive. This is true for me and for the worst person ever to exist.

I can change now; I can start now. If I don't, it doesn't really matter because my distortion must and will change. Only, in the mean time—and that may mean a long time—I will suffer, creating crisis. All distortion is finite and eventually leads to goodness which is infinite.

I will allow myself to believe this. I can already feel my despair abating, perhaps also disappearing.

2) From this new vantage point, I can **disengage** from the problem and observe it. Disengage, but not disconnect. Identify, but not be identified with.

- I separate myself from my problem.
- I assert, affirm myself as a good person.
- I then deal with the problem.

3) **Stasis is illusion:** I realize that, when I was identified with the problem, in despair, I thought that I couldn't possibly

budge, change. I saw the problem as a deadness, as inanimate as a mineral object devoid of consciousness.

But is the mineral kingdom inanimate? The atom contains immense power. So does an electric current. It has all this power and still it is incapable of saying "I am," of being conscious of itself.

How much more powerful, how much more potential must I, therefore, have by possessing the faculty of being conscious of myself? Of being as far more alive as I am?

What I think, feel must have even more power than this. **I see now that I have made my problem—my harmful—static, unchanging, dead.**

4) **Change is reality:** I can change my reality. Nothing is fixed. Everything evolves and is malleable, in flux. I am malleable, I can mould myself into any shape I want to have. I can flow like water into any difficulty and dissolve it. I can melt or erode the most stubborn of static walls.

I seek the places of stasis, stagnation and despair within me. I want to confront the worst, penetrate its despair and introduce it to life, love, beauty, power and freedom. I can accept and dissolve the worst in me.

5) **I connect my hopelessness, my self-condemnation and my guilt to the false belief that what was harmful in me was static, immutable, permanent.** Should I dislike this fault in myself? *Yes.* Should I condemn myself to having it perpetually? *No.*

6) **I see that by denying and repressing, I identified my innermost self with it.** So by revealing it, I stop this self-identification with it. And to reveal it, I must identify with the rest of myself first.

7) I see that by denying and identifying with the harmful, I had no choice but to want to keep it and make it permanent. Since it is my real self, I cannot want to dissolve it. I must

hold onto it. It is life for me, my life. I must give it the infinity and the permanency of God. And that's how it gave me the illusion of permanency. I put it there. And that's how I despaired and suffered! And that's why I couldn't change! I didn't want to! I thought it was death!

My fear of death is my fear of change and my fear of life.

8) **I respect life:** I lovingly recognize its Absolute Power, its ever changing quality, its magnificent beauty, its generous abundance.

My life renews itself. I am immortal. Nothing in me is fixed, not my personality, not my character traits, not my body, not my cruelty, not my stubbornness, not my laziness. Even my love, intelligence and will are continuously changing, adapting to the new, creating the new, and regenerating itself.

I have neglected life. I now commit to respecting and giving to it. Even if I don't completely trust it, I can start giving some to it. It will reward me in kind, giving back to me partially. But if or when I give to it all of myself, it will give to me all of **itself,** and it is far greater than I am. So, I will be benefitting in an infinite way.

9) **I am life. Life is eternal. I am eternal.** The new and liberated potentials have always been there, blocked by me. I can see this now. Life, being eternal is new and old at the same time. So am I—new and old for eternity.

10) **I respect and give to myself:** Having identified my distortions, I no longer feel guilty about them. If guilt occurs, I understand where it is coming from. So, I don't have to be timid. I can claim what is mine. I give what belongs to others. That frees me to claim what belongs to me. I generously give to my clients. They respond in kind.

I am willing to pay fair price for value. That frees me to claim what is fairly mine. Only if I don't cheat can I claim honesty from others. Only if I don't cheat do I love myself enough, respect myself. I can then give to myself.

If I don't have anything to give, I must realize that I always have an infinite treasure: truth, my honesty. That's the one gift no one can take from me.

I must commit myself to have it and to share it. That will open all doors for me.

Chapter 38
Harmful Superstition;
Dare to Believe in Goodness

- *Therefore I say unto you, what things soever you desire, when you pray, believe that you receive them, and you shall have them.*
  —Mark 11:24

- *Superstition sets the whole world on fire. Philosophy quenches the flames.*
  —Voltaire, 1694-1778, *Dictionnaire Philosophique*, 1764, under "Superstition."

I have betrayed the love of at least one of my parents. This has made me deeply ashamed of my own capacity to love and to manifest my real, my best self. (See my sermons: "Betrayal of Love" and "Releasing Your Capacity to Love.")

I no longer trust in the best in myself. I haven't trusted it since the early days of my betrayal of the love of my parent(s).

I have, therefore, created a lot of defeats and frustrations. Not trusting—shame of—my loving and of my best made me hide it. I have operated with a part of my best, expecting it to give me all.

As a consequence of not manifesting my loving and best

self, I have been defeated, frustrated in so many attempts. I have been left with the bitterness of not having what I should, not accomplishing all I could, unable to have all I can have.

* *Jesus says: "It is not possible for someone to enter the house of a strong man and do him violence if he has not tied his hands: [only] then will he plunder his house."*
—Gospel of Thomas, saying #40

As protection against this continuous pain, I have adopted a false modesty, a false timidity, a false resignation. I now expect little or nothing so as not to be disappointed. I expect poverty so as not to feel the full pain of not having abundance.

Thus, I deprive myself of all the goodness of life by not wishing for them. I have convinced myself that if I don't wish them, I'll never feel the pain of not having them.

I now superstitiously prevent myself from wishing, visualizing even in reality, even what should be mine.

I presume the worst so as to be pleasantly surprised when anything good materializes.

I retrace my steps now:

1) I betrayed the love of at least one parent.

2) As a result, I concealed my love and with it the best of myself.

3) I have become ashamed of it.

4) I have instead operated with only part of me. I have loved in a limited fashion, making myself and others believe that it was all my love. I have given in a limited way, making believe that I have given totally.

5) Thus, I have been frustrated, receiving partially of love and of all other goodness. It has hurt me all my life.

6) To protect myself, I have developed a harmful superstition in which I expect nothing, or the worst, or very

little so as not to be disappointed. I call it the **pseudo-safety of pessimism,** or the **glamour of pessimism,** or the glamour of poverty, of meekness.

7) This additional stinginess is diminishing me even more.

Presumption of the Harmful

1) Look deeply inside of yourself for an volitional belief in the harmful out of fear of the pain of disappointment. "By believing that the good will occur, I set myself up for pain if it doesn't. Out of self-protection, I will remove my belief that the best will occur, and replace it with a **presumption of the harmful.**"

2) Also look for the irrational belief that the **expectation of the good itself will ward the good off.**

3) Yet also look for the pseudo-comfort you find in putting yourself down, **forbidding yourself the belief that you are worthy of the best,** making yourself believe that only badness will ever come to you, never any goodness.

4) See where you have decided that you won't change, always stay static, squeeshy squashying yourself through life.

5) In those places you also reinforce the belief that your problems are unsurmountable, that you'll never resolve them.

The Glamour of False Modesty

"It's kind of cute to be shuffling and humble. It's unpretentious and nonthreatening. At least I won't be called arrogant and boastful, and everybody will be my friend, including God, who, most of all, I try to manipulate with this game of false modesty." This is the attitude which supports the glamour of the miserable sinner, so dear to those who call themselves Christians.

The result is the formation of an unnecessary and additional block to beneficial occurrences, to goodness. Only the belief in goodness makes room for it. Only the dignity of self-assertion actualizes the goodness to which we are entitled.

The Good Is Taboo

The word taboo is defined in Webster's as *a native, South Pacific term among primitive peoples, a sacred prohibition making certain people or things untouchable.* It has also come to mean "any conventional social restriction." Thus, the verb to taboo is to prohibit or forbid.

Well, see within your primitive self where there is a deep prohibition against believing beneficially. You'll find it to be a deeply acquired Pavlovian response which immediately equates expectation of the good with a) the pain of disappointment b) arrogance and social unacceptability, being contrary to the expectation of self- deprecation.

Check here in sports where it is unacceptable to claim that you have been at your best, that you can and will be so in the future. This belief is a manipulation ploy through which you try to get approval.

So, two layers supporting each other:

1) The primitive taboo prohibiting the belief in the good.

2) The superimposed glamour of the meekness which is supposed to placate and seduce everyone, including God.

And, on top, an expectation that, because you are so meek and good, a messiah, or God will rescue you without your having to exert yourself. This then facilitates the belief that your problems are insurmountable, that you are a victim of them, that God gave them to you for testing purposes, and of course, that you couldn't possibly have created them. In other words, aside from being a wretched, unhappy individual, you are also powerless.

1) In order to protect myself from the pain of frustration, I will not expect the good. I will presume the harmful.

2) Now, I am creating harmful energy forms with my presumption of the harmful.

3) Thus, I attract distortion, painful life occurrences.

4) I have justified the presumption of the harmful through the Law of Cause and Effect; this law works for goodness and for harmfulness, depending on where we apply it.

5) Now, what I made myself temporarily say for protection against pain has become a permanent belief. I now believe in the harmful, and I have "proof," it seems.

Transformation

You are playing games with yourself. All game playing, whether with the self or with others constitutes abuse of the power in the word, and therefore, breeds unhappiness and pain.

This superstition of self-protection, of the harmful must first be identified inside yourself. You have made it largely unconscious.

1) **First, let it emerge in your consciousness.** Take each life area at a time, and listen to the harmful self-protection within:

- I'll never have abundance.
- I'll never have an honest and loving relationship.
- I'll never succeed in anything.
- I'll never be brilliant.

You have brainwashed yourself in that way.

2) If you do this, **you will feel the way it has limited you.** You will start saying "why couldn't I have abundance, an honest and loving relationship, etc.? The possibility of those will start dawning on you. "Why not?"

3) "Why not?" Simply because you have betrayed the love of at least one parent. Which one? How? Open your heart to

him/her. Change your mind and realize what you have missed in terms of tenderness, affection, love. Then see how this has lead to your denial of your own capacity to love, to being ashamed of it and to thus repress, demean and deny it, tying your hands behind your back. (Gospel of Thomas #40.) For further in-depth teachings about this point, again see, "The Betrayal of Love" and "Releasing Your Capacity to Love."

4) **Convert the "why not" into a yes:** Assert and affirm the beneficial. Dare to do it. Go counter the taboo of the good. Take the Kingdom of God. Claim it as yours. **Risk defeat.** Do this with the support of the liberated love of your rejected parent. If you experience this lost love, you will feel the necessary self-confidence to risk defeat.

Whenever the superstition of the harmful re-emerges, remind yourself of its consequences. Without repressing it, talk to it, suggest to it that the games it plays create the very harmfulness that it is trying to avert.

Promise the following to yourself; "I will only say to myself what I honestly mean, what I really wish."

Dare to Believe in the Best

"I am the source of infinite resources. My life provides countless possibilities for fulfillment. I can create all that I can imagine. I will imagine the best of my best."

Sustain this assertion, hold it steady in the light until it becomes a reality.

The little child tyrant who wants instant results will tempt you into returning to the mind games of belief in the harmful. It will want to demonstrate to you that it doesn't work. And your mind has been allowed to obey this tyrant.

Retrain your mind. Allow the rediscovered natural thoughts of faith, to become familiar and comfortable in your soul essence, once again. Plant them there and let them grow roots. The good must grow roots before it bears fruit.

Two Balances

1) **Between owning up to distortions and expecting it to always be there:** When you first own up to your harmfulness, you are motivated to change it. You are feeling the pain of it, and it is that pain that urges you to change it.

When you superstitiously hold onto your distortion in order not to be disappointed in your wish of the good, you are numb. You do not feel the pain of it. In fact, there is a sick, grey enjoyment of it, the sickly sweetness of the miserable sinner in conventional churches; the hypocritical false modesty of false devotion.

Remind yourself that you have revealed the harmful in order to transform it into the good, not in order to remain stuck in it and glorify it to attract a saviour.

First, you had to dissolve the dishonest denial of the existence of distortion within yourself. Then you owned up to that distortion. Now you hold on to it for protection against the frustration of your desire for the good. You now expect this distortion to permanently keep you in mediocrity. So, dare to believe in goodness. Risk the possibility of rejection for the sake of achieving goodness.

Goodness will not come by itself. Only you can create it, elevate yourself to its level in order to claim it.

In the harmful, you keep yourself from what you really want all the time, at 100% in order to protect yourself from the possibility of rejection. What is the percentage of this possibility? Actually measure it. "What percentage of success do I have if I try?" "If I don't, I have 100% possibility of failure. If I try, whatever the chances of success, I am better off than not trying. I have given myself a chance. And if I lose, I'll try again."

What possibility of success do I have by believing at 100% in my failure? I am keeping myself permanently disappointed so as not to risk the occasional disappointment of defeat. That's not very smart.

Get smart. Dare to risk. It makes a lot more sense.

2) **Between daring to believe in goodness and wishful thinking.** Daring to believe in goodness transforms the harmful cowardice that blocks. It is, in itself, the distortion itself turned around. Wishful thinking, on the contrary, escapes and perpetuates the harmful by taking premature pleasure by being content with the mere pleasure of daydreaming. It represses the harmful by compensating for it. It superimposes itself on the harmful while denying it. Thus, it guarantees the perpetual existence of the harmful.

Wishful thinking must be unrealistic and wild, so as to counter the cowardly self-protection of the harm.

Daring to believe in goodness can't afford to be unrealistic since it is the transformation of the cowardly self-protection itself.

The coward is gradually acquiring courage and is daring to claim life. It cannot be anything else bu realistic. It is too timid yet to be anything else. Any measure of courage it obtains is real and has the potential to become more and more real.

The Glamour of the Harmful
and the Taboo of the Good

Here are two mutually supportive distortions:

1) When I don't want to resolve what in me is harmful, I proceed to glamourize it. I idealize my distortion by for example calling cruelty strength, or victimization virtue, martyrdom. This aids to support

2) The taboo of the good in which I protect myself from

the risk to expect and desire the good. In turn, the expectation of the harmful encourages its glamourization in #1, a vicious circle has been again formed.

****

Create your own reality. Remove the **glamour of the harmful** and **the taboo of the good.** Be God.

Chapter 39
Kant's Categorical and Practical Imperatives

We start with two quotes by him:

- *Act in such a way that you will be worthy of being happy.*
  —"Critique of Pure Reason."

- *There is only one (true) religion; but there can be many different kinds of belief.*
  —"Religion within the Bounds of Mere Reason."

Immanuel Kant, a German philosopher, who lived in Konigsberg, in Germany from 1724 to 1804, never traveled more than 100 miles in his life. His life was a model of impeccable order. He devised, among other things, an ethical system of life. He expresses his fundamental requisite for an ethical life through his imperatives.

The Categorical Imperative
It is expressed as follows: **act as if the maxim of your act were to become, by your will, a Universal Law of nature.**
Maxim is defined in Webster's Dictionary as *a concisely expressed principle or rule of conduct, or a statement of a*

general truth; a precept. Thus, **volition is key.** What is behind every thought, feeling and act for you? What is the maxim that animates them? What is the rule of conduct that leads you to having that thought, that feeling or to doing that act?

Once you have found that volition, can it become a Universal Law of nature, a Spiritual Law, a Law of God? If it cannot, then the volition is harmful and, according to Kant, you are **lying**. Here we are given a sure way to detect all within us that is devoid of integrity, that leads us to duplicity.

A lie is an example of this duplicity. When you lie, you create that which is against the truth. Since the truth can never die, as long as you lie, you make yourself the enemy of Eternal Life, i.e., you are dying. **Lying is dying.**

Kant also points out that a lie sets up an unjust double standard. Indeed, it requires that others sincerely believe us in our insincerity. In that condition, it is impossible for anyone to be aligned with, nor to benefit from, Spiritual Law.

Another way of expressing the categorical imperative is **"live by the same rules your act requires of others."** We recognize here the Christ's command "love thy neighbour as thyself."

The most apparently innocent way that we violate the categorical imperative is when we look for the best possible deal while intending to pay the least—the worst—possible. In business, we see this as shrewd. In marriage, we see it as success. In religion, we seek to be saved without changing. In positive thinking or in so-called prosperity churches, the perfunctory mouthing of platitudinal affirmations is supposed to be enough effort and giving of yourself to open the doors to anything you can possibly desire.

How can any of this have behind it a maxim that can become Spiritual Law? The underlying maxim behind all of this is "cheating is the easy way to get what I want" or "cheating is the only way to get what I want." Not only does it not work, but it regresses. It also sets up the situation where, perforce, being a cheater, I become blind to being cheated.

This reinforces the desire to give up on the world, which happens to be the reason why I started cheating in the first place.

Use this tool to discover your motives and to clean them up.

The Practical Imperative

The above leads us to study Kant's practical imperative, which in his terms was: *Treat every man as an end in himself and never as a means only.* We extend this in our faith to:

Treat everything as an end, not as a means. Don't use anything as a means. Even when you use a tool, respect the tool for its own sake. The tool itself is an end, receiving your respect through its proper use.

It has a task, and therefore, a sovereign self. By proper use, you merely help it in its sovereignty. In no way is this tool your slave.

Now, extend this thought to people. Are they means or ends? Do you use them, or are you concerned about their well-being? Do you respect their sovereignty? Their dignity? Their task?

Make a list of those around you. Determine how they are your tool, how you allow them to make you theirs, and the why—the purpose, the volition—behind this.

Then, one at a time, consider the possibility of changing this. It will involve a risk for the sake of love.

The Wrong Way

I use myself to obtain approval. I sell out my integrity to

keep my job. Eventually, in order to justify this behaviour, I will unconsciously attract jobs which require that I sell out in order to make a living.

I will sell out by appearing to be somebody else, and, that way, attract a relationship. I will use my partner for my ends and he will use me for his.

I use my business to make money. My business is merely a means, not an end. Therefore, I don't value and respect it. I don't perfect it. I don't seek excellence in it. Thus, it loses its value and diminishes its earning power.

I use myself as a means to obtain money or sex or security. I am not any longer an end, but a means. Thus, I value myself less than I value the end, be it money, sex or other. I can only, in this way, obtain partial satisfaction since I create pain to myself in the pursuit of that which is pleasurable.

So, I push some more, use myself more, demean myself more. But end up enjoying less. Thus, I create:

- The glamour of the end.
- The denigration of the means, myself.
- An increasingly ruthless greed, insensitive to pain—my distorted self.
- An addiction to the end.

Therefore, the self-centered "I'm number one" philosophy, which is supposed to bring self-esteem, brings instead self-loathing.

Another conclusion here: respecting the other's sovereignty is, therefore, the only possible way to self-esteem.

The Right Way

Everything is an end, to be loved and respected in its sovereignty. This instantly unifies duality. For example, if a salesperson considers a prospect an end, he won't want to use him as a tool for making money. He will treat him with respect and dignity. He will not try to impose on him something that is not needed. He will not charge anything else but what is fair.

A buyer, on the other hand, who considers a purchase, will not want to pay less than fair market value because he sees both seller and purchased service or goods as ends, not means, ends to be respected. Thus, buying loses its desire me arrogance and selling loses its pressure and pushiness. Buying and selling become one.

Consider this principle in your past, present and future. Apply it to everything you have done, are doing or contemplate in the future:

- Marriage proposals.
- Marriage, itself.
- Mate, him/herself.
- Job; raise; promotion, demotion, being fired, looking for employment.
- Career and change.
- Church.
- Donations.
- Giving and receiving, and how they unify in that principle.

Consider the sovereignty of your thoughts, feelings and opinions. How have you violated them by selling them out, i.e., using them as means, tools, not as ends, respected, autonomous entities? Consider the objects you own, big and small. How have you used them as tools, disrespecting their sovereignty and their task? How does that lead to abuse? To overspending? To accumulation of useless objects?

Divine Self, Distorted Self and Deified Self
The distorted self uses parts of the Divine Self as means to its selfish, egocentric ends. They thus become part of the deified self, petrify and burn out, being disconnected from the

Divine Self, the source of life.

Unless the distorted self is directly confronted for its errors, unless it is convinced that what it is doing is wrong, it will not burn out, because it is connected to the Divine Self, directly receiving and distorting its energies.

Say, for instance, that I have a talent for medicine, or law, or math. This talent is part of my Divine Self. If I use it as a means to make money, I will deplete it, darken it and eventually lose it and the money it can make me.

But, if I develop and pursue it as an end, for its own sake, I will never burn out. My distorted self is never involved. The talent will forever remain connected to the Divine Self. It will forever grow, create, heal.

Actually, each of us has different degrees of distorted self involvement in what we do. That degree eventually determines the necessity for a destructive crisis in which the burned out aspect is abandoned, albeit temporarily.

Aladdin, the Genie and the Practical Imperative

This concept of Kant's further illuminates the allegory of Aladdin and the genie.

Aladdin uses the genie as a means to his ends. He doesn't love and respect the genie. The genie is not an end on to himself. Think here of all those you used. Think of material used for your ends. Think of this material, for instance, and how it is used as means, not as an end. This needs to be reversed. If it isn't, you would be regressing into guilt, egocentricity and self-diminishment.

Remember, Aladdin uses the genie to cheat, to by-pass the labour of obtaining what he wants the old fashioned way—earning it. By using the genie, he constantly debilitates himself. If he were to respect the genie and his power, perhaps he would accept the genie as his teacher rather than his abused saviour. Here, we learn that we could also change our attitude towards Christ and God as well as towards our teachers, learning how to acquire their power for ourselves rather than abusing it through them.

Conversely, the genie uses Aladdin as a means, a tool, not an end. By fulfilling Aladdin's every whim, the genie's end is not Aladdin's happiness, but his own. **He** wants to finally achieve freedom from the lamp, from slavery. This is also true of the permissive parent, or of the parent obsessed with being perfect with his children, doing everything right for them. This obsession, far from being loving and altruistic, conceals a guilt for not loving which results in a false sense of obligation. The parent is using the child as well as what he provides the child as means, tools to assuage his own guilt. He can't wait to be free of his obligations to his children. He actually wants to get rid of them.

The Hegelian master-slave relationship is one of mutual using as means, not of love.

Group Implications; The Cultural Imperative

Imagine a community which operates according to this principle. All members have raised their consciousness to that level of ends. All participate in harmony and respect for Universal Law. Everyone is both king and subject, leader and follower. Everyone recognizes both in themselves and each other.

The result must be that ethics, equal rights, justice become the implicit consequence of such consciousness.

Let's use this tool for our growth and our community. Let's be respectful of each other and of everything as a created end, thus emulating God.

Chapter 40
The Tibetan Meets Kant;
The Way to Wisdom

- *All men naturally desire knowledge.*
  —Aristotle, 384-322 B.C., Greek philosopher.

- *People of quality know everything without having learned anything.*
  —Moliere, 1622-1673, French dramatist, "Les Précieuses Ridicules."

- *A knowledgeable fool is more of a fool than an ignorant fool.*
  —Moliere, "Les Femmes Savantes."

- *The desire of knowledge, like the thirst for riches, increases ever with the acquisition of it.*
  —Lawrence Sterne, 1713-1768, English novelist and clergyman, *Tristram Shandy.*

The Tibetan Master D.K., and his work dictated through Alice A. Bailey contains some wonderful material on the acquisition of knowledge. In this sermon I have blended some of these with Kant's philosophy.

According to the Tibetan, the great initiations are reached by accomplishing the little daily ones. Both great and small ones, however, require the transformation of knowledge into wisdom. This then becomes the key to growth, which is initiation, great or small. And here, the Tibetan and Kant meet.

****

To transform knowledge to wisdom, the following requirements must be fulfilled:

I. The Knowledge Must Be Deliberately Wanted

This means that it must be pursued for its own sake, as an end in and by itself, with respect for its sovereignty and for its task. This means that we must find and remove any and all ways that we have wanted this knowledge as a means to an end. Here, the Tibetan meets Kant's practical imperatives: **Treat every man as an end in himself and never as a means only.** We extend this in our faith to: **Treat everything as an end, not as a means**.

For example, the study of medicine, law, engineering or of these here teachings should be done for their own sovereign sake and for the furthering of their task. The acquisition of this knowledge should not be for money, power, position, or the conquest of others through seduction.

Now, what if I am a doctor who has acquired knowledge of medicine for money, power or seduction? Must I give it all up?

Not necessarily. Many enter into a profession or acquire knowledge initially for the wrong reasons. If and when they enter this faith, they become conscious of their wrong motives. This usually occurs through a crisis brought about by the abuse of the knowledge carried out by the wrong motives behind it. At this juncture, the person can, through this spiritual training, remove the wrong motive. He can, for instance, no longer practice medicine with greed. The removal of his greed requires the steps offered by this faith. To meet the Tibetan again, the Law of Repulse must be used. It is the point of outrage reached when it occurs to us that we have created ugliness, harmfulness, by deviating from the light. The Law of Repulse at this point activates the forces which will help us relinquish the harmful creation.

If the harm can be removed, the knowledge regains its sovereignty, creating only happiness for the individual. In spite of a temporary loss, he will experience more abundance this way than the way of greed.

Sometimes, however, the profession itself, or the knowledge itself is so enmeshed with the wrong motives that both must be given up, albeit temporarily, until the person is free of the wrong motives, allowing him to pursue the knowledge for its own sake. There are two possibilities here:

1) The individual within himself has so loaded the profession with his harmful volition, using it and abusing it as a means, that it must be given up.

2) The profession itself has been corrupted. The individual hooks in to this corruption with his own. All professions, particularly the established ones, are, to some extent, corrupt. The more established, the more tempting it is for a profession to corrupt itself. This is done in the same way as with the individual—by violating Kant's imperatives.

Your corruption or your profession's are an opportunity for change, individually or in group fashion. Group initiation is also available.

When that is done, knowledge is transformed into wisdom, and experience into quality.

II. The Knowledge, Thus Sought,
Must Be Selflessly Applied to Life

Again, this is true of **all** knowledge, including knowledge of this faith. If this knowledge is respected in its sovereign state, it will naturally apply to life. The life application will be clear to the person following I. and II.

Wrong. Involutionary motives of greed, power hunger or abuse of knowledge as a means, reverse the way of nature, imploding it, inverting it. This creates distortions, unhappiness and blindness. The person squanders his energies into exhausting mediocrity, having to learn every little thing, feeling pressured and mired in detail and unnecessary self-protection, paranoia and bad pain.

Let me repeat: "exhausting mediocrity." Brilliance, always being new, is connected to the Cosmic Life Force and the Cosmic Consciousness, and therefore, never tires, always regenerating itself, always creating anew.

Withdrawing from life by desiring to own and enslave knowledge, he loses the meaning of it. Every time you intend to use knowledge as a means, not an end, every time you enslave knowledge, you cut yourself off from life. Life then becomes meaningless. So do your possessions, mental or material. So do your emotional connections. The knowledge then becomes a detriment being used as a defense. The person is better off ignorant.

If you use knowledge as a means, you and it will lose the sense of meaning. If you use knowledge as an end, you will transform it into wisdom. It will yield infinite meaning.

If you find yourself inordinately busy, crazily imprisoned by obligations, every single one of which being a matter of survival, you have violated this principle. You are not applying your knowledge to life. You have made it into a means, a prisoner, a genie in a bottle, without dignity, sovereignty, in slavery, and it is eroding you.

You must rethink your life and redress it. Two examples come to mind:

1) **Immanuel Kant:** who realized that he wouldn't discover anything new by traveling. He lived a life of ecstasy and serenity within 100 kilometers of Konigsberg, in spite of his world fame. He was repeatedly offered better posts elsewhere, with more of everything. He refused them all, remaining at home in more ways than one.

One thing he traveled for daily, however, was his lunch. Every day, he went out to lunch, using different restaurants to avoid the hounding curiosity of those who wanted to have contact with him.

He did not use geography to solve his problems. He was committed to his word, to which he gave selflessly. It is this commitment that got him to shape his life to his liking.

2) **Me:** I had, at some point, a job that required world travel. Yet, I never missed one of my teacher's lectures or lessons. (I missed one, later after that job, out of pure greedy sexual acting out.) My commitment and devotion to this faith always found a way to resolve the conflict, which themselves were always a manifestation of my distorted self, the part of me that didn't want to be there.

III. A Genuine Desire to Use The Knowledge to Serve

And not to be served by it. Strangely enough, as I said repeatedly, **that's** how you will reap the greatest benefits, on all levels.

So, serve your knowledge. Give it lovingly, but not freely. Don't throw pearls to swine. Give it to those who want it and who demonstrate gratitude and respect for it.

Don't give it otherwise, or you will be a slave, and a slave always intends to become the tyrant. Working for nothing is slavery. And slavery is against the law, any law on any level.

It is part of your giving:

A) To respect your work and your knowledge,

B) To see to it that the condition of your imparting it be respect for it as well.

Observe the games you play when you overzealously spend longer hours at work than you should. You are not really doing it for the sake of the work as an end. You are doing it for selfish purposes:

- To get your boss's approval.
- To justify your demand for more money.
- To beat someone with whom you compete.
- To escape going home to your family.
- To justify your case against the Universe.

This is the kind of hard work that will burn you out quickly.

You owe this respect to your work and knowledge; you owe to it its sovereignty and its task.

IV. An Intelligent Volition to Use Your Knowledge, to Further the Good, the Beautiful and the True

And not to use its power for anti-life, destructive purposes. All knowledge, being power, has the potential for abuse by the individual's and humanity's lower nature. It doesn't have to be abused. It is not meant to be.

If it is acquired clearly, no abuse will ensue. If the individual is aware of his uncleanliness, and if he follows this faith, he won't abuse his knowledge, or will abuse it less, depending on his degree of evolution. Here we meet Kant's categorical imperative: **Act as if the maxim of your act were to become, by your will, a Universal Law of nature.** What is the maxim governing your decision to acquire knowledge? Any knowledge? Can it become a principle governing the

Universe? If yes, your knowledge will become wisdom and you will be blessed, initiated. Work for that gradually. If not, you will alienate yourself and reach the point of outrage in which you will relinquish and destroy all of your achievements. The same applies to humanity or to a group. Here, we find Kant's social contract.

If knowledge is abused, it will destroy his abuser. That's why your Divine Self, which is a lot wiser than you, is preventing you from acquiring too much knowledge.

That's why also, the distorted self is dumb and getting dumber. The Nazis increasingly got dumber as World War II progressed. Despite their overwhelming technical superiority, they ended up blocking the light to a considerable extent, committing huge blunders and losing the war.

Commit your knowledge to the good of the world. That's the road to wisdom, among other bonuses. Also, do it willingly, lovingly, freely, not in a forced and coerced way, not in pretense which will do more harm than good.

Knowledge And Experience in Evolution

Ordinary Humanity		Our Faith
Ignorance → Knowledge	→	Wisdom
Experience → Faculty	→	Quality

The Tibetan says that in ordinary humanity ignorance becomes knowledge and experience, faculty, while in our faith, knowledge becomes wisdom and experience, quality.

Let's compare the definitions of faculty and quality:

A **faculty** is an aptitude. It is owned by someone who uses it without necessarily identifying with it.

A **quality**, however, is *that which makes something what it is,* according to Webster.

Thus, outside of our faith, a person is disconnected from the experience and its results. Even if there is a partial connection, the experience becomes a skill, a faculty.

By contrast, in this faith, experience extends beyond faculty to quality. The person is identified **by** his experiences. He integrates them completely. He truly **becomes** a doctor, personifying the best essence of the profession, through his respect of it, as in I., II., III. above.

Are you your profession? As menial as it may be, you must first personify its best before you can complete your task through and with it.

It is, in a way, becoming an instrument of the profession, serving it, being it.

It is the same in a marriage, a relationship or a citizenship. You become it. You don't dualize and abuse. You don't disconnect and use as means.

If anything **you** become **its** means, the means through which the profession can accomplish its task.

Here, we are reversing Kant's practical imperative, or taking them a point further:

I become a means through which others may achieve, others being humans, professions, causes, concepts, knowledge. Become the tool through which knowledge can manifest, and you will acquire wisdom.

****

I am the means through which the Universe can evolve. That's how I help knowledge in its evolution to wisdom. That's how I am increasingly entrusted with more of it, which is initiation. And thus, I stand, at-one with God.

Chapter 41

Love Through the History of Humanity

- *Love is moral even without legal marriage, but marriage is immoral without love.*
  —Ellen Key, 1849-1926, Swedish feminist, *The Morality of Women.*

- *History is philosophy teaching from examples.*
  —Dionysius of Helicarnassus, 30-7 B.C., *Ars Rhetorica.*

The most obvious demonstration of selfless love expresses itself by a mother to her baby. I thought it might be a good idea for Mother's Day to study the progress of the many facets of love throughout history. Of course, this is not complete. It is merely a stroll. So, come with me as we visit the blossoming of love in our Western Civilization, with an occasional sidestep to the East.

The ancients viewed love as an aesthetic concern. They saw it as an aspiration to beauty, a movement towards it, a worshiping of it. Through the search for beauty, the true was also sought, for anything beautiful must be true. The same can be found with beauty's connection to the good, goodness. Thus, the Good, the Beautiful and the True were pursued, even in pagan times.

God responded to this longing by sending the Christ to us. The movement upward of the seeking of divine beauty, goodness and truth, got its response when Christ became human. His descent could not have been possible without the ascent of longing for beauty.

Christ taught us the other side of the equation: love everybody and everything, even the ugly, the enemy and the untrue. Love the goodness in all and renounce and denounce the evil in all, with a sword, if need be.

Disconnected from each other, each one of these acquired their oft-mentioned distortions.

The pagan seeking for beauty became:

- Heartless and materialistic.
- Cruel to the old and the disadvantaged.
- Materialistic.
- Self-indulgent and abusive of sex, each other, etc.
  Then Christians receiving the Christ:
- Denied the physical.
- Denigrated sex.
- Worshiped poverty.
- Denied science and learning.
- Created the dark ages.

They completely reversed the teachings of Christ, propelling the West into the dark ages. The Arabs, in contrast, who had no civilization in the 8th Century, skyrocketed to great heights by the year 800. At that time, Bagdad had street lights and a high level of literacy, with debate societies and great amount of freedom of expression. That same year, 800, saw the coronation of the illiterate Christian emperor of the West, Charlemagne, the first "Holy Roman Emperor."

Haroun El Rashid, the Khalif of Bagdad, sent Charlemagne a gift for his coronation. Charlemagne didn't know what it was when first he saw it. It happened to be the first mechanical clock in the West.

****

Let's trace, with more detail, some of the aspects involving the development of the consciousness of love.

For **Hesiod**, a Greek philosopher of the 8th Century. The power of **Eros** drew order out of chaos. Eros, the in-love state, later personified as Cupid, raises physical love—sexuality—to the higher spheres of love, i.e., selfless giving. Well, it makes sense that it also elevates through longing, the unhappy state of chaos to the happy state of order. We can see here the genesis of the guided teachings concerning Eros as elevating people from crass sexuality to selfless love.

Have you lost touch with your desire for order? That desire is an expression of love. Don't forget that when you look for it, because if you do, you'll never find it.

Consider the order needed to keep track of all the details of having a baby. The mother can't afford to be in chaos when it comes to bottles, feeding times, diapers. It all has to be in impeccable order. And, it is motivated by **selfless giving, love.**

Empedocles, 490-430 B.C.: Introduces love as **philia** which he sees as attraction, the force that ends strife (neixos) or conflict. He describes an amazingly wise system of love, originally binding all aspects and attributes. Then, strife—evil—splits them apart. But philia comes back and puts it all together again.

Plato, 427?-347? B.C.: Develops the concept of Eros to the search for perfect beauty, only found in the abstract. For us, it demonstrates that falling in love is a God given faculty given to us to recover our longing for Him, through union with a mate.

This concept became platonic love, i.e., love without sexuality but with the in-love state.

Aristotle, 384-322 B.C.: Develops the idea of love as **movement** from imperfection to perfection, an oft-forgotten but essential aspect. How have you separated movement from love, seeing yourself as its static victim? Love is given to you for change to the better, for evolution. No evolution is possible without love. No improvement is valid without love. Tell it to the yuppies who are so busy making a killing.

Aristotle also develops philia as love for our fellow men, brotherly love, anticipating Christ's "love they neighbour as thyself." This is a step forward from Empedocles, who saw philia as attraction, as the end of strife.

Confucius, 551-479 B.C.: Develops the equivalent of philia, **Jen,** which he takes beyond love of fellow men, into the realm of ethics. Through Jen—love—one enters the Way—Tao—and develops truthfulness, productivity, commitment, generosity and intelligence.

Remember, it is with the motivating power of love that all of this becomes available.

Christianity: Brings **Agápe,** the selfless love of God, which should be practiced and given unconditionally and Universally, to everyone, beautiful or not. The free giving of love also is directed at the imperfect, the enemy. It is the response of perfection, a movement, therefore, towards imperfection, giving to it.

Our way of cleansing is such a movement. It focuses on the imperfection in an attempt to illuminate it and liberate it from its own distortions. That then was the goal of Christianity. The downward movement of God's love also is practical in teaching. The Second Ray of Love is the Ray of the teacher. Christ is the greatest teacher.

Neo-Platonism: Combines the Christian movement "downward" with the Greek movement "upward." This combinations represents, as said in the beginning of this sermon, our philosophy. Neo-Platonism:

- Flourishes in Alexandria.
- Illuminates Augustine, at some point in his life.
- Resurges in Bagdad during the golden age (9th Century).
- And persists there and in Spain through so many eminent Arab thinkers: Al-Kindi (813-873), Al Farabi (10th Century), Avicenna (980-1037), Averroës (Ibn Rushd, 1126-1198) in Cordoba, and Avicebron (Suleiman Ibn Gobrial), a Jew in Malaga (1020-1070).
- We find it in the Irish, John Scotus Erigena (810-877) who actually did most of his work in France.
- We find it in the German Meister Eckhart, (1260-1327), who under pressure from the bigoted but powerful Vatican, sold out to stay alive. This was the beginning of humanism which is rooted in Neo-Platonism.
- We find it re-emerging in the West in the Florentine academy in the Fifteenth Century, the one founded by the Medici
- We find it in the 16th Century with Paracelsus, who combines Gnosticism to it.
- We find it in the 17th Century in Cambridge, with the Cambridge Platonists.
- We find it in the 19th Century with Hegel and Schelling.
- And finally in our own century with our and so many other teachings.
- We do not find it in the darkness of bigoted Christianity. Yet, without it, democracy, freedom of speech, freedom of thought, and their results—civilization as we know it in the West—would not exist. It is not Christianity that authored our civilization—not the distorted Christianity of

organized religion. It is the blending of it with Platonic philosophy, as found in "Neo-Platonism." This blending and unity is effected by the true love, as it is known in its many names.

Let's see what is happening to love in Christian theology:

St. Augustine, 354-430: Brings love and light together. That's great. However, he unfortunately gets lost in trying to distinguish love from lust, which he sees as being blurred in a fog.

We can solve it for him. Lust is a distortion of Divine sexuality. His problem—shared today by so many bigots who call themselves Christians—is his inability to legitimize sexuality. He, along with so many other "founding fathers of Christianity," is stuck in his latency period of late childhood, the pre-adolescent stage wherein the opposite sex is denigrated and sexuality denied. Let's not make the same mistake.

Antipathy for sex today can be found, for instance, in Ken Starr, who seems to be stuck in this latency period and who is waging a holy war on Clinton's sexual addiction. Starr does this under the banner of the law upholder. Did you hold such extreme views in your latency period, i.e., before puberty? How about now?

Baruch Spinoza, 1632-1677: According to him, loving God intellectually was the highest achievement of life. Today, we might say, "God as we understand Him." I can't help but think, though that was Spinoza meant by "intellectual" was pure and truthful. He was confused about physical and emotional love, not seeing the divinity in them. He restricted divinity to the intellect. That's a mistake.

However, for us, could we consider the meaning of intellectually loving God? We would learn a lot by this exercise in our age of computers, of the global village, and of denigration of the intellect.

Nicolas Malebranche, 1638-1715: According to whom altruistic love establishes and nurtures our relationship to God.

Then, there is a return to the "bottom," as it were with **Sigmund Freud**, who explains everything through sexual love. In his atheism and its exclusivity, he commits the same error—in reverse—as the religious fanatics in their antipathy for sex. On the way, though, he liberates very powerful concepts of love as it gets distorted in family settings.

****

We are for the rich balance of the blending of our longing for God and His consequent and subsequent response. Let's find and nurture love as truth, good will, intelligence, beauty, knowledge, faith and order. All of these are one. Let's mend the differences that we have created between them.

In that blessed unity we will find God.

Bibliography

The works of the Tibetan and Alice A. Bailey, New York, Lucis Publishing Company. (Available on CD-ROM: Bailey, Alice A., *The Twenty Four Books of Esoteric Philosophy*, 1998)

Reese, William L., *Dictionary of Philosophy and Religion*, New Jersey, Humanities Press, 1996, 856 pp.

Jeffares, Norman A. and Gray, Martin, *A Dictionary of Quotations*, Barnes and Nobles Books, 1997, 1027 pp.

Maslow, A. H., *Motivation and Personality*, New York, Harper and Brothers Publishers, 1954.

Index

For More Information

Please visit our website at:

www.austin360.com/community/churchpath

or

email us at:

ChurchofthePath@worldnet.att.net

Reverend Albert Gani
Church of the Path
207 South Commons Ford Road
Austin, Texas 78733
512-263-9435